Harry Stillwell Edwards

Sons and Fathers

Harry Stillwell Edwards

Sons and Fathers

ISBN/EAN: 9783743303720

Manufactured in Europe, USA, Canada, Australia, Japa

Cover: Foto ©Thomas Meinert / pixelio.de

Manufactured and distributed by brebook publishing software
(www.brebook.com)

Harry Stillwell Edwards

Sons and Fathers

SONS AND FATHERS

BY

HARRY STILLWELL EDWARDS.

CHICAGO AND NEW YORK:

RAND, McNALLY & COMPANY,

MDCCCXCVI.

He was already heading for the sidewalk; his company was as sunlight and Morgan was tempted to stay in the sunlight.

"Then I will go," he said. "You are very kind."

A four-seated vehicle stood outside and by it a little old negro, who laughed as Montjoy rapidly approached.

"Well, Isam," he said, tossing his bag in, "how are all at home?"

"Dey's all well."

"By the way, Mr. Morgan, we will probably have to leave your trunks, but I can supply you with everything for a 'one-night stand.'"

"I have a valise that will answer if there is room."

"Plenty. Let Isam have the check and he will get it." While Morgan was feeling for his bit of brass Isam continued:

"Miss Annie will be mighty glad to see you. Sent me in here now goin' on fo' times an' gettin' madder——"

"That's all right; here's the check; hurry up." The negro started off rapidly.

"Drive by the club, Isam," he said, when the negro had resumed the lines. "I reckon we'll be too late for supper at home; better get it in town."

"Miss Mary save supper for you, sho', Marse Norton."

"Save the mischief! Go ahead!" The single horse moved forward on a dignified trot.

As they entered the club several young men were grouped near a center table. There was a vista of open doors, a glimmer of cards and the crash of billiards. Montjoy walked up and dropped his hat on the table, then followed a general exclamation and handshaking. Edward Morgan noticed that they greeted him with general cordiality. Then he saw his manner change and he turned with a show of formality.

"Gentlemen, this is my friend, Mr. Morgan, a nephew of Col. John Morgan." He rapidly pronounced the names of those present, and each shook the newcomer's hand. At the same time Morgan felt their sudden scrutiny, but it was brief. Montjoy rung the bell.

"What are you going to have, gentlemen? John," to the old waiter, "how are you, John?"

"First rate, Marse Norton; first rate." The old man bowed and smiled, well pleased.

"Take these orders, John. Five toddies, one Rhine wine, and hurry, John! Oh, John!" The worthy came back. "There is only one mistake you can make with mine; take care about the water!"

"All right, sah, all right. Dere won't be any."

Montjoy ordered a tremendous supper, as he called it, and while waiting the half-hour for its preparation, several of the party repeated the order for refreshments, it appeared to the stranger, with something like anxiety. It was as though they feared an opportunity to return the courtesies they had accepted would not be given. None joined them at supper, but when the newcomers were seated one of the gentlemen lounged near and dropping into a seat renewed the conversation that had been interrupted. Champagne had been added to the supper and this gentleman yielded at length to Montjoy's demand and joined them.

The conversation ran upon local politics until Morgan began to feel the isolation. He took to studying the new man and presently felt the slight, inexplicable prejudice that he had formed upon the introduction wearing away. The man was tall, dark and straightly built, probably thirty years of age, with fine eyes and unchanging countenance. He did but little talking, and when he spoke it was with great deliberation and positiveness. If there were an unpleasant shading of character written there it was in the mouth, which, while not ill-formed, seemed to promise a relentless disposition. But the high and noble forehead redeemed it all. This man was now addressing him:

"You will remain some time in Macon, Mr. Morgan?"

The voice possessed but few curves; it grated a trifle upon the stranger.

"I cannot tell as yet," he said; "I do not know what will be required of me."

"Well, I will be pleased to see you at my place of business whenever you find an opportunity of calling. Norton, bring Mr. Morgan down to see me."

He laid his card by Edward and bade them good-evening. Looking over his plate, the latter read H. R. Barksdale, president A. F. & C. railroad. He had not caught the name in the general introduction. "Good fellow," said Montjoy, between mouthfuls; "talked more to-night than I ever heard him, and never knew him to pull a card before."

The night was dark. The road ran over hills, but sometimes was sandy enough to reduce the horse to his slowest gait. "From this point," said Montjoy, looking back, "you can see the city five miles away, rather a good view in the daytime, but now only the scattered electric lights show up."

"It looks like the south of France," said Morgan. Montjoy revealed the direction of his thoughts.

"You will find things at home very different from what they once were," he put in. "With free labor the plantations have run down, and it is very hard for the old planters to make anything out of land now. The negroes won't work and it hardly pays to plant cotton. I wish often that father could do something else, but he can't change at his time of life."

"Could not the young men do better with the plantations?"

"Young men! My dear sir, the young men can't afford to work the plantations; it is as much as they can do to make a living in town—most of them."

"Is there room for all?"

"No, indeed! They are having a hard time of it, I reckon, and salaries are getting smaller every year."

"I have heard," said Morgan, slowly, "that labor is the wealth of a country. It seems to me that if they expect to make anything out of this, they must labor in the productive branches. Where does the support for all come from?"

"From the farms—from cotton, mostly."

"The negro is, then, after all, the productive agent."

Montjoy thought a moment, then replied:

"Yes, as a rule. Manufacturing is increasing and there is some development in mining, but as a matter of fact the negroes and the poor whites of the country keep the balance up. Somebody has got to sweat it out between

the plow handles, but you can bet your bottom dollar
that Montjoy is out. I couldn't make $100 a year on the
best plantation in Georgia, but I can make $5,000 selling
clothing."

The dignified horse had climbed his last hill for the
night and was just turning into an avenue, when a dark
form came plunging out of the shadow and collided with
him violently. Morgan beheld a rider almost unhorsed
and heard an oath. For an instant only he saw the
man's face, white and malignant, and then it disappeared
in the darkness. To Montjoy's greeting, good-naturedly
hurled into the night, there came no reply.

"My wife's cousin," he said, laughing. "I am glad it
is not my horse he is riding to-night."

They came up in front of a large house with Corinth-
ian columns and many lights. There was a sudden movement of chairs upon the long veranda and then a young
woman came slowly down to the gate and lifted her
face to Montjoy's kiss. A pretty boy of five climbed
into his arms. Morgan stood silent, touched by the
scene. He started violently as Norton Montjoy, remembering his presence, called his name. The woman extended her hand.

"I am very glad to see you," she said, accenting the
adjective. Morgan, sensitive to fine impressions, did not
like the voice, although the courtesy was perfect.

They advanced to the porch. An old gentleman was
standing at the top of the steps. In the light streaming
from the hallway Morgan saw that he was tall and soldierly and with gray hair pressed back in great waves
from the temples. He put one arm around his son and
the other around his grandson, but did not remove his
eyes from the guest. While he addressed words of welcome and chiding to the former, he was slowly extending
his right hand, seeing which the son said, gaily:

"Mr. Morgan, father—a nephew of Col. John Morgan."
The light fell upon the half-turned face of the old gentleman and showed it lighted by a mild and benevolent
expression and a dawning smile.

"Indeed! Come in, Mr. Morgan, come in; I am glad
to see you."

The words were cordial and tone of voice perfect, but to Edward there seemed a shading of surprise in the prolonged gaze that rested upon him.

Norton had passed on to the further end of the porch, where an elderly lady sat upright, prevented from rising by a little girl asleep in her lap. There were sounds of repeated kisses as she embraced her overgrown boy, and then her voice:

"The Duchess tried to keep her eyes open for you, but she could not. Why are you so late?" Her voice was as the winds in the pines, and the hand she gave to Morgan a moment later was as cool as chamois and as soft.

A young girl had come to the doorway. She was simply dressed in white and her abundant hair was twisted into the Grecian knot that makes some women appear more womanly. She put her arms about the big brother and gave her little hand to Morgan. For a moment their eyes met, and then, gently disengaging her hand, she went to lean against her father's chair, softly stroking his white hair, while the conversation went round.

"Mary," said the older woman, presently, "Mr. Morgan and Norton have had a long ride and must be hungry."

"No," said the latter, checking the girl's sudden movement, "we have had something to eat in town."

"You should have waited, my son; it was a needless expense," said the mother, gently. "But I am afraid you will never practice economy." Norton laughed and did not dispute the proposition. The young mother and children disappeared, and Norton gave a spirited account of the quarantine incident without securing applause.

"I understand," said the colonel to his guest presently, when conversation had lulled, "that you are a nephew of John Morgan. I did not know that he had brothers or sisters——"

"I am not really a nephew," said Morgan, quietly, "but a distant relative and always taught to regard him as uncle." Something in his voice made the young girl lift her eyes. His figure in the half-light where he sat was immovable. Against the white column beyond, his head, graceful in its outlines, was sharply silhouetted.

It was bent slightly forward; and while they remained upon the porch, ever at the sound of his voice she would turn her eyes slowly and let them rest upon the speaker. But she was silent.

CHAPTER III.

A BREATH FROM THE OLD SOUTH.

The room in which Edward Morgan opened his eyes next morning was large and the ceiling low. The posts of the bed ran up to within a foot of the latter and supported a canopy. There was no carpet, the curtains were of chintz and the lambrequins evidently home made. The few pictures on the wall were portraits, in frames made of pine cones, with clusters of young cones at the corners. There were home-made brackets, full of swamp grasses. The bureau had two miniature Tuscan columns, between which was hung a swivel glass. All was homely but clean and suggestive of a woman's presence. And through the open windows there floated a delicious atmosphere, fresh, cool and odorous, with the bloom-breath of tree and shrub.

He stepped out of bed and looked forth. For a mile ran the great fields of cotton and corn, with here and there a cabin and its curl of smoke. A flock of pigeons were walking about the barn doors, and a number of goats waited at the side gate, which led into a broad back yard. In the distance he could see negroes in the fields, hear their songs and the "clank" of a little grist-mill in the valley.

But sweeping all other sounds from mind, he heard also another musical voice calling "Chick! chick! chickee, chickee!" and caught a glimpse of fowls hurrying from every direction toward the back yard. He plunged his head into a basin of cool water, and presently he was dressed.

The front door was open, as it had remained all night, the chairs on the porch, with here and there books and papers, when Edward Morgan walked out. The yard was spacious and full of plants. Sunflowers and poke-berries were growing along the front fence, and mocking birds, cardinals and jays, their animosities suspended, were breakfasting side by side. His walk carried him to the side of the house, and, looking across the low picket fence, he saw Mary. Her sleeves were rolled up above the elbows and her arms covered with dough from a great pan into which, from time to time, she thrust a hand. A multitude of ducks, chickens and turkeys and guineas scrambled about her, and a dozen white pigeons struggled for standing-room upon her shoulders.

"May I come in?" he called.

"If you can stand it, Mr. Morgan." There was not the slightest embarrassment; the brown eyes were frank and encouraging; he placed his hands upon the fence and leaped lightly over.

"What a family you have!" he said. She smiled, turn-ing her face to him as she scattered dough and gently pushed away the troublesome birds.

"Many birds' mouths to fill; and they will have to fill some mouths, too, one of these days, poor things."

"That is but fair."

"I suppose so; but what a mission in life—just to fill somebody's mouth."

"The mission of many poor men and women I have seen," he said, gravely, "is merely to fill mouths. And sometimes they get so poor they can't do that."

"And sometimes chickens get the same way," she said, sagely, at which both laughed outright. Her face resumed its placid expression almost instantly. "It must be sad to be very poor; how I wish they could arrange for all of the poor people to come out here and find homes; there seems to be so much land wasted."

"They would not stay long anywhere away from the city," he said; "but do you never sigh for city life?"

"I prefer it," she replied, simply, "but we cannot afford it. And there is no one to take care of this place. It is harder on Annie, brother's wife. She simply detests the country. When I graduated——"

2

"You graduated!" he exclaimed, almost incredulously. She looked at him surprised.

"Yes, I am young, seventeen this month, but that is not extraordinary. Mamma graduated at the same age, sixteen, forty years ago." A servant approached, spoon in hand.

"Want some more lard, missy." She took her bunch of keys, and selecting one that looked like the bastile memento at Mount Vernon, unlocked the smoke-house door and waited. "Half of that will do, Gincy," she said, never looking around as she talked with Morgan, and the woman returned half.

"Now," she continued to him, "I must go see about the milking."

"I will go, too, if you do not object! This is all new and enjoyable." They came to where the women were at work. As they stood looking on, a calf came up and stood by the girl's side, letting her rub its sensitive ears. A little kid approached, too, and bleated.

"Aunt Mollie," Mary asked, "has its mother come up yet?"

"No, ma'am. Spec' somep'n done cotch her!"

"See if he will drink some cow's milk—give me the cup." She offered him a little, and the hungry animal drank eagerly. "Let him stay in the yard until he gets large enough to feed himself." Then turning to Morgan, laughing, she said: "I expect you are hungry, too; I wonder why papa does not come."

"Is he up?"

"Oh, yes; he goes about early in the morning—there he comes now!" The soldierly form of the old man was seen out among the pines. "Bring in breakfast, Gincy," she called, and presently several negroes sped across the yard, carrying smoking dishes into the cool basement dining-room. Then the bell rung.

At the top of the stairway Morgan had an opportunity to better see his hostess. The lady was slender and moved with deliberation. Her gray hair was brushed down over her temples, and her faded face was brightened by eyes that seemed to swim with light and sympathy. The dress was a black silk, old in fashion and texture, but there was real lace at the throat and wrists, and a little lace headdress. She smiled upon the young man and gave him her plump hand as he offered to assist her.

"I hope you slept well," she said; "no ghosts! That part of the house you were in is said to be one hundred years old, and must be full of memories."

They stood for grace, and then Mary took her place behind the coffee pot and served the delicious beverage in thin cups of china. The meal consisted of broiled chicken, hot, light biscuits, bread of cornmeal, and eggs that Morgan thought delicious, corn cakes, bacon and fine butter. A little darky behind an enormous apron, but barefooted, stood by the coffee pot and with a great brush of the gorgeous peacock feathers kept the few flies off the tiny caster in the middle of the table, while his eyes followed the conversation around. Presently there was a clatter on the stairs and the little boy came down and climbed into his high chair. He was barefooted and evidently ready for breakfast, as he took a biscuit and bit it. The colonel looked severely at him.

"Put your biscuit down," he said, quietly but sternly, "and wait outside now until the others are through. You came in after grace and you have not said good-morning." The boy's countenance clouded and he began to pick at his knife handle; the grandmother said, gently:

"He'll not do it again, grandpa, and he is hungry, I know. Let him off this time." Grandpa assumed a very severe expression as he replied, promptly:

"Very well, madam; let him say grace and stay, under those circumstances." The company waited on him, he hesitated, swelled up as if about to cry and said, earnestly: "Gimme somep'n to eat, for the Lord's sake, amen." Grandma smiled benignly, but Mary and grandpa were convulsed. Then other footfalls were heard on the stairs outside, as if some one were coming down by placing the same foot in front each time. Presently in walked a blue-eyed, golden-haired, barefooted girl of three, who went straight to the colonel and held up her arms. He lifted her and pressed the little cheek to his.

"Ah," he said, "here comes the Duchess." He gave her

a plate next to his, and taking her fork she ate demurely, from time to time watching Morgan.

"Papa ain't up yet," volunteered the boy. "He told mamma to throw his clothes in the creek as he wouldn't have any more use for them—ain't going to get up any more."

"Mamma, does your eye hurt you?" said Mary, seeing the white hand for the second time raised to her face.

"A little. The same old pain."

"Mamma," she explained to Morgan, "has lost one eye by neuralgia. She still suffers dreadfully at times from the same trouble."

Presently the elder lady excused herself, the daughter watching her anxiously as she slowly disappeared.

It was nearly noon when Norton Montjoy and Edward Morgan reached the law office of Ellison Eldridge. As they entered Morgan saw a clean-shaven man of frank, open expression. Norton spoke:

"Judge, this is Mr. Edward Morgan—you have corresponded with him." Morgan felt the sudden penetrating look of the lawyer. Montjoy was already saying au revoir and hastening out, waving off Edward's thanks as he went.

"Will see you later," he called back from the stairway, "and don't forget your promise to the old folks."

"You got my letter, Mr. Morgan. Please be seated."

"Yes; three days since, in New York, through Fuller & Fuller. You have, I believe, the will of the late John Morgan."

"A copy of it. The will is already probated." He went to his safe and returned with a document and a bunch of keys. "Shall I read it to you?"

"If you please."

The lawyer read, after the usual recitation that begins such documents, as follows: "Do create, name and declare Edward Morgan of the city of New York my lawful heir to all property, real and personal, of which I may die possessed. And I hereby name as executor of this my last will and testament, Ellison Eldridge of —— state aforesaid, relieving said Ellison Eldridge of bond as executor and giving him full power to wind up my estate, pay all debts and settle with the heir as named, without the order of or returns to any court, and for his services in this connection a lien of $10,000 in his favor is hereby created upon said estate, to be paid in full when the residue of property is transferred to the said Edward Morgan," etc.

"The property, aside from Ilexhurst, his late home," continued Judge Eldridge, "consists of $630,000 in government bonds. These I have in a safety-deposit company. I see the amount surprises you."

"Yes," said the young man; "I am surprised by the amount." He gave himself up to thought for a few moments.

"The keys," said Eldridge, "he gave me a few days before his death, stating that they were for you only, and that the desk in his room at home, which they fitted, contained no property."

"You knew Mr. Morgan well, I presume?" said the young man.

"Yes, and no. I have seen him frequently for a great many years, but no man knew him intimately. He was eccentric, but a fine lawyer and a very able man. One day he came in here to execute this will and left it with me. He never referred to it again but once and that was when he came to bring your address and photograph."

"Was there—anything marked—or strange—in his life?"

"Nothing beyond what I have outlined. He was a bachelor, and beyond an occasional party to gentlemen in his house, when he spared no expense, and regular attendance upon the theater, he had few amusements. He inherited some money; the balance he accumulated in his practice and by speculation, I suppose. The amount is several times larger than I suspected. His one great vice was drink. He would get on his sprees two or three times a year, but always at home. There he would shut himself up and drink until his housekeeper called in the doctors." Morgan waited in silence; there was nothing else and he rose abruptly.

"Judge, we will wind up this matter in a few days. Here are your letters, and John Morgan's to me, and letters from Fuller & Fuller, who have known me for many years and have acted as agents for both Col. Morgan and myself. If more proof is desired——"

"These are sufficient. Your photograph is accurate. May I ask how you are related to Col. Morgan?"

"Distantly only. The fact is I am almost as near alone in the world as he was. I must have your advice touching other matters. I shall return, very likely, in the morning."

Upon the street Edward Morgan walked as in a dream. Strange to say, the information imparted to him had been depressing. He called a carriage.

"Take me out to John Morgan's," he said, briefly.

"De colonel's done dead, sah!"

"I know, but the house is still there, is it not?"

The driver conveyed the rebuke to his bony horse, in the shape of a sharp lash, and secured a reasonably fair gait. Once or twice he ventured observations upon the character of the deceased.

"Col. Morgan's never asked nobody 'how much' when dey drive 'im; he des fling down half er doller an' go long 'bout es business. Look to me, young marster, like you sorter got de Morgan's eye. Is you kinned to 'im?"

"I employed you to drive, not to talk," said Edward, sharply.

"Dere now, dat's des what Col. Morgan say!"

The negro gave vent to a little pacifying laugh and was silent. The shadow on the young man's face was almost black when he got out of the hack in front of the Morgan house and tossed the old negro a dollar.

"Oom-hoo!" said that worthy, significantly. "Oom-hoo! What I tole you?"

CHAPTER IV.

THE MOTHER'S ROOM.

The house before which Morgan stood overlooked the city two miles away and was the center of a vast estate now run to weeds. It was a fine example of the old style of southern architecture. The spacious roof, embattled, but unbroken by gable or tower, was supported in front by eight massive columns that were intended to be Ionic. The space between them and the house constituted the veranda, and opening from the center of the house upon this was a great doorway, flanked by windows. This arrangement was repeated in the story above, a balcony taking the place of the door. The veranda and columns were reproduced on both sides of the house, running back to two one-story wings. The house was of slight elevation and entered in front by six marble steps, flanked by carved newel posts and curved rails; the front grounds were a hundred yards wide and fifty deep, inclosed by a heavy railing of iron. These details came to him afterward; he did not even see at that time the magnolias and roses that grew in profusion, nor the once trim boxwood hedges and once active fountain. He sounded loudly upon the front door with the knocker.

At length a woman came around the wing room and approached him. She was middle-aged and wore a colored turban, a white apron hiding her dress. The face was that of an octoroon; her figure tall and full of dignity. She did not betray the mixed blood in speech or manner, but her form of address proclaimed her at once a servant. The voice was low and musical as she said, "Good-morning, sir," and waited.

Morgan studied her in silence a moment; his steady glance seemed to alarm her, for she drew back a step and placed her hand on the rail.

"I want to see the people who have charge of this house," said the young man. She now approached nearer and looked anxiously into his face.

"I have the care of it," she answered.

"Well," said he, "I am Edward Morgan, the new owner. Let me have the keys."

"Edward Morgan!" She repeated the name unconsciously.

"Come, my good woman, what is it? Where are the keys?" She bowed her head. "I will get them for you, sir." She went to the rear again, and presently the great doors swung apart and he entered.

The hallway was wide and opened through massive folding doors into the dining-room in the rear, and this dining-room, by means of other folding doors, entering the wing-rooms, could be enlarged into a princely salon. The hall floor was of marble and a heavy frieze and centerpiece decorated walls and ceiling. A gilt chandelier hung from the center. Antique oak chairs flanked this hallway, which boasted also a hatrack, with looking-glass six feet wide. A semicircular stairway led to apartments above, guarded by a carved oak rail, a newel post and a knight in armor. A musty odor pervaded the place.

"Open the house," said Edward; "I must have better air."

And while this was being done he passed through the rooms into which now streamed light and fresh air. On the right was parlor and guest chamber, the hangings and carpets unchanged in nearly half a century. On the left was a more cheerful living-room, with piano and a rack of yellow sheet music, and the library, with an enormous collection of books. There were also cane furniture, floor matting and easy-chairs.

In all these rooms spacious effects were not lessened by bric-a-brac and collections. A few portraits and landscapes, a candelabra or two of brass and glass, brass fire dogs, one or two large and exquisitely painted vases made up the ornamental features. The dining-room proper differed in that its furnishings were newer and more elaborate. The wing-rooms were evidently intended for cards and billiards. Behind was the southern back porch closed in with large green blinds. Over all was the chill of isolation and disuse.

Edward made his way upstairs among the sleeping apartments, full of old and clumsy furniture, the bedding having been removed. Two rooms only were of interest; to the right and rear a small apartment connected with the larger one in front by a door then locked. This small room seemed to have been a boy's. There were bows and arrows, an old muzzle-loading gun, a boat paddle, a dip net, stag horns, some stuffed birds and small animals, the latter sadly dilapidated, a few game pictures, boots, shoes and spurs—even toys. A small bed ready for occupancy stood in one corner and in another a little desk with drop lid. On the hearth were iron fire dogs and ashes, the latter holding fragments of charred paper.

For the first time since entering the house Edward felt a human presence; it was a bright sunny room opening to the western breeze and the berries of a friendly china tree tapped upon the window as he approached it. He placed his hand upon the knob of the door, leading forward, and tried to open it; it was locked.

"That," said the woman's low voice, "is Col. Morgan's mother's room, sir, and nobody ever goes in there. No one has entered that room but him since she died, I reckon more than forty years ago."

Edward had started violently; he turned to find the sad, changeless face of the octoroon at his side.

"And this room?"

"There is where he lived all his life—from the time he was a boy until he died."

Edward took from his pocket the bunch of keys and applied the largest to the lock of the unopened door; the bolt turned easily. As he crossed the threshold a thrill went through him; he seemed to trespass. Here had the boy grown up by his mother, here had been his retreat at all times. When she passed away it was the one spot that kept fresh the heart of the great criminal lawyer, who fought the outside world so fiercely and well. Edward had never known a mother's room, but the scene appealed to him, and for the first time he felt kinship with the man who preceded him, who was never anything but a boy here in these two rooms. Even when he lay dead, back there in that simple bed, over which many a night his mother must have leaned to press her kisses upon his brow, he was a boy grown old and lonely.

One day she had died in this front room! What an agony of grief must have torn the boy left behind! In the dim light of the room he had opened, objects began to appear; almost reverently Edward raised a window and pushed open the shutters. Behind him stood ready for occupancy a snowy bed, with pillows and linen as fresh seemingly as if placed there at morn. By the bedside was a pair of small worn slippers, a rocking chair stood by the east window, and by the chair was a little sewing stand, with a boy's jacket lying there, and threaded needle thrust into its texture. On the little center table was a well-worn bible by a small brass lamp, and a single painting hung upon the wall—that of a little farmhouse at the foot of a hill, with a girl in frock and poke bonnet swinging upon its gate.

There was no carpet on the floor; only two small rugs. It had been the home of a girl simply raised and grown to womanhood, and her simplicity had been repeated in her boy. The great house had been the design of her husband, but here in these two rooms mother and son found the charm of a bygone life delighting in those "vague feelings" which science cannot fathom, but which simpler minds accept as the whisperings of heredity.

One article only remained unexamined. It was a small picture in a frame that rested upon the mantel and in front of which was draped a velvet cloth. Morgan as in a dream drew aside the screen and saw the face of a wondrously beautiful girl, whose eyes rested pensively upon him. A low cry escaped the octoroon, who had noiselessly followed him; she was nodding her head and muttering, all unconscious of his presence. When she saw at length his face turned in wonder upon her she glided noiselessly from the room. He replaced the cloth, closed the window again and tiptoed out, locking the door behind him.

He found the octoroon downstairs upon the back steps. She was now calm and answered his questions clearly. She had not belonged to John Morgan, she said, but had always been a free woman. Her husband had been free, too, but had died early. She had come to keep house at Ilexhurst many years ago, before the war, and had been there always since, caring for everything while Mr. Morgan was in the army, and afterward, when he was away from time to time. No, she did not know anything of the girl in the picture; she had heard it said that he was once to have married a lady, but she married somebody else and that was the end of it. John Morgan had kept the room as it was. No, he was never married. He had no cousins or kinfolks that she had heard of except a sister who died, and her two sons had been killed in battle or lost at sea during the war. Neither of them was married; she was certain of that. She herself cooked and kept house, and Ben, a hired boy, attended to the rest and acted as butler.

Edward was recalled to the present by feeling her eyes fixed upon him. He caught but one fleeting glance at her face before it was averted; it had grown young, almost beautiful, and the eyes were moistened and tender and sad. He turned away abruptly.

"I will occupy an upper room to-night," he said, "and will send new furniture to-morrow." His baggage had come and he went back with the express to the city. He would return, he said, after supper.

Sometimes the mind, after a long strain imposed upon it, relieves itself by a refusal to consider. So with Edward Morgan's. That night he stood by his window and watched the lessening moon rise over the eastern hills. But he seemed to stand by a low picket fence beyond which a girl, with bare arms, was feeding poultry. He felt again the power of her frank, brown eyes as they rested upon him, and heard her voice, musical in the morning air, as it summoned her flock to breakfast.

In New York, Paris and Italy, and here and there in other lands, were a few who called him friend; it would be better to wind up his affairs and go to them. It did not seem possible that he could endure this new life. Already the buoyancy of youth was gone! His ties were all abroad.

Thoughts of Paris connected him with a favorite air. He went to his baggage and unpacked an old violin, and, sitting in the window, he played as a master hand had taught him and an innate genius impelled. It was Schubert's serenade, and as he played the room was no longer lonely; sympathy had brought him friends. It seemed to him that among them came a woman who laid her hand on his shoulder and smiled on him. Her face was hidden, but her touch was there, living and vibrant. On his cheek above the mellow instrument he felt his own tears begin to creep and then—silence. But as he stood calmer, looking down into the night, a movement in the shrubbery attracted him back to earth; he called aloud:

"Who is there?" A pause and the tall figure of the octoroon crossed the white walk.

"Rita," was the answer. "The gate was left open."

CHAPTER V.

THE STRANGER IN THE LIBRARY.

Edward was up early and abroad for exercise. Despite his gloom he had slept fairly well and had awakened but once. But that once! He could not rid himself of the memory of the little picture and it had served him a queer trick. He had simply found himself lying with open eyes and staring at the woman herself; it was the same face, but now anxious and harassed. He was not superstitious and this was clearly an illusion; he rubbed his eyes deliberately and looked again. The figure had disappeared. But the mind that entertains such fancies needs something—ozone and exercise, he thought; and so he covered the hills with his rapid pace and found himself an hour later in the city and with an appetite.

The day passed in the arrangement of those minor requirements when large estates descend to new owners. There was an accounting, an examination of securities, the passing of receipts and a consultation of records. Judge Eldridge gave him assistance everywhere, but there was no time for private and past histories. In passing he dropped in at Barksdale's office and left a card.

One of the distinctly marked features of the day was

his meeting with a lawyer, Amos Royson by name. This man held a druggist's claim of several hundred dollars against the estate of John Morgan for articles purchased by Rita Morgan, the charges made upon verbal authority from the deceased. John Morgan had been absent many months just previous to his death and the account had not been presented.

Edward was surprised to find, upon entering this office, that the lawyer was the man who had collided with Montjoy's horse the night before. Royson saluted him coldly but politely and produced the account already sworn to and ready for filing. It had been withheld at Eldridge's request. As Edward ran his eye over the list he saw that chemicals had been bought at wholesale, and with them had been sent one or two expensive articles belonging to a chemical laboratory. Just what use Rita Morgan might have for such things he could not imagine. He was about to say that he would inquire into the account when he saw that Royson, with a sardonic smile upon his face, was watching him. He had a distinct impression that a natural antipathy to the man was stirring within him; he was about to pay the account and rid himself of the necessity of any further dealings with the man, when, angered by the impudent, irritating manner, he decided otherwise.

"Have you ever shown this account to Rita Morgan?"

"Oh, yes!"

"And she pronounced it correct, I suppose?"

"She did not examine it; she said that you would pay it now that John Morgan is dead."

"If the account is a just charge upon the Morgan estate I certainly will," said Morgan, pocketing the written statement.

"I think after you examine into the matter it will be paid," said Royson, confidently. Edward thought long upon the man's manner and the circumstance, but could make nothing out of them. He would see Rita, and with that resolution he let the incident pass from his mind.

The shadows were falling when he returned to take his first meal in his new home. He descended to the dining-room to find it lighted by the fifty or more jets in the large gilt chandeliers. The apartment literally blazed with light. The sensation under the circumstances was agreeable, and in better spirits he took the single seat provided. Here, as afterward ascertained, had been the lawyer's one point of contact with the social world, and it was here that he had been accustomed, at intervals varying from weeks to years, to entertain his city acquaintances.

The room was not American but continental from its Louvre ceiling of white and gold to its niched half life-size statuary and pictures of fishing and hunting scenes in gilded frames. But the foreign effects ended in this room. Outside all else was American.

Edward was silently served by the butler and was pleased to find his dinner first class in every respect. Then came a box of choice cigars upon a silver tray.

Passing into the library, he seated himself by the reading light near the little side table where a leather chair had been placed, and sought diversion in the papers; but, alas, the European finds but little of home affairs in American papers outside the great cities. A speech in one parliament, a regatta, a horse race, a German-army review, a social sensation—these were all.

He turned from the papers; the truth is the one great overwhelming fact at that moment was that he, a wanderer all of his life, without family or parents, or knowledge of them, had suddenly been transplanted among a strange people and made the master of a household and a vast fortune. On this occasion, as ever since entering the house, he could not rid himself of a suggestion so indefinite as to belong to the region of subconsciousness that he was an interloper, an inferior, and that jealous, unseen eyes were watching him. The room seemed haunted by an unutterable protest. He was not aware then that this is a peculiarity of all old houses.

Something like an oppression seized upon him and he was wondering if this should continue, would it be possible for him to endure the situation long? Upstairs was the little desk, the keys to which he held, and in it information that would lay bare the secret of his life and reveal the mystery of years ago, which would give him the same chance for happiness that other men have. All that was left now for him to do was to ascend the stairs, open the desk and read. He had put it off until a quiet and convenient moment, and that time had come.

But what was contained in that desk? He remembered Hamlet and understood his doubts for the first time. It was the gravity of this doubt, the weight of the revelation to come that caused him to smoke on, cigar after cigar, in silence. It flashed upon him that it might be wiser to take his fortune and return to Europe as he was. But as he smoked his mind rejected its cowardly suggestion.

It was at this stage in his reverie that Edward Morgan received the severest shock of his life. Without having noticed any sound or movement, he presently became conscious that some one besides himself was in the room, and instantly almost his eyes rested on a man standing before the open bookcase. It was a figure, slender and tall, clad in light, well-worn trousers, and short smoking jacket. The face turned from him was lifted toward the shelves, and long black hair fell in shining masses upon his shoulders. The right hand extended upward, touching first one, then another of the volumes as it searched along the line, was white as paraffine and slender as a girl's, and a fold of linen, edged with lace, lay upon the wrists. All the other details of the figure were lost in shadow. While thus Edward sat, his brain whirling and eyes riveted upon the strange figure, the visitor paused in his search as if in doubt, turned his profile and listened, then faced about suddenly and the two men gazed into each other's eyes.

Edward had gained his first full view of the visitor's face. Had it been withdrawn from him in an instant he could at any time thereafter have reproduced it in every line, so vividly was it impressed upon his memory. It was new, and yet strangely, dimly, vaguely familiar! It was oval, pale and lighted by eyes with enormously distended pupils. It seemed to him that they were not mirrors at that moment, but scintillating lights burning within their cavities.

But the first effect, startling though it was, passed away immediately; nothing could have withstood the gentle pleading entreaty that lurked in all the face lines; an expression childish and girlish. The stranger gazed for a moment only on the man sitting bolt upright now in his chair, his hands clutching the arms, and then went quickly forward.

"You are Edward Morgan?" he said, encouragingly. "My uncle told me you would come some day." The deep, indrawn breath that had made the new master's figure rigid for the moment escaped back slowly between the parted lips. He was ashamed that he should have been so startled.

"Yes," he said, presently, "I am Edward Morgan. And you are——"

"Gerald Morgan. But I must say good-by now. I have a matter of utmost importance to conclude." He smiled again, returned to the shelves and this time without hesitation selected a volume and passed out toward the dining-room.

A faint odor of burning material attracted Edward's attention. He looked for his cigar; it lay upon the matting, in a circle as large as his hat. He must have sat there watching the door for fifteen minutes after the singular visitor had passed through. He stamped out the creeping circle of fire and rung the bell. The octoroon entered and stood waiting, her eyes cast down.

"A young man came here a few minutes since and went out through that door," said he, with difficulty suppressing his excitement; "who is he?"

She looked to him astonished.

"Why, that was Mr. Gerald, sir. Don't you know of him? Mr. Gerald Morgan?"

"Absolutely nothing! I have never seen him before nor heard of him—no mention of him has been made in my presence." The woman was clearly amazed.

"Is it possible! Your uncle never wrote you about Gerald Morgan—the lawyers have never told you?"

"No one has told me, I say; the man is as new to me as if he had dropped from the clouds."

She thought a moment. "He must have left papers——"

"Oh!" exclaimed Edward, starting suddenly; "I have not read the papers! I see! I see!"

"You will find it there," she said, relieved. "I thought you knew already. It did not occur to me to tell you about him, sir! We have grown used to not speaking of him. He never goes out anywhere now." Edward was puzzled and then an explanation flashed upon him.

"He is insane!" he exclaimed.

"Oh, no, sir! But he has always been delicate—not like other children; and then the medicine they gave him when he had the pains and was a baby—he has been obliged to keep it up. It is the morphine and opium, sir, that has changed him." Edward nodded his head; the explanation was sufficient.

"He has lived here a long time, I presume?"

"Yes, sir. He smokes and reads and paints and does many curious things, but he never goes out. Sometimes he walks about the place, but generally at night; and once or twice in the last ten years he has gone down-town, but it excites him too much and he is apt to die away."

"Die away?"

"Yes, sir; the attacks come on him at any time, and so we let him live on as he wants to and no one sees him. He cannot bear strangers, but he is not insane, sir. One trouble is, he knows more than his head can hold—he studies too much." She said this very tenderly and her voice trembled a little as she finished and turned her face away. The hands clasped under her apron could be seen to work nervously.

"You have not told me who he is."

"I do not know, sir," and then she added: "He was a baby when I came, and I have done my best by him." She did not meet his eyes. Her suffering and embarrassment touched Edward.

"I will read the papers," he said, gently; "they will tell me all." Taking this as a dismissal the woman withdrew.

CHAPTER VI.

"WHO SAYS THERE CAN BE A 'TOO LATE' FOR THE IMMORTAL MIND?"

Something like fear, a superstitious fear, arose in Edward's heart as he turned down the lid of the old-fashioned desk in the little room upstairs and saw the few papers pigeon-holed there with lawyer-like precision. On the top lay a long envelope sealed and bearing his name. His hand shook as he held it and studied the chirography. The moment was one to which he had looked forward for a lifetime and should contain the explanation of the singular mystery that had environed him from infancy.

As he held the letter, hesitating over the final act, his life passed in review as, it is said, do the lives of drowning persons. The thought that Edward Morgan was dying came in that connection. The orphan, the lonely college boy, the wandering youth, the bohemian of a dozen continental capitals, the musician and half-way metaphysicist and theosophist, the unformed man of an unformed age, was to die and lie out of memory in the past, and in the new sphere, one of quick, earnest, feverish action, the new man, was to spring armed, or hampered by—what? At that moment, by a strange revulsion, the life that he had worn so hardly, so bitterly, even its sadness seemed dear and beautiful. After all it had been a life of ease and many scenes. It had no responsibilities—now it would pass! He tore open the envelope impatiently and read:

"Edward Morgan—Sir: When this letter comes to your knowledge you will have been acquainted with the fact that my will has made you heir to all my property, without legacy or restriction. That document was made brief and simple, partly to avoid complications, and partly to conceal facts with which the public has no reasonable interest. I now, assured of your character in every particular, desire that you retain during the lifetime of Gerald Morgan the residence which has always been his home, providing for his wants and pleasures freely as I have done and leaving him undisturbed in the manner

of his life. I direct, further, that you extend the same
care and kindness to Rita Morgan, my housekeeper,
seeing that she is not disturbed in her home and the
manner of her life. My object is to guard the welfare
of the only people intimately connected with me by ties
of friendship and association, whom I have not already
provided for. Carrying out this intention, you will as
soon as possible, after coming into possession, take precautions looking to the future of Gerald Morgan and
Rita Morgan, my housekeeper, in the event of your own
death; and the plan to be selected in this connection I
leave to your own good sense and judgment, only suggesting as adviser for you Ellison Eldridge, one of the
few lawyers living whose heart is outside of his pocket-
book, and discretion perfect.

"John Morgan."

That was all.

The young man, dumbfounded, turned over the single
sheet of paper that contained the whole message, examined again the envelope, read and reread the communication, and finally laid it aside. Not one word of explanation of his own (Edward's) existence, no claim of
relationship, no message of sympathy, only the curt voice
of an eccentric old man echoing beyond the black wall
of mystery and already sunk into eternal silence. The
old life no longer seemed dear or beautiful. It returned
upon him with the dull weight of oppression he had
known so long. It was a bitter ending, a crushing, overwhelming disappointment.

But Edward Morgan had lost in his training the power
of giving way entirely to moods; he had wrestled with
them, but had never surrendered. Where another man,
sure of sympathy, would have fallen back upon it,
crushed, he smiled at length and lighted another cigar.
His mind reverted to the singular character whose last
expression lay upon the desk. His last act had been to
guard against the curious, and that had included the
beneficiary. He had succeeded in living a mystery, in
dying a mystery, and in covering up his past with a mystery.

"It was well done." Such was Edward's reflection spoken aloud. He recalled the lines: "I now, assured of your character in every particular." Every word in that laconic letter, as also every word in the few communications made to him in life by this man, meant something. What did these mean? "Assured" by whom? Who had spied upon his actions and kept watch over him to such an extent as would justify the sweeping confidences? But he knew that the testator had read him right. A faint wave of pleasure flushed his cheek and warmed his heart when he realized the full significance of this tribute to his true character. He no longer felt like an intruder.

And yet, "assured" by whom? And who was Gerald Morgan? Not a relative or he would have said so; he would have said "my nephew, Gerald Morgan." The same argument shut him (Edward) out. Why this suspicious absence of relationship terms?—and they, both of them, Morgans and heirs to his wealth?

Again he dragged the papers from the desk and ran them over. Manuscripts all, they contained detached accounts of widely separated people and incidents, and moreover they were clearly briefed. "A Dramatic Trial," "The Storm," "A Midnight Struggle," etc. They had no bearing upon his life; they were the unpublished literary remains of John Morgan.

Every paper lay exposed; the mine was exhausted. He again read the letter slowly, idly lifted each paper and returned all to the desk.

The cigar was out again; he tossed it from the window, locked the desk and passed into the mother's room. The action was without forethought, but his new philosophy had taught him the value of human actions as index fingers. What cause then had drawn him into that long-deserted room? As he reflected, his eyes rested upon the picture of the girl in the little frame on the mantel. He started back, amazed and overwhelmed. It was the face that had been turned to him in the library—the face of Gerald Morgan!

Edward was surprised to find himself standing by the open window when he had exhausted the train of thought that the recognition put in motion, and counting his heart-beats, ninety to the minute. By that curious power or weakness of certain minds his thoughts ran entirely from the matter in hand along the lines of a lecture his friend Virdow at Jena had delivered, the theory of which was that organic heart disease, unless fastened to its victim by inheritance, is always a mental result. If a mere thought or combination of thoughts could excite, a thought could depress. It was plain; he would write to Virdow confirming his theory.

Then he became conscious that the moon hung like a plate of silver in the vast sky space of the east and that her light was flashed back by many little points in the city beneath him—a gilt ball, a vane, a set of window glasses, and the dew-wet slates of a modern roof. One white spot was visible in the yard in front, white and pale as the moon when the vapor has not dispersed but set immovably. As he idly sought to unravel its little secret, it simply became a part of the shadow and invisible, but he felt that some one was looking up at him; and suddenly he saw the slender figure of a man pass, cross the gravel walk and vanish in the shrubbery on the left.

Edward did not cry out; he stood musing upon the fact, and lo, there came a glitter of rosy light along the horizon; the moon had vanished overhead, and sound arose in confused murmurs from the dull heaps of houses in the valley. He saw again at that moment, over the eastern hills, the face of a girl as she stood calling her pets, and felt her eyes upon him.

When he awoke that day he found the sun far beyond the zenith and lay revolving in his mind the events of the night; to his surprise much of the weight was gone and in its place an interest the like of which he had never before known. An object in life had suddenly been developed and instinctively he felt that the study of this new mystery would lead to a knowledge of himself and his past.

The first thing to be done was to again see the stranger who had invaded his library, and carry his investigation as far as this person would permit. This in mind, he dressed himself with care and descended into the dining-

room. In a few moments his breakfast was served. Upon
hearing his inquiry for Rita, Ben, the butler, retired and
presently the woman, grave, and after a few words quiet,
took his place.   Before speaking Edward noticed her
closely again. About fifty years of age, perhaps less, she
stood as erect and rigid as an Indian, her black hair without a kink.   There was an easy dignity in her attitude,
hardly the pose of a slave, or one who had been.   But
in her face was the sadness of personal suffering, and in
her voice a tone he had noticed at first, an echo of some
depressing experience, it seemed to him.

Where was Gerald's room? There! · He had not noticed the door; it led out from the dining-room. It was
the wing intended for billiards, but now the retreat of
her poor young master and had been all his life. He did
not like to be disturbed, but perhaps the circumstances
would make a difference.

Edward knocked on the door. Receiving no answer,
he opened it hesitatingly and looked in.   Then he entered.   Gerald greeted him with an encouraging smile
and closing the door behind him, he viewed the interior
with interest.   The walls were hung with pictures,
swords, guns, pistols and other weapons, and between
them on every available spot were books, books, books
and periodicals. In the far corner was a cabinet and by
it a blackboard. A broad center table held writing ma-
terials and manuscripts, and upon a long table by two
open windows were bottles of many colors and all the
queer paraphernalia of a chemical laboratory. Against the
opposite wall was a spacious divan, and seated upon it,
wrapped in a singular-looking dressing-gown, a fez upon
his head and smoking a chibouk as he read, was the
strange being for whom Edward searched.

"I was expecting you," the young man said; "where
have you been?" The naturalness of the words confused
the visitor for a moment. No seat had been offered him,
but he drew one near the divan.

"I suppose I may smoke?" he said, smiling, ignoring
the query, but the intent look of Gerald caused him to
add: "I slept late; how did you rest?"

"Do you know," said Gerald, his expression changing,

"strange as it may seem, I have seen you before, but where, where——" The long lashes dropped above the eyes; he shook his head sadly, "but where, no man may say."

"It hardly seems possible," said Edward, gravely. "I have never been here before, and you, I believe, have never been absent."

"So they say; so they say. Mere old-nurse talk! I have been to many places." Edward turned his head in sadness. Man or woman the person was crazy. He looked again; it was the face of the girl in the picture frame, grown older, with time and suffering.

"It is an odd room," he said, presently; "do you sleep here?"

Gerald nodded to the other door.

"Would you like to see? Enter."

To Edward's amazement he found himself in a conservatory, a glass house about forty by twenty feet, arranged for sliding curtains at sides and top. There was little to be seen besides a small bed and necessary furniture. But an easel stood near the center and on it a canvas ready for painting. In a corner was a large portfolio for drawings, closed.

"I cannot sleep unless I see the stars," said Gerald, joining him. "And there is an entrance to the grounds!" He threw open a glass door, exposing an oleander avenue. "This is my favorite walk." The scene seemed to strike him anew. He stood there lost in thought a moment and returned to his divan. Edward found him absorbed in a volume. He had studied him there long and keenly and reached a conclusion that would, he felt, be of value in his future associations with this eccentric mind; it was a mind reversed, living in abstract thought. Its visions of real life were only glimpses. Therefore, he reasoned, to keep company with such a mind, one must be prepared for its eccentricities and avoid discord.

It was a keen diagnosis and he acted upon it. He went about noiselessly examining the furnishings of the room without further speech. The young man was writing as he passed him. Looking over his shoulder, Edward read a few lines of what was evidently a thesis:

"The mind can therefore have no conscious memory. Memory being a function of the brain and physical structure, and mind being endowed with a capacity for wandering, it follows that it can bring back no record of its experience since no memory function went with it. It may, indeed, be true that the mind can itself be shaped and biased anew by its detached experiences, but who can ever read its history backward? Unless somewhere arises a mind brilliant enough to find the alphabet, to connect the mind's hidden storehouse with consciousness, the mystery of mind—life (that is, higher dream life)— must remain forever unread."

"It has been found," said Edward, as though Gerald had stated a proposition aloud.

"How? Where?" Gerald did not look up, but merely ceased writing a moment.

"Music is the connecting link. Music is the language of the mind. Vibration is the secret of creation and along its lines will all secrets be revealed." The book closed slowly in the reader's hands, his thesis slipped to the floor. He sat in deep thought. Then a light gleamed in his face and eyes.

"It is true," he said, with agitation, as he arose. "It is a great thought; a great discovery. I must learn music." He rang his bell violently; the door opened at once and Rita stood waiting. "Bring me musical instruments—what?" He turned impatiently to Edward. The latter shook his head.

"'Tis a lifetime study," he said, sadly, "and then—failure. No man has yet reached the end."

"I will reach it."

"It calls for labor day and night—for talent—for teachers."

"I will have all."

"It calls for youth, for a mind young and fresh and responsive. You are old in mind. It is too late."

"Too late! Too late! Never, never, never too late. Who says there can be a 'too late' for the immortal mind? I will begin! I will labor! I will succeed! If not in this life, then in the next, or the next; ay, at the foot of Buddha, if need be, I will press to read all to the strains of music. Oh, blind! Blind! Blind!" He strode about the room in an ecstasy of excitement.

"Prove to me it is too late here," shrieked the unhappy being, "and I will end this existence; will go back a thousand cycles, if necessary, carrying with me the impression of this truth, and begin, an infant, to lisp in numbers."

He had snatched a poniard from the wall and was gesticulating frantically. Edward was about to speak when he saw the enthusiast's eyes lose their frenzy and fix upon the woman's. He dropped the weapon and plunged face downward in despair among the pillows. Like a statue the woman stood gazing upon him.

"My violin," said Edward. She disappeared noiselessly.

CHAPTER VII.

"BACK! WOULD YOU MURDER HER?"

When Edward Morgan went to Europe from Columbia college it was in obedience to a mandate of John Morgan through the New York lawyers. He went, began there the life of a bohemian. Introduced by a chance acquaintance, he fell in first with the art circles of Paris, and, having a fancy and decided talent for painting, he betook himself seriously to study. But the same shadow, the same need of an overpowering motive, pursued him. With hope and ambition he might have become known to fame. As it was, his mind drifted into subtleties and the demon change came again. He closed his easel. Rome, Athens, Constantinople, the occident, all knew him, gave him brief welcome and quick farewells.

The years were passing; as he had gone from idleness to art, from art to history, and from history to archaeology by easy steps, so he passed now, successively to religion, to philosophy, and to its last broad exponent, theosophy.

The severity of this last creed fitted the crucifixion of his spirit. Its contemplation showed him vacancies in his education and so he went to Jena for additional study. This decision was reached mainly through the suggestion of a chance acquaintance named Abingdon, who had come into his life during his first summer on the continent. They met so often that the face of this man had become familiar, and one day, glad to hear his native tongue, he addressed him and was not repelled.

Abingdon gave to Edward Morgan his confidence; it was not important; a barrister in an English interior town, he crossed the channel annually for a ramble in the by-ways of Europe. It had been his unbroken habit for many years.

From this time the two men met often and journeyed much together, the elder seeming to find a pleasure in the gravity and earnestness of the young man, and he in turn a relief in the nervous, jerky lawyer, looking always through small, half-closed eyes and full of keen conceptions. And when apart, occasionally he would get a characteristic note from Abingdon and send a letter in reply. He had so much spare time.

This man had once surprised him with the remark:

"If I were twenty years younger I would go to Jena and study vibration. It is the greatest force of the universe. It is the secret of creation." The more Edward dwelt upon this remark, in connection with modern results and invention, the more he was struck with it. Why go to Jena to study vibrations was something that he could not fathom, nor in all probability could Abingdon. America was really the advanced line of discovery, but nevertheless he went, and with important results; and there in the old town, finding the new hobby so intimately connected with music, to which he was passionately devoted, he took up with renewed energy his neglected violin. With feverish toil he struggled along the border land of study and speculation, until he felt that there was nothing more possible for him—in Jena.

In Jena his solitary friend had been the eminent Virdow and to him he became an almost inseparable companion.

The confidence and speculations of Virdow, extending
far beyond the limits of a lecture stand, carried Edward
into dazzling fields. The intercourse extended through
the best part of several years. On leaving Jena he was
armed with a knowledge of the possibilities of the vast
field he had entered upon, with a knowledge of thorough
bass and harmony, and with a technique that might have
made him famous had he applied his knowledge. He
did not apply it!

His final stand had been Paris. Abingdon was there.
Abingdon had discovered a genius and carried Edward
to see him. He had been passing through an obscure
quarter when he was attracted by the singular pathos
of a violin played in a garret. To use his expression,
"the music glorified the miserable street." Everybody
there knew Benoni, the blind violinist. And to this man,
awed and silent, came Edward, a listener.

No words can express the meaning that lay in the
blind man's improvisations; only music could contain
them. And only one man in Paris could answer! When
having heard the heart language, the heart history and
cravings of the player expressed in the solitude of that
half-lighted garret, Edward took the antique instrument
and replied, the answer was overwhelming. The blind
man understood; he threw his arms about the player
and embraced him.

"Grand!" he cried. "A master plays, but it is incomplete; the final note has not come; the harmony died
where it should have become immortal!" And Edward
knew it.

From that meeting sprung a warm friendship, the
most complete that Morgan had ever known! It made
the old man comfortable, gained him better quarters and
broadened the horizon toward which his sun of life was
setting. It would go down with some of the colors of
its morning.

It became Edward's custom to take his old friend to
hear the best operas and concerts, and one night they
heard the immortal Cambia sing. It was a charity concert and her first appearance in many years.

When the idol of the older Paris came to the footlights

for the sixth time to bow her thanks for the ovation given her, she smiled and sung in German a love song, indescribable in its passion and tenderness. It was a burst of melody from the heart of some man, great one moment in his life at least. Edward found himself standing when the tumult ceased. Benoni had sunk from his chair to his knees and was but half-conscious. The excitement had partially paralyzed him. The lithe fingers of the left hand were dead. They would never again rest upon the strings of his great violin—the Cremona to which in sickness and poverty, although its sale would have enriched him, he clung with the faith and instinct of the artist.

There came the day when Edward was ready to depart to America. He went to say good-by, and this is what happened: The old man held Edward's hands long in silence, but his lips moved in prayer; then lifting the instrument, he placed it in the young man's arms.

"Take it," he said. "I may never meet you again. It is the one thing that I have been true to all my life. I will not leave it to the base and heartless." And so Edward, to please him, accepted the trust. He would return some day; many hours should the violin sing for the old man. As he stood he drew the bow and played one strain of Cambia's song and the blind man lifted his face in sudden excitement. As Edward paused he called the notes until it was complete. "Now again," he said, singing:

> "If thou couldst love me
> As I do love thee,
> Then wouldst thou come to me,
> Come to me.
> Never forsaking me,
> Never, oh, never
> Forsaking me.
> Oceans may roll between,
> Thine home and thee
> Love, if thou lovest me
> Lovest me,
> What care we, you and I?
> Through all eternity,
> I love thee, darling one,
> Love me; love me."

"You have found the secret," said Benoni; "the chords on the lower octaves make the song."

And so they had parted! The blind man to wait for the final summons; the young man to plunge into complications beyond his wildest dreams.

"A man," said Virdow once, "is a tribe made up of himself, his family and his friends." And this was the history in outline of the man to whom Rita Morgan handed the violin that fateful day when Gerald lay face down among the pillows of his divan.

Recognizing in the delicate and excitable organism before him the possibilities of emotion and imagination, Edward prepared to play. Without hesitation he drew the bow across the strings and began a solemn prelude to a choral. And as he played he noticed the heaving form before him grow still. Then Gerald lifted his face and gazed past the player, with an intensity of vision that deepened until he seemed in the grasp of some stupendous power or emotion. Edward played the recital; the story of Calvary, the crucifixion and the mourning women, and the march of soldiers. Finally there came the tumult of bursting storm and riven tombs. The climax of action occurred there; it was to die away into a movement fitted to the resurrection and the peaceful holiness of Christ's meeting with Mary. But before this latter movement began Gerald leaped upon the player with the quickness and fury of a tiger and by the suddenness of the onset nearly bore him to the floor. This mad assault was accompanied by a shriek of mingled fear and horror.

"Back—would you murder her?" By a great effort Edward freed himself and the endangered violin, and forced the assailant to the divan. The octoroon was kneeling by his side weeping.

"Leave him to me," she said. Stunned and inexpressibly shocked Edward withdrew. The grasp on his throat had been like steel! The marks remained.

"I have," he writes that night in a letter to Virdow, "heard you more than once express the hope that you would some day be able to visit America. Come now, at once! I have here entered upon a new life and need your help. Further, I believe I can help you."

After describing the circumstances already related, the letter continued: "The susceptibility of this mind to music I regard as one of the most startling experiences I have ever known, and it will afford you an opportunity for testing your theories under circumstances you can never hope for again. Let me say to you here that I am now convinced by some intuitive knowledge that the assault upon me was based upon a memory stirred by the sound of the violin; that vibration created anew in that delicate mind some picture that had been forgotten and brought back again painful emotions that were ungovernable. I cannot think but that is to have a bearing upon the concealed facts of my life; the discovery of which is my greatest object now, as in the past. And I cannot but believe that your advice and discretion will guide me in the treatment and care of this poor being, perhaps to the extent of effecting a radical change, and leave him a happier and a more rational being.

"Come to me, my friend, at once! I am troubled and perplexed. And do not be offended that I have inclosed exchange for an amount large enough to cover all expenses. I am now rich beyond the comprehension of your economical German mind, and surely I may be allowed, in the interests of science, of my ward and myself to spend from the abundant store. I look for you early. In the meantime, I will be careful in my experiments. Come at once! The mind has an independent memory and you can demonstrate it."

Edward knew that there was more in that concluding sentence than in the rest of the letter and exchange combined, and half-believing it, he stated it as a prophecy. He was preparing to retire, when it occurred to him that the strange occupant of the wing-room might need his attention. Something like affection had sprung up in his heart for the unfortunate being who, with chains heavier than his own, had missed the diversion of new scenes, the broadening, the soothing of great landscapes and boundless oceans. A pity moved him to descend and to knock at the door. There was no answer. He entered to find the apartment deserted, but the curtain was drawn from the doorway of the glass-room and he passed in. Upon the bed in the yellow light of the moon lay the slender figure of Gerald, one arm thrown around the disordered hair, the other hanging listless from his side.

He approached and bent above the bed. The face turned upward there seemed like wax in the oft-broken gloom. The sleeper had not stirred. It was the vibration of chords in harmony, then, that had moved him. Would it have power again? He hesitated a moment, then returned quickly to the wing-room and secured his instrument. Concealing himself he waited. It was but a moment.

The wind brought the branches of the nearest oleanders against the frail walls, and the play of lightning had become continuous. Then began in earnest the tumult of the vast sound waves as they met in the vapory caverns of the sky. The sleeper tossed restlessly upon his bed; he was stirred by a vague but unknown power; yet something was wanting.

At this moment Edward lifted his violin and, catching the storm note, wove a solemn strain into the diapason of the mighty organ of the sky. And as he played, as if by one motion, the sleeper stood alone in the middle of the room. Again Edward saw that frenzied stare fixed upon vacancy, but there was no furious leap of the agile limbs; by a powerful effort the struggling mind seemed to throw off a weight and the sleeper awoke.

The bow was now suspended; the music had ceased. Gerald rushed to his easel and, standing in a sea of electric flame, outlined with swift strokes a woman's face and form. She was struggling in the grasp of a man and her face was the face of the artist who worked. But such expression! Agony, horror, despair!

The figure of the man was not complete from the waist down; his face was concealed. Between them, as they contended, was a child's coffin in the arms of the woman. Overhead were the bare outlines of an arch.

The artist hesitated and added behind the group a

tree, whose branches seemed to lash the ground. And there memory failed; the crayon fell from his fingers; he stood listless by the canvas. Then with a cry he buried his face in his hands and wept.

As he stood thus, the visitor, awed but triumphant, glided through the door and disappeared in the wing-room. He knew that he had touched a hidden chord; that the picture on the canvas was born under the flash-light of memory! Was it brain or mind? Oh, for the wisdom of Virdow!

Sympathy moved him to return again to the glass-room. It was empty!

CHAPTER VIII.

ON THE BACK TRAIL.

Edward found himself next day feverish and mentally disturbed; but he felt new life in the early morning air. There was a vehicle available; a roomy buggy, after the fashion of those chosen by physicians, with covered tops to keep out the sun, and rubber aprons for the rain. And there was a good reliable horse, that had traveled the city road almost daily for ten years.

He finished his meal and started out. In the yard he found Gerald pale and with the distended pupils that betrayed his deadly habit. He was taking views with a camera and came forward with breathless interest.

"I am trying some experiments with photographs on the line of our conversation," he said. "If the mind pictures can be revived they must necessarily exist. Do they? The question with me now is, can any living substance retain a photographic impression? You understand, it seems that the brain can receive these impressions through certain senses, but the brain is transient; through a peculiar process of supply and waste it is always coming and going. If it is true that every atom of our physical bodies undergoes a change at least once in seven years, how can the impressions survive? I have here upon my plate the sensitivefied film of a fish's eye: I caught it this morning. I must establish, first, the proposition that a living substance can receive a photographic image; if I can make an impression remain upon this film I have gained a little point—a little one. But the fish should be alive. There are almost insuperable difficulties, you understand! The time will come when a new light will be made, so powerful, so penetrating as to illumine solids. Then, perhaps, will the brain be seen at work through the skull; then may its tiny impressions even be found and enlarged; then will the past give up its secrets. And the eye is not the brain." He looked away in perplexity. "If I only had brain substance, brain substance—a living brain!" He hurried away and Edward resumed his journey to the city, sad and thoughtful.

"It was not wise," he said, "it was not wise to start Gerald upon that line of thought. And yet why not as well one fancy as another?" He had no conception of the power of an idea in such a mind as Gerald's.

"You did not mention to me," he said an hour later, sitting in Eldridge's office, "that I would have a ward in charge out at Ilexhurst. You naturally supposed I knew it, did you not?"

"And you did not know it?" Eldridge looked at him in unaffected astonishment.

"Positively not until the day after I reached the house! I had never heard of Gerald Morgan. You can imagine my surprise, when he walked in upon me one night."

"You really astound me; but it is just like old Morgan —pardon me if I smile. Of all eccentrics he was the most consistent. Yes, you have a charge and a serious one. I am probably the only person in the city who knows something of Gerald, and my information is extremely limited. With an immense capacity for acquiring information, a remarkable memory and a keen analysis, the young man has never developed the slightest capacity for business. He received everything, but applied nothing. I was informed by his uncle, not long since, that there was no science exact or occult into which Gerald had not

4

delved at some time, but his mind seemed content with simply finding out."

"Gerald has been a most prodigious reader, devouring everything," continued the judge, "ancient and modern, within reach, knows literature and politics equally well, and is master of most languages to the point of being able to read them. I suppose his unfortunate habit—of course you know of that—is the obstacle now. For many years now, I believe, the young man has not been off the plantation, and only at long intervals was he ever absent from it. Ten or fifteen years ago he used to be seen occasionally in the city in search of a book, an instrument or something his impatience could not wait on."

"Ten or fifteen years ago! You knew him then before he was grown?"

"I have known him ever since his childhood!" An exclamation in spite of him escaped from Edward's lips, but he did not give Eldridge time to reflect upon it.

"Is his existence generally known?" asked he, in some confusion.

"Oh, well, the public knows of his existence. He is the skeleton in Morgan's closet, that is all."

"And who is he?" asked Edward, looking the lawyer straight into the eyes.

"That," said Eldridge, gravely, "is what I would ask of you." Edward was silent. He shook his head; it was an admission of ignorance, confirmed by his next question.

"Have you no theory, judge, to account for his existence under such circumstances?"

"Theory? Oh, no! The public and myself have always regarded him simply as a fact. His treatment by John Morgan was one of the few glimpses we got of the old man's rough, kind nature. But his own silence seemed to beg silence, and no one within my knowledge ever spoke with him upon the subject. It would have been very difficult," he concluded, with a smile. "For he was the most unapproachable man, in certain respects, that I ever met."

"You knew him well? May I ask if ever within your

knowledge there was any romance or tragedy in his earlier life?"

"I do not know nor have I ever heard of any tragedy in the life of your relative," said the lawyer, slowly; and then, after a pause: "It is known to men of my age, at least remembered by some, that late in life, or when about forty years old, he conceived a violent attachment for the daughter of a planter in this county and was, it is said, at one time engaged to her. The match was a sort of family arrangement and the girl very young. She was finishing her education at the north and was to have been married upon her return; but she never returned. She ran away to Europe with one of her teachers. The war came on and with it the blockade. No one has ever heard of her since. Her disappearance, her existence, was soon forgotten. I remember her because I, then a young lawyer, had been called occasionally to her father's house, where I met and was greatly impressed by her. But I am probably one of the few who have carried in mind her features. She was a beautiful and lovable young woman, but, without a mother's training, she had grown up self-willed and the result was as I have told you." Edward had risen and was walking the floor. He paused before the speaker.

"Judge Eldridge," he said, his voice a little unsteady, "I am going to ask you a question, which I trust you will be free to answer—will answer, and then forget." An expression of uneasiness dwelt on the lawyer's face, but he answered:

"Ask it; if I am free to answer, and can, I will."

"I will ask it straight," said Edward, resolutely: "Have you ever suspected that Gerald Morgan is the son of the young woman who went away?"

Eldridge's reply was simply a grave bow. He did not look up.

"You do not know that to be a fact?"

"I do not."

"What, then, is my duty?"

"To follow the directions left by your relative," said Eldridge, promptly.

Edward reflected a few moments over the lawyer's answer.

"I agree with you, but time may bring changes. May I ask what is your theory of this strange situation—as regards my ward?" He could not bring himself to betray the fact of his own mystery.

"I suppose," said Eldridge, slowly, "that if your guess is correct the adventure of the lady was an unfortunate one, and that, disowned at home, she made John Morgan the guardian of her boy. She, more than likely, is long since dead. It would have been entirely consistent with your uncle's character if, outraged in the beginning, he was forgiving and chivalrous in the end."

"But why was the silence never broken?"

"I do not know that it was never broken. I have nothing to go upon. I believe, however, that it never was. The explanations that suggest themselves to my mind are, first, a pledge of silence exacted from him, and he would have kept such a pledge under any circumstances. Second, a difficulty in proving the legitimacy of the boy. You will understand," he added, "that the matter is entirely supposititious. I would prefer to think that your uncle saw unhappiness for the boy in a change of guardianship, and unhappiness for the grandfather, and left the matter open. You know he died suddenly."

There was silence of a few moments and Eldridge added: "And yet it does seem that he would have left the old man something to settle the doubt which must have rested upon his mind; it is an awful thing to lose a daughter from sight and live out one's life in ignorance of her fate." And then, as Edward made no reply, "You found nothing whatever to explain the matter?"

"Nothing! In the desk, to which his note directed me, I found only a short letter of directions; one of which was that I should arrange with you to provide for Gerald's future in case of my death. The desk contained nothing else except some manuscripts—fragmentary narratives and descriptions, they seemed." Eldridge smiled.

"His one weakness," he said. Years ago John Morgan became impressed with the idea that he was fitted for literary work and began to write short stories for magazines, under a nom de plume. I was the only person who shared his secret and together we told many a good story of bench, bar and practice. Neither of us had much invention and our career—you see I claim a share—our career was limited to actual occurrences. When our stock of ammunition was used up we were bankrupt. But it was a success while it lasted. Mr. Morgan had a rapid, vivid style of presenting scenes; his stories were full of action and dramatic situations and made quite a hit. I did not know he had any writings left over. He used to say, though, as I remember now, speaking in the serio-comic way he often affected, that the great American novel, so long expected, lay in his desk in fragments. You have probably got among these.

"And by the way," continued the judge, impressively, "he was not far wrong in his estimate of the literary possibilities of this section. The peculiar institutions of the south, its wealth, its princely planters, and through all the tangle of love, romance, tragedy and family secrets. And what a background! The war, the freed slaves, the old regime—courtly, unchanged, impractical and helpless. Turgeneff wrote under such a situation in Russia, and called his powerful novel 'Fathers and Sons.' Mr. Morgan used to say that he was going to call his 'Sons and Fathers.' Hold to his fragments; he was a close observer, and if you have literary aspirations they will be suggestive." Edward shook his head.

"I have none, but I see the force of your outline. Now about Gerald; I trust you will think over the matter and let me know what your judgment suggests. I promised Mr. Montjoy to drop in at the club. I will say good-morning."

"No," said Eldridge, "it is my lunch hour and I will go with you."

Together they went to a business club and Edward was presented to a group of elderly men who were discussing politics over their glasses. Among them was Col. Montjoy, in town for a day, several capitalists, a planter or two, lawyers and physicians. They regarded the newcomer with interest and received him with perfect courtesy. "A grand man your relative was, Mr. Morgan, a grand man; perfect type, sir, of the southern gentleman! The community, sir, has met with an irreparable loss. I trust you will make your home here, sir. We need good men, sir; strong, brainy, energetic men, sir."

So said the central figure, Gen. Albert Evan.

"Montjoy, you remember cousin Sam Pope of the Fire-Eaters—died in the ditch at Marye's Heights near Cobb; perfect likeness of Mr. Morgan here; same face, same figure—pardon the personal allusion, Mr. Morgan, but your prototype was the bravest of the brave. You do each other honor in the resemblance, sir! Waiter, fill these glasses! Gentlemen," cried the general, "we will drink to the health of our young friend and the memory of Sam Pope. God bless them both."

Such was Edward's novel reception, and he would not have been human had he not flushed with pleasure. The conversation ran back gradually to its original channel.

"We have been congratulating Col. Montjoy, Mr. Morgan," said one of the party in explanation to Morgan, "upon the announcement of his candidacy for congress."

"Ah," said the latter, promptly bowing to the old gentleman, "let me express the hope that the result will be such as will enable me to congratulate the country. I stand ready, colonel, to lend my aid as far as possible, but I am hampered somewhat by not knowing my own politics yet. Are you on the democratic or republican ticket, colonel?"

This astonishing question silenced the conversation instantly and drew every eye upon him. But recovering from his shock, Col. Montjoy smiled amiably, and said:

"There is but one party in this state, sir—the democratic. I am a candidate for nomination, but nomination is election always with us." Then to the others present he added: "Mr. Morgan has lived abroad since he came of age—I am right, am I not, Mr. Morgan?"

"Quite so. And I may add," continued Edward, who was painfully conscious of having made a serious blunder, "that I have never lived in the south and know nothing of state politics." This would have been sufficient, but unfortunately Edward did not realize it. "I know, how-ever, that you have here a great problem and that the world is watching to see how you will handle the race question. I wish you success; the negro has my sym-pathy and I think that much can be safely allowed him in the settlement."

He remembered always thereafter the silence that fol-lowed this earnest remark, and he had cause to remem-ber it. He had touched the old south in its rawest point, and he was too new a citizen. Eldridge joined him in the walk back, but Edward let him talk for both. The direc-tion of his thoughts was indicated in the question he asked at parting.

"Judge Eldridge, did you purposely withhold the girl's name—my uncle's fiancee? If so, I will not ask it, but——"

"No, not purposely, but we handle names reluctantly in this country. She was Marion Evan, and you but re-cently met her father."

CHAPTER IX.

THE TRAGEDY IN THE STORM!

Edward returned to Ilexhurst that evening conscious of a mental uneasiness. He could not account for it ex-cept upon the hypothesis of unusual excitement. His mind had simply failed to react. And yet to his sensitive nature there was something more. Was it the conver-sation with Eldridge and the sudden dissipation of his error concerning Gerald, or did it date to the meeting in the club? There was a discord somewhere. He be-came conscious after awhile that he had failed to har-monize with his new acquaintances and that among these was Col. Montjoy. He seemed to feel an ache as though a cold wind blew upon his heart. If he had not made that unfortunate remark about the negro! He acquitted himself very readily, but he could not forget that terrible silence. "I have great sympathy for the negro," he had said. What he meant was that, secure in her power and intelligence, her courage and advancement, the south could safely concede much to the lower class. That is what he felt and believed, but he had not said it that way. He would say it to-morrow to Col. Montjoy and explain. Relief followed the resolution.

And then, sitting in the little room, which began to exert a strange power over him, he reviewed in mind the strange history of the people whose lives had begun to touch his. The man downstairs, sleeping off the effects of the drug, taken to dull a feverish brain that had all day struggled with new problems; what a life his was! Educated beyond the scope of any single university, Eldridge had said, and yet a child, less than a child! What romance, what tragedies behind those restless eyes! And sleeping down yonder by the river, in that eternal silence of the city of the dead, the old lawyer, a mystery living, a mystery dead! What a depth of love must have stirred the bosom of the man to endure in silence for so many years for the sake of a fickle girl! What forgiveness! Or was it revenge? This idea flashed upon Edward with the suddenness of an inspiration. Revenge! What a revenge! And the woman, was she living or dead? And if living, were her eyes to watch him, Edward Morgan, and his conduct? Where was the father and why was the grandfather ignorant or silent? Then he turned to his own problem. That was an old story. As he sat dreaming over these things his eyes fell upon the fragmentary manuscripts, and almost idly he began to read the briefs upon them.

One was inscribed, "The Storm," and it seemed to be the bulkiest. Opening it he began to read; before he knew it he was interested. The chapter read:

"Not a zephyr stirred the expectant elms. They lifted their arms against the starlit sky in shadowy tracery, and motionless as a forest of coral in the tideless depths of a southern sea.

"The cloud still rose.

"It was a cloud indeed. It stretched across the west, far into north and south, its base lost in the shadow, its upper line defined and advancing swiftly, surely, flanking the city and shutting out the stars with its mighty wings. Far down the west the lightning began to tear the mass, but still the spell of silence remained. When this strange hush is combined with terrific action, when the vast forces are so swift as to outrun sound, then, indeed, does the chill of fear leap forth.

"So came on the cloud. Now the city was half surrounded, its walls scaled. Half the stars were gone. Some of the flying battalions had even rushed past!

"But the elms stood changeless, immovable, asleep!

"Suddenly one vivid, crackling, tearing, deafening flash of intensest light split the gloom and the thunder leaped into the city! It awoke then! Every foundation trembled! Every tree dipped furiously. The winds burst in. What a tumult! They rushed down the parallel streets and alleys, these barbarians; they came by the intersecting ways! They fought each other frantically for the spoils of the city, struggling upward in equal conflict, carrying dust and leaves and debris. They were sucked down by the hollow squares, they wept and mourned, they sobbed about doorways, they sung and cheered among the chimneys and the trembling vanes. They twisted away great tree limbs and hurled them far out into the spaces which the lightning hollowed in the night! They drove every inhabitant indoors and tugged frantically at the city's defenses! They tore off shutters and lashed the housetops with the poor trees!

"The focus of the battle was the cathedral! It was the citadel! Here were wrath and frenzy and despair! The winds swept around and upward, with measureless force, and at times seemed to lift the great pile from its foundations. But it was the lashing trees that deceived the eye; it stood immovable, proud, strong, while the evil ones hurled their maledictions and screamed defiance at the very door of God's own heart.

"In vain. In a far up niche stood a weather-beaten saint—the warden. The hand of God upheld him and kept the citadel while unseen forces swung the great bell to voice his faith and trust amid the gloom!

"Then came the deluge, huge drops, bullets almost,

in fierceness, shivering each other until the street-lamps seemed set in driving fog through which the silvered missiles flashed horizontally—a storm traveling within a storm.

"But when the tempest weeps, its heart is gone. Hark! 'Tis the voice of the great organ; how grand, how noble, how triumphant! One burst of melody louder than the rest breaks through the storm and mingles with the thunder's roar.

"Look! A woman! She has come, whence God alone may know! She totters toward the cathedral; a step more and she is safe, but it is never taken! One other frightened life has sought the sanctuary. In the grasp of the tempest it has traveled with wide-spread wings; a great white sea bird, like a soul astray in the depths of passions. It falls into the eddy, struggles wearily toward the lights, whirls about the woman's head and sinks, gasping, dying at her feet. The God-pity rises within her, triumphing over fear and mortal anguish. She stands motionless a moment; she does not take the wanderer to her bosom, she cannot! The winds have stripped the cover from the burden in her arms! It is a child's coffin, pressed against her bosom. The moment of safety is gone! In the next a man, the seeming incarnation of the storm itself, springs upon her, tears the burden from her and disappears like a shadow within a shadow!

"Within the cathedral they are celebrating the birth of Christ. Without the elements repeat the scene when the veil of the temple was rended.

*   *   *   *

"The storm had passed. The lightning still blazed vividly, but silently now, and at each flash the scene stood forth an instant as though some mighty artist was making pictures with magnesium. A tall woman, who had crouched as one under the influence of an overpowering terror near the inner door, now crept to the outer, beneath the arch, and looked fearfully about. She went down the few steps to the pavement. Suddenly in the transient light a face looked up into hers, from her feet; a face that seemed not human. The features were convulsed, the eyes set. With a low cry the woman slipped her arms under the figure on the pavement, lifted it as though it were that of a child and disappeared in the night. The face that had looked up was as white as the lily at noon; the face bent in pity above it was dark as the leaves of that lily scattered upon the sod."

Edward read this and smiled, as he laid it aside, and continued with the other papers. They were brief sketches and memoranda of chapters; sometimes a single sentence upon a page, just as his friend De Maupassant used to jot them down one memorable summer when they had lingered together along the Riviera, but they had no connection with "The Storm" and the characters therein suggested. If they belonged to the same narrative the connections were gone.

Wearied at last he took up his violin and began to play. It is said that improvisers cannot but run back to the music they have written. "Calvary" was his masterpiece and soon he found himself lost in its harmonies. Then by easy steps there rose in memory, as he played, the storm and Gerald's sketch. He paused abruptly and sat with his bow idle upon the strings, for in his mind a link had formed between that sketch and the chapter he had just read. He had felt the story was true when he read it. The lawyer had said John Morgan wrote from life. Here was the first act of a drama in the life of a child, and the last, perhaps, in the life of a woman.

And that child under the influence of music had felt the storm scene flash upon his memory and had drawn it. The child was Gerald Morgan.

Edward laid aside the violin for a moment, went into the front room, threw open the shutters and loosened his cravat. Something seemed to suffocate him, as he struggled against the admission of this irresistible conclusion. Overwhelmed with the significance of the discovery, he exclaimed aloud: "It was an inherited memory."

But if the boy had been born under the circumstances set forth in the sketch, who was the man, and why should he have assaulted the woman who bore the child's coffin? And what was she doing abroad under such circumstances? The man and the woman's object was hidden perhaps forever. But not so the woman; the artist had given her features, and as for the other woman, the author had said she was dark. How curiously the testimony fitted in! There was in Gerald's mind picture no dark woman; only the girl with the coffin, the arch above and the faint outlines of bending trees!

CHAPTER X.

"GOD PITY ME! GOD PITY ME!"

Edward was sitting thus lost in the contemplation of the circumstances surrounding him, when by that subtle sense as yet not analyzed he felt the presence of another person in the room, and looked over his shoulder. Gerald was advancing toward him smiling mysteriously. Edward noticed his burning eyes and saw intense mental excitement gleaming beyond. The man's mood was different from any he had before revealed.

"So you have been out among the friends of your family," he said, with his queer smile. "How did you like them?" Edward was distinctly offended by the supercilious manner and impertinent question, but he remembered his ward's condition and resentment passed from him.

"Pleasant people, Gerald, but I am not gifted with the faculty of making friends easily. How come on your experiments?"

The visitor's expression changed. He looked about him guardedly. "They advance," he replied, in a whisper; "they advance!"

Whatever his motive for entering that room—a room unfamiliar to him, for his restless eyes had searched it over and over in the few minutes he had been in it—was forgotten in the enthusiasm of the scientist. "I have mapped out a course and am working toward it," he said; and then presently: "You remember that pictures can now be transmitted by electricity across great stretches of space and flashed upon a disk? So goes the scene from the convex surface of the eye along a thread-like nerve, so flashes the picture in the brain. But somewhere there it remains. How to prove it, to prove it, that is the question! Oh, for a brain, a brain to dissect!" He glared at Edward, who shuddered under the wildness of the eyes bent upon him. "But time enough for that; I must first ascertain if a picture can be imprinted upon any living substance by light, and remain. This I can do in another way."

"How?" Edward was fascinated.

"It is a great idea. The fish's eye will not do; it is itself a camera and the protecting film is impression-proof. It lacks the gelatine surface, but over some fish is spread the real gelatine—in fact, the very stuff that sensitive plates rely upon. In our lake is a great bass, that swims deep. I have caught them weighing ten and twelve pounds. They are pale, greenish white until exposed to the light, when they darken. If the combined action of the light and air did not actually destroy this gelatine, they would turn black. The back, which daily receives the downward ray direct, is as are the backs of most fishes, dark; it is a spoiled plate. But not so the sides. It is upon this fish I am preparing to make pictures."

"But how?" Gerald smiled and shook his head.

"Wait. It is too important to talk about in advance."

Edward regarded him long and thoughtfully and felt rising within him a greater sympathy. It was pitiful that such a mind should die in the embrace of a mere drug, dragged down to destruction by a habit. "Beyond the scope of any single university," but not beyond the slavery of a weed.

"I have been thinking, Gerald," he said, finally, fixing a steady gaze upon the restless eyes of his visitor, "that the day is near at hand when you must bring to your rescue the power of a great will."

Gerald listened, grew pale and remained silent. Presently he turned to the speaker.

"You know, then. Tell me what to do."

"You must cease the use of morphine and opium."

Gerald drew a deep breath and smiled good-naturedly.

"Oh, that is it," he said; "some one has told you that I am a victim of morphine and opium. Well, what would you think if I should tell you he is simply mistaken?"

His face was frank and unclouded. Edward gazed upon him, incredulous. After a moment's pause, during which Gerald enjoyed his astonishment, he continued:

"I was once a victim; there is no doubt of that; but now I am cured. It was a frightful struggle. A man who has not experienced it or witnessed it can form no conception of what it means to break away from habitual use of opium. Some day you may need it and my experience will help you. I began by cutting my customary allowance for a day in half, and day after day, week after week, I kept on cutting it in half until the time came when I could not divide it with a razor. Would you believe it, the habit was as strong in the end as in the beginning? I lay awake and thought of that little speck by the hours; I tossed and cried myself to sleep over it! I slept and wept myself awake. The only remedy for this and all habits is a mental victory. I made the fight—I won!

"I can never forget that day," and he smiled as he said it; "the day I found it impossible to divide the speck of opium; a breath would have blown it away, but I would have murdered the man who breathed upon it. I swallowed it; the touch of that atom is yet upon my tongue; I swallowed it and slept like a child; and then came the waking! For days I was a maniac—but it passed.

"I grew into a new life—a beautiful, peaceful world. It had been around me all the time, but I had forgotten how it looked; a blissful world! I was cured.

"Years have passed since that day, and no taste of the hateful drug has ever been upon my tongue. Not for all the gold in the universe, not for any secrets of science, not for a look back into the face of my mother," he cried, hoarsely, rising to his feet; "not for a smile from heaven would I lay hands upon that fiend again!"

He closed abruptly, his hand trembling, the perspiration beading his brow. His eyes fell and the woman Rita stood before them, a look of ineffable sadness and tenderness upon her face.

"Will you retire now, Master Gerald?" she said, gently. Without a word he turned and left the room. She was about to follow when Edward, excited and touched by the scene he had witnessed and full of his discoveries, stopped her with an imperious gesture.

For a moment he paced the room. Rita was motionless, awaiting with evident nervousness his pleasure. He came and stood before her, and, looking her steadily in the face, said, abruptly:

"Woman, what is the name of that young man, and what is mine?"

She drew back quickly and her lips parted in a gasp.

"My God!" he heard her whisper.

"I demand an answer! You carry the secret of one of us—probably both. Which is the son of Marion Evan?"

She sunk upon her knees and hid her face in her apron.

It was all true, then. Edward felt as though he himself would sink down beside her if the silence continued.

"Say it," he said, hoarsely; "say it!"

"As God is my judge," she answered, faintly, "I do not know."

"One is?"

"One is."

"And the other—who is he?"

"Mine." The answer was like a whisper from the pines wafted in through the open window. It was loud enough. Edward caught the chair for support. The world reeled about him. He suffocated.

Rita still knelt with covered head, but her trembling form betrayed the presence of the long-restrained emotions. He walked unsteadily to the mantel, and, drawing the cover from the little picture, went to the mirror and placed it again by his face. At length he said in despair:

"God pity me! God pity me!"

The woman arose then and took the picture and gazed long and earnestly upon it. A sob burst from her lips. Lifting it again to the level of the man's face, he watching her with a fascination he could not resist, she looked from one to the other.

"Enough!" he said, reading it aright.

Despair had settled over his own face. She handed back the little likeness, and, clasping her hands, stood in simple dignity awaiting his will. He noticed then, as he studied her countenance closely, the lines of suffering there; the infallible record that some faces carry, which, whether it stands for remorse, for patience, for pure, unbroken sorrow, is always a consecration.

"Master, it must have come some time," she said, at length, "but I have hoped it would not be through me." Her voice was just audible.

"Be seated," said Morgan. "If your story is true, and it may be so, you should not stand." He turned away from her and walked to the window; she was seeking for an opening to begin her story. He began for her:

"You crouched in a church door to avoid the storm; a woman seeking shelter there appeared just outside. She was attacked by a man and fell to the ground unconscious; you carried her off in your arms; her child was born soon after, and what then?"

Amazed she stared at him a moment in silence.

"And mine was born! The fright, the horror, the sickness! It was a terrible dream; a terrible dream! But a month afterward, I was here alone with two babies at my breast and the mother of one was gone. God help me, and help her! But in that time Master John says I lost the memory of my own child! Master Gerald I claimed, but his face was the face of Miss Marion, and he was white and delicate like her. And you, sir, were dark. And then I had never been a slave; John Morgan's father gave me my liberty when I was born. I lived with him until my marriage, then after my husband's death, which was just before this storm, they brought me here and I waited. She never came back. Master Gerald was sickly always and we kept him, but they sent you away. Master John thought it was best. And the years have passed quickly."

"And Gen. Evan—did he never know?"

"No, sir; I would not let them take Master Gerald, because I believed he was my child; and Master John, I suppose, would not believe in you. The families are proud; we let things rest as they were, thinking Miss Marion would come back some day. But she will not come now; she will not come!"

The miserable secret was out. After a long silence Edward lifted his head and said with deep emotion: "Then, in your opinion, I am your son?" She looked at him sadly and nodded.

"And in the opinion of John Morgan, Gerald is the son of Marion Evan?" She bowed.

"We have let it stand that way. But you should never have known! I do not think you were ever to have known." The painful silence that followed was broken by his question:

"Gerald's real name?"

"I do not know! I do not know! All that I do know I have told you!"

"And the child's coffin?" She pressed her hand to her forehead.

"It was a dream; I do not know!"

He gazed upon her with profound emotion and pity.

"You must be tired," he said, gently. "Think no more of these troubles to-night."

She turned and went away. He followed to the head of the stairs and waited until he heard her step in the hall below.

"Good-night," he had said, gravely. And from the shadowy depths below came back a faint, mournful echo of the word.

When Edward returned to the room he sat by the window and buried his face upon his arm. Hour after hour passed; the outer world slept. Had he been of the south, reared there and a sharer in its traditions, the secret would have died with him that night and its passing would have been signaled by a single pistol shot. But he was not of the south, in experience, association or education.

It was in the hush of midnight that he rose from his seat, took the picture and descended the steps. The wing-room was never locked; he entered. Through the drawn curtains of the glass-room he saw the form of Gerald lying in the moonlight upon his narrow bed. Placing the

5

picture beside the still, white face of the sleeper, he was shocked by the likeness. One glance was enough. He went back to his window again.

One, two, three, four o'clock from the distant church steeple.

How the solemn numbers have tolled above the sorrow-folds of the human heart and echoed in the dewless valleys of the mind, the depths to which we sink when hope is gone!

But with the dawn what shadows flee!

So came the dawn at last; the pale, tremulous glimmer on the eastern hills, the white light, the rosy flush and then in the splendor of fading mists the giant sun rolled up the sky.

A man stood pale and weary before the open window at Ilexhurst. "The odds are against me," he said, grimly, "but I feel a power within me stronger than evidence. I will match it against the word of this woman, though every circumstance strengthened that word. The voice of the Caucasian, not the voice of Ethiopia, speaks within me! The woman does not believe herself; the mother's instinct has been baffled, but not destroyed!"

And yet that fatal likeness—and the fatal absence of likeness!

And yet again, the patrician bearing, the aristocrat! Such was Gerald.

"We shall see," he said, between his teeth. "Wait until Virdow comes!"

Nevertheless, when, not having slept, he arose late in the day, he was almost overwhelmed with the memory of the revelation made to him, and the effect it must have upon his future.

At that moment there came into his mind the face of Mary.

CHAPTER XI.

IN THE CRIMSON MISTS OF SUNSET.

Edward left the house without any definite idea of how he would carry on the search for the truth of his own history, but his determination was complete. He did not enter the dining-room, but called for his buggy and drove direct to the city. He wished to see neither Rita nor Gerald until the tumult within him had been stilled. His mind was yet in a whirl when without previous resolution he turned his horse in the direction of "the Hall" and let it choose its gait. The sun was low when he drew up before the white-columned house and entered the yard. Mary stood in the doorway and smiled a welcome, but as he approached she looked into his face in alarm.

"You have been ill?" she said, with quick sympathy.

"Do I look it?" he asked; "I have not slept well. Perhaps that shows upon me. It is rather dreary work this getting acquainted." He tried to deceive her with a smile.

"How ungallant!" she exclaimed, "to say that to me, and so soon after we have become acquainted."

"We are old acquaintances, Miss Montjoy," he replied, with more earnestness than the occasion justified. "I knew you in Paris, in Rome, even in India—I have known you always." She blushed slightly and turned her face away as a lady appeared leading a little girl.

"Here is Mr. Morgan, Annie; you met him for a moment only, I believe."

The newcomer extended her hand languidly.

"Any one that Norton is so enthusiastic about," she said, without warmth, "must be worth meeting a second time."

Her small eyes rested upon the visitor an instant. Stunned as he had been by large misfortunes, he felt again the unpleasant impression of their first meeting. Whether it was the manner, the tone of voice, the glance or languid hand that slipped limply from his own, or all combined, he did not know; he did not care much at that time. The young woman placed the freed hand over the mouth of the child begging for a biscuit, and without looking down said:

"Mary, get this brat a biscuit, please. She will drive me distracted." Mary stooped and the Duchess leaped into her arms, happy at once. Edward followed them with his eyes until they reached the turn of the porch and Mary turned a moment to receive additional directions from the young mother. He knew, then, where he had first seen her. She was a little madonna in a roadside shrine in Sicily, distinct and different from all the madonnas of his acquaintance, in that she seemed to have stepped up direct from among the people who knelt there; a motherly little woman in touch with every home nestling in those hills. The young mother by him was watching him with curiosity.

"I have to thank you for a beautiful picture," he said.

"You are an artist, I suppose?"

"Yes; a dilettante. But the picture of a woman with her child in her arms appeals to most men; to none more than him who never knew a mother nor had a home." He stopped suddenly, the blood rushed to his face and brain, and he came near staggering. He had forgotten for the moment.

He recovered, to find the keen eyes of the woman studying him intently. Did she know, did she suspect? How this question would recur to him in all the years! He turned from her pale and angry. Fortunately, Mary returned at this moment, the little one contentedly munching upon its biscuit. The elder Mrs. Montjoy welcomed him with her motherly way, inquiring closely into his arrangements for comfort out at Ilexhurst. Who was caring for him? Rita! Well, that was fortunate; Rita was a good cook and good housekeeper, and a good nurse. He affected a careless interest and she continued:

"Yes, Rita lived for years near here. She was a free woman and as a professional nurse accumulated quite a sum of money. And then, her husband dying, John Morgan had taken her to his house to look after a young relative who had been left to his care. What has become of this young person?" she asked. "I have not heard of him for many years."

"He is still there," said Edward, briefly.

And then, as they were silent, he continued: "This woman Rita had a husband; how did they manage in old times? Was he free also? You see, since I have become a citizen your institutions have a deal of interest for me. It must have been inconvenient to be free and have some one else owning the husband."

He was not satisfied with the effort; he could not restrain an inclination to look toward the younger Mrs. Montjoy. She was leaning back in her chair, with eyes half-closed, and smiling upon him. He could have strangled her cheerfully. The elder lady's voice recalled him.

"Her husband was free also; that is, it was thought that she had bought him," and she smiled over the idea.

A slanting sunbeam came through the window; they were now in the sitting-room and Mary quickly adjusted the shade to shield her mother's face.

"Mamma is still having trouble with her eyes," she said; "we cannot afford to let her strain the sound one."

"My eyes do pain me a great deal," the elder Mrs. Montjoy said. "Did you ever have neuralgia, Mr. Morgan? Sometimes I think it is not neuralgia. I must have Dr. Campbell down to look at my eyes. I am afraid——" she did not complete the sentence, but the quick sympathy of the man helped him to read her silence aright. Mary caught her breath nervously.

"Mary, take me to my room; I think I will lie down until tea. Mr. Morgan will be glad to walk some, I am sure; take him down to the mill." She gave that gentleman her hand again; a hand that seemed to him eloquent with gentleness. "Good-night, if I do not see you again," she said. "I do not go to the table now on account of the lamp." He felt a lump in his throat and an almost irresistible desire to throw himself upon her sympathy. She would understand. But the next instant the idea of such a thing filled him with horror. It would banish him forever from the portals of that proud home.

And ought he not to banish himself? He trembled over

the mental question. No! His courage returned. There
had been some horrible mistake! Not until the light of
day shone on the indisputable fact, not until proof irresistible had said: "You are base-born! Depart!" When
that hour came he would depart! He saw Mary waiting
for him at the door; the young mother was still watching
him, he thought. He bowed and strode from the room.

"What is it?" said the girl, quickly; "you seem excited."
She was already learning to read him.

"Do I? Well, let me see; I am not accustomed to
ladies' society," he said, lightly; "so much beauty and
graciousness have overwhelmed me." He was outside
now and the fresh breeze revived him instantly.

There was a sun setting before them that lent a glow to
the girl's face and a new light to her eyes. He saw it
there first and then in the skies. Across a gentle slope
of land that came down from a mile away on the opposite
side into their valley the sun had gone behind a shower.
Out on one side a fiery cloud floated like a ship afire, and
behind it were the lilac highlands of the sky. The scene
brought with it a strange solemnity. It held the last
breath of the dying day.

The man and girl stood silent for a moment, contemplating the wonderful vision. She looked into his face
presently to find him sadly and intently watching her.
Wondering, she led the way downhill to where a little
boat lay with its bow upon the grassy sward which ran
into the clear water. Taking one seat, she motioned
him to the other.

"We have given you a Venetian water-color sunset,"
she said, smiling away her embarrassment, "and now for
a gondola ride." Lightly and skillfully plying the paddle
the little craft glided out upon the lake, and presently,
poising the blade she said, gayly:

"Look down into the reflection, and then look up!
Tell me, do you float upon the lake or in the cloudy regions of heaven?" He followed her directions. Then,
looking steadily at her, he said, gently:

"In heaven!" She bent over the boat side until her face
was concealed, letting her hand cool in the crimson water.

"Mr. Morgan," she said after awhile, looking up from

under her lashes, "are you a very earnest man? I do not think I know just how to take you. I am afraid I am too matter-of-fact."

He was feverish and still weighed down by his terrible memory. "I am earnest now, whatever I may have been," he said, softly, "and believe me, Miss Montjoy, something tells me that I will never be less than earnest with you."

She did not reply at once, but looked off into the cloud-lands.

"You have traveled much?" she said at length, to break the awkward silence.

"I suppose so. I have never had what I could call a home and I have moved about a great deal. Men of my acquaintance," he continued, musingly, "have been ambitious in every line; I have watched them in wonder. Most of them sacrificed what it has been my greatest pleasure to possess—mother and sister and home. I cannot understand that phase of life; I suppose I never will."

"Then you have never known a mother?"

"Never." There was something in his voice that touched her deeply.

"To miss a mother's affection," she said, with a holy light in her brown eyes, "is to miss the greatest gift heaven can bestow here. I suppose a wife somehow takes a mother's place, finally, with every man, but she cannot fill it. No woman that ever lived can fill my mother's place."

Loyal little Mary! He fancied that as she thought upon her own remark her sensitive lips curved slightly. His mind reverted to the sinister face they had left in the parlor.

"Your mother!" he exclaimed, fervently; "would to heaven I had such a mother!" He paused, overcome with emotion. She looked upon him with swimming eyes.

"You must come often, then," she said, softly, "and be much with us. I will share her with you. Poor mamma! I am afraid—I am afraid for her!" She covered her face with her hands suddenly and bowed her head.

"Is she ill, so ill as all that?" he asked, greatly concerned.

"Oh, no! That is, her eyesight is failing; she does not realize it, but Dr. Campbell has warned us to be careful."

"What is the trouble?" He was now deeply distressed.

"Glaucoma. The little nerve that leads from the cornea to the brain finally dies away; there is no connection, and then——" she could not conclude the sentence.

Edward had never before been brought within the influence of such a circle. Her words thrilled him beyond expression. He waited a little while and said:

"I cannot tell you how much my short experience here has been to me. The little touch of motherly interest, of home, has brought me more genuine pleasure than I thought the world held for me. You said just now that you would share the dear little mamma with me. I accept the generous offer. And now you must share the care of the little mamma with me. Do not be offended, but I know that the war has upset your revenues here in the south, and that the new order of business has not reached a paying basis. By no act of mine I am independent; I have few responsibilities. Why may not I, why may not you and I take the little mamma to Paris and let the best skill in the world be invoked to save her from sorrow?" He, too, would not, after her failure, say "blindness."

She looked at him through tears that threatened to get beyond control, afraid to trust her voice.

"You have not answered me," he said, gently. She shook her head.

"I cannot. I can never answer you as I would. But it cannot be, it cannot be! If that course were necessary, we would have gone long ago, for, while we are poor, Norton could have arranged it—he can arrange anything. But Dr. Campbell, you know, is famous for his skill. He has even been called to Europe in consultation. He says there is no cure, but care of the general health may avert the blow all her life. And so we watch and wait."

"Still," he urged, "there may be a mistake. And the sea voyage——"

She shook her head. "You are very, very kind, but it cannot be."

It flashed over Edward then what that journey would

have been. He, with that sweet-faced girl, the little madonna of his memory, and the patient mother! In his mind came back all the old familiar places; by his side stood this girl, her hand upon his arm, her eyes upturned to his.

And why not! A thrill ran through his heart; he could take his wife and her mother to Paris! He started violently and leaned forward in the boat, his glowing face turned full upon her, with an expression in it that startled her.

Then from it the color died away; a ghastly look overspread it. He murmured aloud:

"God be merciful! It cannot be." She smiled pitifully.

"No," she said, "it cannot be. But God is merciful. We trust Him. He will order all things for the best!" Seeing his agitation she continued: "Don't let it distress you so, Mr. Morgan. It may all come out happily. See, the skies are quite clear now; the clouds all gone! I take it as a happy augury!"

Ashamed to profit by her reading of his feelings, he made a desperate effort to respond to her new mood. She saw the struggle and aided him. But in that hour the heart of Mary Montjoy went out for all eternity to the man before her. Change, disaster, calumny, misfortune, would never shake her faith and belief in him. He had lost in the struggle of the preceding night, but here he had won that which death only could end, and perhaps not death.

Slowly they ascended the hill together, both silent and thoughtful. He took her little hand to help her up the terraces, and, forgetting, held it until, at the gate, she suddenly withdrew it in confusion and gazed at him with startled eyes.

The tall, soldierly form of the colonel, her father, stood at the top of the steps.

"See," said Edward, to relieve her confusion, "one of the old knights guarding the castle!"

And then she called out, gayly:

"Sir knight, I bring you a prisoner." The old gentleman laughed and entered into the pleasantry.

"Well, he might have surrendered to a less fair captor! Enter, prisoner, and proclaim your colors." Edward started, but recovered, and, looking up boldly, said:

"An honorable knight errant, but unknown until his vow is fulfilled." They both applauded and the supper bell rang.

CHAPTER XII.

THE OLD SOUTH VERSUS THE NEW.

Edward had intended returning to Ilexhurst after tea, but every one inveighed against the announcement. Nonsense! The roads were bad, a storm was possible, the way unfamiliar to him! John, the stable boy, had reported a shoe lost from the horse! And besides, Norton would come out and be disappointed at having missed him! And why go? Was the room upstairs not comfortable? He should have another! Was the breakfast hour too early? His breakfast should be sent to his room!

Edward was in confusion. It was his first collision with the genuine, unanswerable southern hospitality that survives the wreck of all things. He hesitated and explained and explaining yielded.

Supper over, the two gentlemen sat upon the veranda, a cool breeze wandering in from the western rain area and rendering the evening comfortable. Mary brought a great jar of delicious tobacco, home raised, and a dozen corn-cob pipes, and was soon happy in their evident comfort. As she held the lighter over Edward's pipe he ventured one glance upward into her face, and was rewarded with a rare, mysterious smile. It was a picture that clung to him for many years; the girlish face and tender brown eyes in the yellow glare of the flame, the little hand lifted in his service. It was the last view of her that night, for the southern girl, out of the cities, is an early retirer.

"The situation is somewhat strained," said the colonel;

they had reached politics; "there is a younger set coming on who seem to desire only to destroy all the old order of things. They have had the 'new south' dinged into their ears until they have come to believe that the old south holds nothing worth retaining. They are full of railroad schemes to rob the people and make highways for tramps; of new towns and booms, of colonization schemes, to bring paupers into the state and inject the socialistic element of which the north and west are heartily tired. They want to do away with cotton and plant the land in peaches, plums, grapes," here he laughed softly, "and they want to give the nigger a wheeled plow to ride on. It looks as if the whole newspaper fraternity have gone crazy upon what they call intensive and diversified farming. Not one of them has ever told me what there is can be planted that will sell at all times upon the market and pay labor and store accounts in the fall.

"And now they have started in this county the 'no-fence' idea and are about to destroy our cattle ranges," continued the colonel, excitedly. "In addition to these, the farmers have some of them been led off into a 'populist' scheme, which in its last analysis means that the government shall destroy corporations and pension farmers. In national politics we have, besides, the silver question and the tariff, and a large element in the state is ripe for republicanism!"

"That is the party of the north, I believe," said Edward.

"Yes, the party that freed the negro and placed the ballot in his hands. We are so situated here that practically our whole issue is 'white against black.' We cannot afford to split on any question. We are obliged to keep the south solid even at the expense of development and prosperity. The south holds the Saxon blood in trust. Regardless of law, of constitution, of both combined, we say it is her duty to keep the blood of the race pure and uncontaminated. I am not prepared to say that it has been done with entire success; two races cannot exist side by side distinct. But the Spaniards kept their blue blood through centuries!

"The southern families will always be pure in this respect; they are tenderly guarded," the colonel went on.

"Other sections are in danger. The white negro goes away or is sent away; he is unknown; he is changed and finds a foothold somewhere. Then some day a family finds in its folds a child with a dark streak down its spine—have you dropped your pipe? The cobs really furnish our best smokers, but they are hard to manage. Try another—and it was known that somewhere back in the past an African taint has crept in."

"You astound me," said Edward, huskily; "is that an infallible sign?"

"Infallible, or, rather, indisputable if it exists. But its existence under all circumstances is not assured."

"And what, Col. Montjoy, is the issue between you and Mr. Swearingen—I understand that is his name—your opponent in the campaign for nomination?"

"Well, it is hard to say. He has been in congress several terms and thinks now he sees a change of sentiment. He has made bids for the younger and dissatisfied vote. I think you may call it the old south versus the new—and I stand for the old south."

"Where does your campaign open? I was in England once during a political campaign, about my only experience, if you except one or two incipient riots in Paris, and I would be glad to see a campaign in Georgia."

"We open in Bingham. I am to speak there day after to-morrow and will be pleased to have you go with us. A little party will proceed by private conveyance from here—and Norton is probably detained in town to-night by this matter. The county convention meets that day and it has been agreed that Swearingen and I shall speak in the morning. The convention will assemble at noon and make a nomination. In most counties primary elections are held."

"I shall probably not be able to go, but this county will afford me the opportunity I desire. By the way, colonel, your friends will have many expenses in this campaign, will they not? I trust you will number me among them and not hesitate to call upon me for my share of the necessary fund. I am a stranger, so to speak, but I represent John Morgan until I can get my political bearings accurately adjusted." The colonel was charmed.

"Spoken like John himself!" he said. "We are proud, sir, to claim you as one of us. As to the expense, unfortunately, we have to rely on our friends. But for the war, I could have borne it all; now my circumstances are such that I doubt sometimes if I should in perfect honor have accepted a nomination. It was forced on me, however. My friends named me, published the announcement and adjourned. Before heaven, I have no pleasure in it! I have lived here since childhood, barring a term or two in congress before the war and four years with Lee and Johnston, and my people were here before me. I would be glad to end my days here and live out the intervening ones in sight of this porch. But a man owes everything to his country."

He did not comment upon the information; at that moment there was heard the rumble of wheels. Norton, accompanied by a stranger, alighted from a buggy and came rapidly up the walk. The colonel welcomed his son with the usual affection and the stranger was introduced as Mr. Robley of an adjoining county. The men fell to talking with suppressed excitement over the political situation and the climax of it was that Robley, a keen manager, revealed that he had come for $1,000 to secure the county. He had but finished his information, when Norton broke in hurriedly:

"We know, father, that this is all outside your style of politics, and I have told Mr. Robley that we cannot go into any bargain and sale schemes, or anything that looks that way. We will pay our share of legitimate expenses, printing, bands, refreshments and carriage hire, and will not inquire too closely into rates, but that is as far——"

"You are right, my son! If I am nominated it must be upon the ballots of my friends. I shall not turn a hand except to lessen their necessary expenses and to put our announcements before the public. I am sure that this is all that Mr. Robley would consent to."

"Why, of course," said that gentleman. And then he looked helpless. Edward had risen and was pacing the veranda, ready to withdraw from hearing if the conversation became confidential. Norton was excitedly explaining the condition of affairs in Robley's county, and that gentleman found himself at leisure. Passing him Edward attracted his attention.

"You smoke, Mr. Robley?" He offered a cigar and nodded toward the far end of the veranda. "I think you had better let Mr. Montjoy explain matters to his father," he said. Robley joined him.

"How much do you need?" said Edward; "the outside figure, I mean. In other words, if we wanted to buy the county and be certain of getting it, how much would it take?"

"Twenty-five hundred—well, $3,000."

"Let the matter drop here, you understand? Col. Montjoy is not in the trade. I am acting upon my own responsibility. Call on me in town to-morrow; I will put up the money. Now, not a word. We will go back." They strolled forward and the discussion of the situation went on. Robley grew hopeful and as they parted for the night whispered a few words to Norton. As the latter carried the lamp to Edward's door, he said:

"What does this all mean; you and Robley——"

"Simply," said Edward, "that I am in my first political campaign and to win at any cost."

Norton looked at him in amazement and then laughed aloud.

"You roll high! We will win if you don't fail us."

"Then you will win." They shook hands and parted. Norton, passing his sister's room, paused in thought knocked lightly, and getting no reply, went to bed. Edward turned in, not to sleep. His mind in the silent hours rehearsed its horrors. He arose at the sound of the first bell and left for the city, not waiting for breakfast.

CHAPTER XIII.

FEELING THE ENEMY.

Edward Morgan plunged into the campaign with an energy and earnestness that charmed the younger Montjoy and astonished the elder. Headquarters were opened, typewriters engaged, lists of prominent men and party leaders obtained and letters written. Col. Montjoy was averse to writing to his many personal friends in the district anything more than a formal announcement of his candidacy over his own signature.

"That is all right, father, but if you intend to stick to that idea the way to avoid defeat is to come down now." But the old gentleman continued to use his own form of letter. It read:

"My Dear Sir: I beg leave to call your attention to my announcement in the Journal of this city, under date of July 15, wherein, in response to the demands of friends, I have consented to the use of my name in the nomination for congressman to represent this district. With great respect, I am, sir, your obedient servant,
                    "Norton L. Montjoy."

He dictated this letter, gave the list to the typewriter, and announced that when the letters were ready he would sign them. The son looked at him quizzically:

"Don't trouble about that, father. You must leave this office work to us. I can sign your name better than you can. If you will get out and see the gentlemen about the cotton warehouses you can help us wonderfully. You can handle them better than anybody in the world." The colonel smiled indulgently on his son and went off. He was proud of the success and genius of his one boy, when not grieved at his departure from the old-school dignity. And then Norton sat down and began to dictate the correspondence, with the list to guide him.

"Dear Jim," he began, selecting a well-known friend of his father, and a companion in arms. "You have prob-

ably noticed in the Journal the announcement of my candidacy for the congressional nomination. The boys of
the old 'Fire-Eaters' did eat. I am counting on you;
you stood by me at Seven Pines, Fredericksburg, Chan-
cellorsville and a dozen other tight places, and I have no
fear but that your old colonel will find you with him in this
issue. It is the old south against the riffraff combination
of carpetbaggers, scalawags and jaybirds who are trying
to betray us into the hands of the enemy! My opponent,
Swearingen, is a good man in his way, but in devilish
bad company. See Lamar of Company C, Sims, Ellis,
Smith and all the old guard. Tell them I am making the
stand of my life! My best respects to the madam and the
grandchildren! God bless you. Do the best you can.
Yours fraternally,　　　　　　　　N. L. Montjoy."

"P. S. Arrange for me to speak at your court house
some day soon. Get an early convention called. We
fight better on a charge—old Stonewall's way.
　　　　　　　　　　　　　　　　　"N. L. M."

This letter brought down the house; the house in this
instance standing for a small army of committeemen
gathered at headquarters. Norton was encouraged to try
again.

"The Rev. Andrew Paton, D. D.—Dear Andrew: I
am out for congress and need you. Of course we can't
permit you to take your sacred robes into the mire of
politics, but, Andrew, we were boys together, before you
were so famous, and I know that nothing I can bring
myself to ask of you can be refused. A word from you in
many quarters will help. The madam joins me in regard
to you and yours. Sincerely,　　　　N. L. Montjoy."

"P. S. Excuse this typewritten letter, but my hand is
old, and I cannot wield the pen as I did when we put
together that first sermon of yours.　　　　　　M."

This was an addendum in "the colonel's own handwriting" and it closed with "pray for me." The letter was

vociferously applauded and passers-by looked up in the headquarters windows curiously. These addenda in the colonel's own handwriting tickled Norton's fancy. He played upon every string in the human heart. When he got among the masons he staggered a little, but managed to work in something about "upright, square and level." "If I could only have got a few signals from the old gentleman," he said, gayly, "I would get the lodges out in a body."

Norton was everywhere during the next ten days. He kept four typewriters busy getting out "personal" letters, addressing circulars and marking special articles that had appeared in the papers. One of his sayings that afterward became a political maxim was: "If you want the people to help you, let them hear from you before the election." And in this instance they heard.

Within a few days a great banner was stretched across the street from the headquarters window, and a band wagon, drawn by four white horses, carried a brass band and flags bearing the legend:

> "Montjoy at the Court House
> Saturday Night."

Little boys distributed dodgers.

Edward, taking the cue, entered with equal enthusiasm into the comedy. He wanted to do the right thing, and he had formed an exaggerated idea of the influence of money in political campaigns. He hung a placard at the front door of the Montjoy headquarters that read:

"One thousand dollars to five hundred that Montjoy is nominated."

He placed a check to back it in the secretary's hands. This announcement drew a crowd and soon afterward a quiet-appearing man came in and said:

"I have the money to cover that bet. Name a stake-holder."

One was named. Edward was flushed with wine and

6

enthused by the friendly comments his bold wager had drawn out.

"Make it $2,000 to $1,000?" he asked the stranger.

"Well," was the reply, "it goes."

"Make it $10,000 to $5,000?" said Edward.

"No!"

"Ten thousand to four thousand?"

"No!"

"Ten thousand to three thousand?"

"No!" The stranger smiled nervously and, saluting, withdrew. The crowd cheered until the sidewalk was blockaded. The news went abroad: "Odds of 300 to 100 have been offered on Montjoy, and no takers."

Edward's bet had the effect of precipitating the campaign in the home county; it had been opening slowly, despite the rush at the Montjoy headquarters. The Swearingen men were experienced campaigners and worked more by quiet organization than display. Such men know when to make the great stroke in a campaign. The man who had attempted to call young Morgan's hand had little to do with the management of the Swearingen campaign, but was engaged in a speculation of his own, acting upon a hint.

But the show of strength at the Montjoy headquarters was at once used by the Swearingen men to stir their friends to action, lest they be bluffed out of the fight. Rival bands were got out, rival placards appeared and handbills were thrown into every yard.

And then came the first personalities, but directed at Edward only. An evening paper said that "A late citizen, after half a century of honorable service, and although but recently deceased, seemed to have fallen into betting upon mundane elections by proxy." And elsewhere: "A certain class of people and their uncle's money are soon divorced." Many others followed upon the same line, clearly indicating Edward Morgan, and with street-corner talk soon made him a central figure among the Montjoy forces. Edward saw none of these paragraphs, nor did he hear the gossip of the city.

This continued for days; in the meantime Edward took Norton home with him at night and generally one or two others accompanied them. Finally it came to be settled that Norton and Edward were old friends, and the friends of Montjoy senior looked on and smiled.

The other side simply sneered, swore and waited.

Information of these things reached Mary Montjoy. Annie, the sister-in-law, came into the city and met her cousin, Amos Royson, the wild horseman who collided with the Montjoy team upon the night of Edward's first appearance. This man was one of the Swearingen managers. His relationship to Annie Montjoy gave him entrance to the family circle, and he had been for two years a suitor for Mary's hand.

Royson took a seat in the vehicle beside his cousin and turned the horse's head toward the park. Annie Montjoy saw that he was in an ugly mood, and divined the reason. She possessed to a remarkable degree the power of mind-reading and she knew Amos Royson better than he knew himself.

"Tell me about this Edward Morgan, who is making such a fool of himself," he said, abruptly. "He is injuring Col. Montjoy's chances more than we could ever hope to, and is really the best ally we have!"

She smiled as she looked upon him from under the sleepy lids. "Why, then, are you not pleased?"

"Oh, well, you know, Annie, the unfortunate fact remains that you are one of the family. I hate to see you mixed up in this matter and a sharer in the family's downfall."

"You do not think enough of me to keep out of the way."

"I cannot control the election, Annie; Swearingen will be elected with or without my help. But you know my whole future depends upon Swearingen. Who is Edward Morgan?"

"Oh, Edward Morgan! Well, you know, he is old John Morgan's heir, and that is all I know; but," and she laughed maliciously, "he is what Norton calls 'a rusher,' not only in politics but elsewhere. He has seen Mary, and—now you know why he is so much interested in this election." Amos turned fiercely upon her and involuntarily drew the reins until the horse stopped. He felt the innuendo and forgot the thrust.

"You cannot mean——" he began, and then paused, for in her eyes was a triumph so devilish, so malicious, that even he, knowing her well, could not bring himself to gratify it. He knew that she had never forgiven him for his devotion to Mary.

"Yes, I mean it! If ever two people were suddenly, hopelessly, foolishly infatuated with each other that same little hypocritical chit and this stranger are the two. He is simply trying to put his intended father-in-law into congress. Do you understand?"

The man's face was white and only with difficulty could he guide the animal he was driving. She continued, with a sudden exhibition of passion: "And Mary! Oh, you should just hear her say 'Ilexhurst'! She will queen it out there with old Morgan's money and heir, and we——" she laughed bitterly, "we will stay out yonder, keep a mule boarding house and nurse sick niggers—that is all it amounts to; they raise corn half the year and hire hands to feed it out the other half; and the warehouses get the cotton. In the meantime, I am stuck away out of sight with my children!" Royson thought over this outburst and then said gravely:

"You have not yet answered my question. Who is Edward Morgan—where did he come from?"

"Go ask John Morgan," she said, scornfully and maliciously. He studied long the painted dashboard in front of him, and then, in a sort of awe, looked into her face:

"What do you mean, Annie?" She would not turn back; she met his gaze with determination.

"Old Morgan has educated and maintained him abroad all his life. He has never spoken of him to anybody. You know what stories they used to tell of John Morgan. Can't you see? Challenged to prove his legal right to his name he couldn't do it." The words were out. The jealous woman took the lines from his hands and said, sneeringly: "You are making a fool of yourself, Amos, by your driving, and attracting attention. Where do you want to get out? I am going back uptown." He did not reply. Dazed by the fearful hint he sat looking ahead.

When she drew rein at a convenient corner he alighted. There was a cruel light in his gray eyes.

"Annie," he said, "the defeat of Col. Montjoy lies in your information."

"Let it," she exclaimed, recklessly. "He has no more business in congress than a child. And for the other matter, I have myself and my children's name to protect."

And yet she was not entirely without caution. She continued:

"What I have told you is a mere hint. It must not come back to me nor get in print." She drove away. With eyes upon the ground Royson walked to his office.

Amos Royson was of the new south entirely, but not its best representative. His ambition was boundless; there was nothing he would have left undone to advance himself politically. His thought as he walked back to his office was upon the words of his cousin. In what manner could this frightful hint be made effective without danger of reaction? At this moment he met the man he was plotting to destroy, walking rapidly toward the postoffice with Norton Montjoy. The latter saluted him, gayly, as he passed:

"Hello, Amos! We have you on the run, my boy!" Amos made no reply to Norton, nor to Edward's conventional bow. As they passed he noted the latter's form and poetical face, then somewhat flushed with excitement, and seemed to form a mental estimate of him.

"Cold-blooded devil, that fellow Royson," said Norton, as he ran over his letters before mailing them; "stick a knife in you in a minute."

But Royson walked on. Once he turned, looked back and smiled sardonically. "They are both in a bad fix," he said, half-aloud. "The man who has to look out for Annie is to be pitied."

At home Annie gave a highly colored account of all she had heard in town about Edward, made up chiefly of boasts of friends who supposed that her interest in Col. Montjoy's nomination was genuine, of Norton's report and the sneers of enemies, including Royson. These lost nothing in the way of color at her hands. Mary sought her room and after several efforts sealed for Edward this letter:

"You can never know how grateful we all are for your interest and help, but our gratitude would be incomplete if I failed to tell you that there is danger of injuring yourself in your generous enthusiasm. You must not forget that papa has enemies who will become yours. This we would much regret, for you have so much need of friends. Do not put faith in too many people, and come out here when you feel the need of rest. I cannot write much that I would like to tell you. Your friend,

"Mary Montjoy."

"P. S. Amos Royson is your enemy and he is a dangerous man."

When Edward received this, as he did next day by the hand of Col. Montjoy, he was thrilled with pleasure and then depressed with a sudden memory. That day he was so reckless that even Norton felt compelled, using his expression, "to call him down."

CHAPTER XIV.

THE OLD SOUTH DRAWS THE SWORD.

When Royson reached his office he quietly locked himself in, and, lighting a cigar, threw himself into his easy-chair. He recalled with carefulness the minutest facts of his interview with Annie Montjoy, from the moment he seated himself beside her, until his departure. Having established these in mind he began the course of reasoning he always pursued in making an estimate of testimony. The basis of his cousin's action did not call for much attention; he knew her well. She was as ambitious as Lucifer and possessed that peculiar defect which would explain so many women if given proper recognition—lack of ability to concede equal merit to others. They can admit no uninvited one to their plane; not even an adviser. They demand flattery as a plant demands nitrogen, and cannot survive the loss of attention.

And, reading deeper, Royson saw that the steadfast, womanly soul of the sister-in-law had, even in the knowledge of his cousin, overshadowed hers until she resented even the old colonel's punctilious courtesy; that in her heart she raged at his lack of informality and accused him of resting upon the young girl. If she had been made much of, set up as a divinity, appealed to and suffered to rule, all would have been fair and beautiful. And then the lawyer smiled and said aloud to that other self, with whom he communed: "For a while." Such was the woman.

Long he sat, studying the situation. Once he arose and paced the floor, beating his fist into his hand and grinding his teeth.

"Both or none!" he cried, at last. "If Montjoy is nominated I am shelved; and as for Mary, there have been Sabine women in all ages."

That night the leaders of the opposition met in secret caucus, called together by Royson. When, curious and attentive, they assembled in his private office, he addressed them:

"I have, gentlemen, to-day found myself in a very embarrassing position; a very painful one. You all know my devotion to our friend; I need not say, therefore, that here to-night the one overpowering cause of the action which I am about to take is my loyalty to him. To-day, from a source I am not at liberty to state here, I was placed in possession of a fact which, if used, practically ends this campaign. You must none of you express a doubt, nor must any one question me upon the subject. The only question to be discussed is, shall we make use of the fact—and how?" He waited a moment until the faces of the committee betrayed their deep interest.

"Whom do you consider in this city the most powerful single man behind the movement to nominate Montjoy?"

"Morgan," said one, promptly. It was their unanimous judgment.

"Correct! This man, with his money and zeal, has

made our chances uncertain if not desperate, and this
man," he continued, excitedly, "who is posing before the
public and offering odds of three to one against us with
old Morgan's money, is not a white man!"

He had leaned over the table and concluded his re-
marks in almost a whisper. A painful silence followed,
during which the excited lawyer glared inquiringly into
the faces turned in horror upon him. "Do you understand?" he shouted at last. They understood.

A southern man takes a hint upon such a matter readily. These men sat silent, weighing in their minds the
final effect of this announcement. Royson did not give
them long to consider.

"I am certain of this, so certain that if you think best
I will publish the fact to-morrow and assume the whole
responsibility." There was but little doubt remaining
then. But the committee seemed weighed upon rather
than stirred by the revelation; they spoke in low tones
to each other. There was no note of triumph in any voice.
They were men.

Presently the matter took definite shape. An old man
arose and addressed his associates:

"I need not say, gentlemen, that I am astonished by
this information, and you will pardon me if I do say I
regret that it seems true. As far as I am concerned I am
opposed to its use. It is a very difficult matter to prove.
Mr. Royson's informant may be mistaken, and if proof
was not forthcoming a reaction would ruin our friend."
No one replied, although several nodded their heads. At
length Royson spoke:

"The best way to reach the heart of this matter is to
follow out in your minds a line of action. Suppose in
a speech I should make the charge—what would be the
result?"

"You would be at once challenged!" Royson smiled.
"Who would bear the challenge?"

"One of the Montjoys would be morally compelled to."

"Suppose I convince the bearer that a member of his
family was my authority?" Then they began to get a
glimpse of the depth of the plot. One answered:

"He would be obliged to withdraw!"

"Exactly! And who else after that would take Mont-joy's place? Or how could Montjoy permit the duel to go on? And if he did find a fool to bring his challenge, I could not, for the reason given in the charge, meet his principal!"

"A court of honor might compel you to prove your charge, and then you would be in a hole. That is, unless you could furnish proof."

"And still," said Royson, "there would be no duel, be-cause there would be no second. And you understand, gentlemen," he continued, smiling, "that all this would not postpone the campaign. Before the court of honor could settle the matter the election would have been held. You can imagine how that election would go when it is known that Montjoy's campaign manager and right-hand man is not white. This man is hail-fellow-well-met with young Montjoy; a visitor in his home and is spend-ing money like water. What do you suppose the country will say when these facts are handled on the stump? Col. Montjoy is ignorant of it, we know, but he will be on the defensive from the day the revelation is made.

"I have said my action is compelled by my loyalty to Swearingen, and I reiterate it, but we owe something to the community, to the white race, to good morals and posterity. And if I am mistaken in my proofs, gentlemen, why, then, I can withdraw my charge. It will not affect the campaign already over. But I will not have to with-draw."

"As far as I am concerned," said another gentleman, rising and speaking emphatically, "this is a matter upon which, under the circumstances, I do not feel called to vote! I cannot act without full information! The fact is, I am not fond of such politics! If Mr. Royson has proofs that he cannot use publicly or here, the best plan would be to submit them to Col. Montjoy and let him withdraw, or pull off his lieutenant." He passed out and several with him. Royson argued with the others, but one by one they left him. He was bursting with rage.

"I will determine for myself!" he said; "the victory shall rest in me!"

Then came the speech of the campaign at the court

house. The relations of Col. Montjoy, his family friends, people connected with him in the remotest degree by marriage, army friends, members of the horticultural and agricultural societies, masons, members of the bar, merchants, warehousemen and farmers generally, and a large sprinkling of personal and political enemies of Swearingen made up the vast crowd.

In the rear of the hall, a smile upon his face, was Amos Royson. And yet the secret glee in his heart, the knowledge that he, one man in all that throng, by a single sentence could check the splendid demonstration and sweep the field, was clouded. It came to him that no other member of the Montjoy clan was a traitor. Nowhere is the family tie so strong as in the south, and only the power of his ambition could have held him aloof. Swearingen had several times represented the district in congress; it was his turn when the leader moved on. This had been understood for years by the political public. In the meantime he had been state's attorney and there were a state senatorship, a judgeship and possibly the governorship to be grasped. He could not be expected to sacrifice his career upon the altar of kinship remote. Indeed, was it not the duty of Montjoy to stand aside for the sake of a younger man? Was it not true that a large force in his nomination had been the belief that Swearingen's right-hand man would probably be silenced thereby? It had been a conspiracy.

These thoughts ran through his mind as he stood watching the gathering.

On the stage sat Edward Morgan, a prominent figure and one largely scanned by the public; and Royson saw his face light up and turn to a private box; saw his smile and bow. A hundred eyes were turned with his, and discovered there, half concealed by the curtains, the face of Mary Montjoy. The public jumped to the conclusion that had previously been forced on him.

Over Royson's face surged a wave of blood; a muttered oath drew attention to him and he changed his position. He saw the advancing figure of Gen. Evan and heard his introductory speech. The morning paper said it was the most eloquent ever delivered on such an occasion; and all that the speaker said was:

"Fellow-citizens, I have the honor to introduce to you this evening Col. Norton Montjoy. Hear him."

His rich bass voice rolled over the great audience; he extended his arm toward the orator of the evening, and retired amid thunders of applause.

Then came Col. Montjoy.

The old south was famous for its oratory. It was based upon personal independence, upon family pride and upon intellect unhampered by personal toil in uncongenial occupations; and lastly upon sentiment. Climate may have entered into it; race and inheritance undoubtedly did. The southern orator was the feature of congressional displays, and back in congressional archives lie orations that vie with the best of Athens and of Rome. But the flavor, the spectacular effects, linger only in the memory of the rapidly lessening number who mingled deeply in ante-bellum politics. No pen could have preserved this environment faithfully.

So with the oration that night in the opening of the Montjoy campaign. It was not transmissible. Only the peroration need be reproduced here:

"God forbid!" he said in a voice now husky with emotion and its long strain, "God forbid that the day shall come when the south will apologize for her dead heroes! Stand by your homes; stand by your traditions; keep our faith in the past as bright as your hopes for the future! No stain rests upon the honor of your fathers! Transmit their memories and their virtues to posterity as its best inheritance! Defend your homes and firesides, remembering always that the home, the family circle, is the fountain head of good government! Let none enter there who are unclean. Keep it the cradle of liberty and the hope of the English race on this continent, the shrine of religion, of beauty, of purity!"

He closed amid a tumult of enthusiasm. Men stood on chairs to cheer; ladies wept and waved their handkerchiefs, and then over all arose the strange melody that no southern man can sit quiet under. "Dixie" rung out amid a frenzy of emotion. Veterans hugged each other.

The old general came forward and clasped hands with his comrade, the band changing to "Auld Lang Syne." People crowded on the stage and outside the building the drifting crowd filled the air with shouts.

The last man to rise from his seat was Edward Morgan. Lost in thought, his face lowered, he sat until some one touched him on the shoulder and called him back to the present. And out in the audience, clinging to a post to resist the stream of humanity, passing from the aisles, his eyes strained forward, heedless of the banter and jeers poured upon him, Royson watched as best he could every shade upon the stranger's face. A cry burst from his lips. "It was true!" he said, and dashed from the hall.

CHAPTER XV.

"IN ALL THE WORLD, NO FAIRER FLOWER THAN THIS!"

The city was in a whirl on election day; hacks and carriages darted here and there all day long, bearing flaming placards and hauling voters to the polls. Bands played at the Montjoy headquarters and everything to comfort the inner patriot was on hand.

Edward had taken charge of this department and at his own expense conducted it. He was the host. All kinds of wines and liquors and malt drinks, a constantly replenished lunch, that amounted to a banquet, and cigars, were at all hours quickly served by a corps of trained waiters. In all their experience, old election stagers declared never had this feature of election day been so complete. It goes without saying that Montjoy's headquarters were crowded and that a great deal of the interest which found expression in the streets was manufactured there.

It was a fierce struggle; the Swearingen campaign in the county had been conducted on the "still-hunt" plan, and on this day his full strength was polled. It was Montjoy's home county, and if it could be carried against him, the victory was won at the outset.

On the other hand, the Montjoy people sought for the moral effect of an overwhelming victory. There was an expression of general relief in the form of cheers, when the town clocks struck 5 and the polls windows fell. Anxiety followed, and then bonfires blazed, rockets exploded and all night long the artillery squad fired salutes. Montjoy had won by an unlooked-for majority and the vote of the largest county was secure.

Edward had resolutely refused to think upon the discovery unfolded to him. With reckless disregard for the future he had determined to bury the subject until the arrival of Virdow. But there are ghosts that will not come down at the bidding, and so in the intervals of sleep, of excitement, of politics, the remembrance of the fearful fate that threatened him came up with all the force and terror of a new experience.

Ilexhurst was impossible to him alone and he had held to Norton as long as he could. There was to be a few days' rest after the home election, and the younger Montjoy seized this opportunity to run home and, as he expressed it, "get acquainted with the family." Edward, without hesitation, accepted his invitation to go with him. They had become firm friends now and Edward stood high in the family esteem. Reviewing the work that had led up to Col. Montjoy's magnificent opening and oration, all generously conceded that he had been the potent factor.

It was not true, in fact; the younger Montjoy had been the genius of the hour, but Edward's aid and money had been necessary. The two men were received as conquering heroes. As she held his hand in hers old Mrs. Montjoy said:

"You have done us a great service, Mr. Morgan, and we cannot forget it," and Mary, shy and happy, had smiled upon him and uttered her thanks. There was one discordant note, the daughter-in-law had been silent until all were through.

"And I suppose I am to thank you, Mr. Morgan, that Norton has returned alive. I did not know you were such high livers over at Hexhurst," she smiled, maliciously. "Were you not afraid of ghosts?"

Edward looked at her with ill-disguised hatred. For the first time he realized fully that he was dealing with a dangerous enemy. How much did she know? He could make nothing of that serenely tranquil face. He bowed only. She was his friend's wife.

But he was not at ease beneath her gaze and readily accepted Mary's invitation to ride. She was going to carry a note from her father to a neighbor, and the chance of seeing the country was one he should not neglect. They found a lazy mule and ancient country buggy at the door. He thought of the outfit of the sister-in-law. "Annie has a pony phaeton that is quite stylish," said Mary, laughingly, as they entered the old vehicle, "but it is only for town use; this is mine and papa's!"

"Certainly roomy and safe," he said. She laughed outright.

"I will remember that; so many people have tried to say something comforting about my turnout and failed; but it does well enough." They were off then, Edward driving awkwardly. It was the first time he had ever drawn the reins over a mule.

"How do you make it go fast?" he asked, finally, in despair.

"Oh, dear," she answered, "we don't try. We know the mule." Her laugh was infectious.

They traveled the public roads, with their borders of wild grape, crossed gurgling streams under festoons of vines and lingered in shady vistas of overhanging boughs. Several times they boldly entered private grounds and passed through back yards without hailing, and at last they came to their destination.

There were two huge stone posts at the entrance, with carved balls of granite upon them. An iron gate of Moorish fretwork hung between. A thick tangle of muscadine and Cherokee roses led off from them right and left, hiding the trail of the long-vanished rail fence. In front was an avenue of twisted cedars, and, closing the perspective, a glimpse of white columns and green blinds.

The girl's face was lighted with smiles; it was for her

a new experience, this journeying with a man alone; his voice melodious in her hearing; his eyes exchanging with hers quick understandings, for Edward was happy that morning—happy in his forgetfulness. He had thrown off the weight of misery successfully, and for the first time in his life there was really a smile in his heart. It was the dream of an hour; he would not mar it. Her voice recalled him.

"I have always loved 'The Cedars.' It wears such an air of gentility and refinement. It must be that something of the lives gone by cling to these old places."

"Whose is it?" She turned in surprise.

"Oh, this is where we were bound—Gen. Evan's. I have a note for him."

"Ah!" The exclamation was one of awe rather than wonder. She saw him start violently and grow pale. "Evan?" he said, with emotion.

"You know him?"

"Not I." He felt her questioning gaze and looked into her face. "That is, I have been introduced to him, only, and I have heard him speak." After a moment's reflection: "Sometime, perhaps, I shall tell you why for the moment I was startled." She could not understand his manner. Fortunately they had arrived at the house. Confused still, he followed her up the broad steps to the veranda and saw her lift the antique knocker.

"Yes, ma'am, de general's home; walk in, ma'am; find him right back in the library." With that delightful lack of formality common among intimate neighbors in the south, Mary led the way in. She made a pretty picture as she paused at the door. The sun was shining through the painted window and suffused her form with roseate light.

"May I come in?"

"Well! Well! Well!" The old man rose with a great show of welcome and came forward. "May I come in? How d'ye do, Mary, God bless you, child; yes, come clear in," he said, laughing, and bestowed a kiss upon her lips. At that moment he caught sight of the face of Edward, who stood behind her, pale from the stream of light that came from a white crest in the window. The two men gazed steadily into each other's eyes a moment only. The girl began:

"This is Mr. Morgan, general, who has been such a friend to father."

The rugged face of the old soldier lighted up, he took the young man's hands in both of his and pressed them warmly.

"I have already met Mr. Morgan. The friend of my friend is welcome to 'The Cedars.'" He turned to move chairs for them.

The face of the young man grew white as he bowed gravely. There had been a recognition, but no voice spoke from the far-away past through his lineaments to that lonely old man. During the visit he was distrait and embarrassed. The courtly attention of his host and his playful gallantry with Mary awoke no smile upon his lips. Somewhere a barrier had fallen and the waters of memory had rushed in. Finally he was forced to arouse himself.

"John Morgan was a warm friend of mine at one time," said the old general. "How was he related to you?"

"Distantly," said Edward quietly. "I was an orphan, and indebted to him for everything."

"An eccentric man, but John had a good heart—errors like the rest of us, of course." The general's face grew sad for the moment, but he rallied and turned the conversation to the political campaign.

"A grand speech that, Mr. Morgan; I have never heard a finer, and I have heard great speakers in my day! Our district will be well and honorably represented in congress. Now, our little friend here will go to Washington and get her name into the papers."

"No, indeed. If papa wins I am going to stay with mamma. I am going to be her eyes as well as her hands. Mamma would not like the city."

"And how is the little mamma?"

She shook her head. "Not so well and her eyes trouble her very much."

"What a sweet woman she is! I can never forget the night Norton led her to the altar. I have never seen a fairer sight—until now," he interpolated, smiling and saluting Mary with formal bow. "She had a perfect figure and her walk was the exposition of grace." Mary surveyed him with swimming eyes. She went up and kissed him lightly. He detained her a moment when about to take her departure.

"You are a fortunate man, Morgan. In all the world you will find no rarer flower than this. I envy you your ride home. Come again, Mary, and bring Mr. Morgan with you." She broke loose from him and darted off in confusion. He had guessed her secret and well was it that he had!

The ride home was as a dream. The girl was excited and full of life and banter and Edward, throwing off his sadness, had entered into the hour of happiness with the same abandon that marked his campaign with Norton.

But as they entered the long stretch of wood through which their road ran to her home, Edward brought back the conversation to the general.

"Yes," said Mary, "he lives quite alone, a widower, but beloved by every one. It is an old, sad story, but his daughter eloped just before the war broke out and went abroad. He has never heard from her, it is supposed."

"I have heard the fact mentioned," said Morgan, "and also that she was to have married my relative."

"I did not know that," she said, "but it is a great sorrow to the general, and a girl who could give up such a man must have been wrong at heart or infatuated."

"Infatuated, let us hope."

"That is the best explanation," she said gently.

He was driving; in a few moments he would arrive at the house. Should he tell her the history of Gerald and let her clear, honest mind guide him? Should he tell her that Fate had made him the custodian of the only being in the world who had a right to that honorable name when the veteran back yonder found his last camp and crossed the river to rest in the shade with the immortal Jackson? He turned to her and she met his earnest gaze with a winning smile, but at the moment something in his life cried out. The secret was as much his duty as the ward himself and to confess to her his belief that Gerald was the son of Marion Evan was to confess to himself

7

that he was the son of the octoroon. He would not. Her
smile died away before the misery in his face.

"You are ill," she said in quick sympathy.

"Yes," he replied, faintly; "yes and no. The loss of
sleep—excitement—your southern sun——" The world
grew black and he felt himself falling. In the last moment
of his consciousness he remembered that her arm was
thrown about him and that in response to her call for help
negroes from the cotton fields came running.

He opened his eyes. They rested upon the chintz curtains of the room upstairs, from the window of which he
had heard her voice calling the chickens. Some one
was bathing his forehead; there were figures gliding here
and there across his vision. He turned his eyes and saw
the anxious face of Mrs. Montjoy watching him.

"What is it?" He spoke in wonder.

"Hush, now, my boy; you have been very ill; you must
not talk!" He tried to lift his hand. It seemed made of
lead and not connected with him in any way. Gazing
helplessly upon it, he saw that it was thin and white—the
hand of an invalid.

"How long?" he asked, after a rest. The slight effort
took his strength.

"Three weeks." Three weeks! This was more than
he could adjust in the few working sections of his brain.
He ceased to try and closed his eyes in sleep.

———

CHAPTER XVI.

BEYOND THE SHADOW OF A DOUBT.

It had been brain fever. For ten days Edward was
helpless, but under the care of the two loving women
he rapidly recovered. The time came when he could sit
in the cool of the evening upon the veranda and listen to
the voices he had learned to love—for he no longer disguised the truth from himself. The world held for him
but one dream, and through it and in the spell of his first

home life the mother became a being to be reverenced. She was the fulfilled promise of the girl, all the tender experiences of life were pictured in advance for him who should win her hand and heart.

But it was only a dream. During the long hours of the night as he lay wakeful, with no escape from himself, he thought out the situation and made up his mind to action. He would go to Col. Montjoy and confess the ignorance of his origin that overwhelmed him and then he would provide for his ward and go away with Virdow to the old world and the old life.

The mental conclusion of his plan was a species of settlement. It helped him. Time and again he cried out, when the remembrance came back to him, but it was the honorable course and he would follow it. He would go away.

The hours of his convalescence were the respite he allowed himself. Day by day he said: "I will go to-morrow." In the morning it was still "to-morrow." And when he finally made his announcement he was promptly overruled. Col. Montjoy and Norton were away, speaking and campaigning. All primaries had been held but two. The colonel's enemies had conceded to him of the remaining counties the remote one. The other was a county with a large population and cast four votes in the convention. It was the home of Swearingen, but, as frequently happens, it was the scene of the candidate's greatest weakness. There the struggle was to be titanic. Both counties were needed to nominate Montjoy.

The election took place on the day of Edward's departure for Ilexhurst. That evening he saw a telegram announcing that the large county had given its vote to Montjoy by a small majority. The remote county had but one telegraph office, and that at a way station upon its border. Little could be heard from it, but the public conceded Col. Montjoy's nomination, since there had been no doubt as to this county. Edward hired a horse, put a man upon it, sent the news to the two ladies and then went to his home.

He found awaiting him two letters of importance. One from Virdow, saying he would sail from Havre on the

25th; that was twelve days previous. He was therefore
really due at Ilexhurst then. The other was a letter
he had written to Abingdon soon after his first arrival,
and was marked "returned to writer." He wondered at
this. The address was the same he had used for
years in his correspondence. Although Abingdon was
frequently absent from England, the letters had always
reached him. Why, then, was this one not forwarded?
He put it aside and ascertained that Virdow had not arrived at the house.

It was then 8 o'clock in the evening. By his order a
telephone had been placed in the house, and he at once
rung up the several hotels. Virdow was found to be at
one of these, and he succeeded in getting that distinguished gentleman to connect himself with the American
invention and explained to him the situation.

"Take any hack and come at once," was the message
that concluded their conversation, and Virdow came! In
the impulsive continental style, he threw himself into Edward's arms when the latter opened the door of the carriage.

Slender, his thin black clothes hanging awkwardly upon
him, his trousers too short, the breadth of his round German face, the knobs on his shining bald forehead exaggerated by the puffy gathering of the hair over his ears,
his candid little eyes shining through the round, double-
power glasses, his was a figure one had to know for a long
time in order to look upon it without smiling.

Long the two sat with their cigars and ran over the old
days together. Then the professor told of wondrous experiments in sound, of the advance of knowledge into
the regions of psychology, of the marvels of heredity. His
old great theme was still his ruling passion. "If the
mind has no memory, then much of the phenomena of life
is worse than bewildering. Prove its memory," he was
wont to say, "and I will prove immortality through that
memory."

It was the same old professor. He was up now and
every muscle working as he struggled and gesticulated,
and wrote invisible hieroglyphics in the air about him and

made geometrical figures with palms and fingers. But the professor had advanced in speculation.

"The time will come, my young friend," he said at last, "when the mind will give us its memories complete. We will learn the secrets of creation by memory. In its perfection we will place a man yonder and by vibration get his mind memory to work; theoretically he will first write of his father and then his grandfather, describing their mental lives. He will go back along the lines of his ancestry. He will get into Latin, then Greek, then Hebrew, then Chaldean, then into cuneiform inscriptions, then into figure representation He will be an artist or a musician or sculptor, and possibly all if the back trail of his memory crosses such talents. "Ay," he continued, enthusiastically, "lost nations will live again. The portraits of our ancestors will hang in view along the corridors of all times! This will come by vibratory force, but how?"

Edward leaned forward, breathless almost with emotion.

"You say the time is come; what has been done?"

"Little and much! The experiments——"

"Tell me, in all your experiments, have you known where a child, separated from a parent since infancy, without aid of description, or photograph, or information derived from a living person, could see in memory or imagination the face of that parent, see it with such distinctness as to enable him, an artist, to reproduce it in all perfection?"

The professor wiped his glasses nervously and kept his gaze upon his questioner.

"Never."

"Then," said Edward, "you have crossed the ocean to some purpose! I have known such an instance here in this house. The person is still here! You know me, my friend, and you do not know me. To you I was a rich young American, with a turn for science and speculation. You made me your friend and God bless you for it, but you did not know all of that mystery which hangs over my life never to be revealed perhaps until the millennium of science you have outlined dawns upon us. The man who educated me, who enriched me, was not my parent or relative; he was my guardian. He has made me the guardian of a frail, sickly lad whose mystery is, or was, as complete as mine. Teach us to remember." The words burst from him. They held the pent-up flood that had almost wrecked his brain.

Rapidly he recounted the situation, leaving out the woman's story as to himself. Not to his Savior would he confess that.

And then he told how, following his preceptor's hints about vibration, he had accidentally thrown Gerald into a trance; its results, the second experiment, the drawing and the woman's story of Gerald's birth.

During this recital the professor never moved his eyes from the speaker's face.

"You wish to know what I think of it? This: I have but recently ventured the proposition publicly that all ideal faces on the artist's canvas are mind memories. Prove to me anew your results and if I establish the reasonableness of my theory I will have accomplished enough to die on."

"In your opinion, then, this picture that Gerald drew is a mind memory?"

"Undoubtedly, from the information as given."

"And if we can produce under these rare circumstances those faces, could we not produce others in the same line of succession, supposing Gerald to have descended from one of these women—a grandparent, for example?"

"Undoubtedly. But you will perceive that the more distant, the older the experience, we may say, the less likelihood of accuracy."

"It would depend, then, you think, upon the clearness of the original impression?"

"That is true! The vividness of an old impression may also outshine a new one."

"And if this young man recalls the face of a woman, whom we believe it possible—nay, probable—is his mother, and then the face of one we know to be her father, as a reasonable man, would you consider the story of this negro woman substantiated beyond the shadow of a doubt?"

"Beyond the shadow of a doubt."

"We will try," said Edward, and then, after a moment's silence: "He is shy of strangers and you may find it difficult to get acquainted with him. After you have succeeded in gaining his confidence we will settle upon a way to proceed. One word more, he is a victim of morphia. Did I tell you that?"

"No, but I guessed it."

"You have known such men before, then?"

"I have studied the proposition that opium may be a power to effect what we seek, and, in connection with it, have studied the hospitals that make a specialty of such cases."

There was a long silence, and presently Edward said: "Will you say good-night now?"

"Good-night." The professor gazed about him. "How was it you used to say good-night, Edward? Old customs are good. It is not possible that the violin has been lost." He smiled and Edward got his instrument and played. He knew the old man's favorites; the little folk-melodies of the Rhine country, bits of love songs, mostly, around which the loving players of Germany have woven so many beautiful fancies. And in the playing Edward himself was quieted.

The light from the hall downstairs streamed out along the gravel walk, and in the glare was a man standing with arms folded and head bent forward. A tall woman came and gently laid her hand upon him. He started violently, tossed his arms aloft and rushed into the darkness. She waited in silence a moment and then slowly followed him.

CHAPTER XVII.

"IF I MEET THE MAN!"

When Edward opened the morning paper, which he did while waiting for the return of the professor, who had wandered away before breakfast, he was shocked by the announcement of Montjoy's defeat. The result of the vote in the remote county had been secured by horseback

service organized by an enterprising journal, and telegraphed. The official returns were given.

Already the campaign had drifted far into the past with
him; years seemed to have gone by when he arose from
the sick-bed and now it scarcely seemed possible that he,
Edward Morgan, was the same man who labored among
the voters, shouted himself hoarse and kept the headquarters so successfully. It must have been a dream.

But Mary! That part was real. He wrote her a few
lines expressing his grief.

And then came the professor, with his adventure! He
had met a young man out making photographs and had
interested him with descriptions of recent successful attempts to photograph in colors. And then they had gone
to the wing-room and examined the young man's results
from efforts to produce pictures upon living substances.
"He has some of the most original theories and ideas
upon the subject I have heard," said the German. "Not
wild beyond the possibilities of invention, however, and
I am not sure but that he has taught me a lesson in common sense. 'Find how nature photographs upon living
tissue,' said the young man, 'and when you have reduced
your pictures to the invisible learn to re-enlarge them;
perhaps you will learn to enlarge nature's invisibles.'

"He has discovered that the convolutions of the human
brain resemble an embryo infant and that the new map
which indicates the nerve lines centering in the brain
from different parts of the body shows them entering
the corresponding parts of the embryo. He lingers upon
the startling idea that the nerve is a formative organ, and
that by sensations conveyed, and by impressions, it actually shapes the brain. When sensations are identical
and persistent they establish a family form. The brain is
a bas-relief composite picture, shaped by all the nerves.
Theoretically a man's brain carefully removed, photo-
graphed and enlarged ought to show the outlines of a
family form, with all the modifications.

"You will perceive that he is working along hereditary
lines and not psychologic. And I am not sure but that in
this he is pursuing the wisest course, heredity being the
primer."

"You believe he has made a new discovery, then?"

"As to that, no.   The speculative mind is tolerant.   It accepts nothing that is not proved; it rejects nothing that has not been disproved.   The original ideas in most discoveries in their crude forms were not less wild than this. All men who observe are friends of science."

The incident pleased Edward.   To bring the professor and Gerald together he had feared would be difficult. Chance and the professor's tact had already accomplished this successfully.

"I will leave you and Gerald to get thoroughly acquainted.   When you have learned him you can study him best.   I have business of importance."

He at once went to the city and posted his letter.   Norton's leave had been exhausted and he had already departed for New York.

At the club and at the almost forsaken headquarters of the Montjoy party all was consternation and regret.   The fatal overconfidence in the backwoods county was settled upon as the cause of the disaster. And yet why should that county have failed them?   Two companies of Evan's old brigade were recruited there; he had been assured by almost every prominent man in the county of its vote. And then came the crushing blow.

The morning paper had wired for special reports and full particulars, and at 12 o'clock an extra was being cried upon the streets.   Everybody bought the paper; the street cars, the hotels, the clubs, the street corners, were thronged with people eagerly reading the announcement. Under triple head lines, which contained the words "Fraud" and "Slander" and "Treachery," came this article, which Edward read on the street:

"The cause of the fatal slump-off of Col. Montjoy's friends in this county was a letter placed in circulation here yesterday and industriously spread to the remotest voting places.   It was a letter from Mr. Amos Royson to the Hon. Thomas Brown of this county.   Your correspondent has secured and herewith sends a copy:

"'My Dear Sir: In view of the election about to be held in your county, I beg to submit the following facts:

Against the honor and integrity of Col. Montjoy nothing
can be urged, but it is known here so positively that I do
not hesitate to state, and authorize you to use it, that the
whole Montjoy movement is in reality based upon an
effort to crush Swearingen for his opposition to certain
corporation measures in congress, and which by reason
of his position on certain committees, he threatens with
defeat! To this end money has been sent here and is
being lavishly expended by a tool of the corporation.
Added to this is the fact that the man chosen for the business is one calling himself Edward Morgan, the natural
son of a late eccentric bachelor lawyer of this city. The
mother of this man is an octoroon, who now resides with
him at his home in the suburbs. It is certain that these
facts are not known to the people who have him in tow,
but they are easy of substantiation when necessary. We
look to you and your county to save the district. We
were "done up" here before we were armed with this information. Respectfully yours,   Amos Royson.'

"Thousands of these circulars were printed and yesterday put in the hands of every voter. Col. Montjoy's
friends were taken by surprise and their enthusiasm chilled. Many failed to vote and the county was lost by twen-
ty-three majority. Intense excitement prevails here
among the survivors of Evan's brigade, who feel themselves compromised."

Then followed an editorial denouncing the outrage
and demanding proofs. It ended by stating that the limited time prevented the presentation of interviews with
Royson and Morgan, neither of whom could be reached
by telephone after the news was received.

There are moments when the very excess of danger
calms. Half the letter, the political lie alone, would have
enraged Edward Morgan beyond expression. The attack upon his blood was too fierce an assault. He could
not realize nor give expression to his feeling. In fact, he
was stunned. He looked up to find himself in front of the
office of Ellison Eldridge. Turning abruptly he ascended
the steps; the lawyer was reading the article as he appeared, but would have laid aside the paper.

"Finish," said Edward, curtly; "it is upon that publication I have come to advise with you." He stood at the window while the other read, and there as he waited a realization of the enormity of the blow, its cowardliness, its cruelty, grew upon him slowly. He had never contemplated publicity; he had looked forward to a life abroad, with this wearing mystery forever gnawing at his heart, but publication and the details and the apparent truth! It was horrible! And to disprove it—how? The minutes passed! Would the man behind him never finish what he himself had devoured in three minutes? He looked back; Eldridge was gazing over the paper into space, his face wearing an expression of profound melancholy. He had uttered no word of denunciation; he was evidently not even surprised.

"My God!" exclaimed Edward, excitedly; "you believe it—you believe it!" Seizing the paper, he dashed from the room, threw himself into a hack and gave the order for home.

And half an hour after he was gone the lawyer sat as he left him, thinking.

Edward found a reporter awaiting him.

"You have the extra, I see, Mr. Morgan," said he; "may I ask what you will reply to it?"

"Nothing!" thundered the desperate man.

"Will you not say it is false?"

Edward went up to him. "Young man, there are moments when it is dangerous to question people. This is one of them!" He opened the door and stood waiting. Something in his face induced the newspaper man to take his leave. He said as he departed: "If you write a card we shall be glad to publish it." The sound of the closing door was the answer he received.

Alone and locked in his room, Edward read the devilish letter over and over, until every word of it was seared into his brain forever. It could not be denied that more than once in his life the possibility of his being the son of John Morgan had suggested itself to his mind, but he had invariably dismissed it. Now it came back to him with the force almost of conviction. Had the truth been stated at last? It was the only explanation that fitted the full circumstances of his life—and it fitted them all. It was true and known to be true by at least one other. Eldridge's legal mind, prejudiced in his favor by years of association with his benefactor, had been at once convinced; and if the statement made so positively carried conviction to Eldridge himself, to his legal friend, how would the great sensational public receive it?

It was done, and the result was to be absolute and eternal ruin for Edward Morgan. Such was the conclusion forced upon him.

Then there arose in mind the face of the one girl he remembered. He thought of the effect of the blow upon her. He had been her guest, her associate. The family had received him with open arms. They must share the odium of his disgrace, and for him now what course was left? Flight! To turn his back upon all the trouble and go to his old life, and let the matter die out!

And then came another thought. Could any one prove the charge?

He was in the dark; the cards were held with their backs to him. Suppose he should bring suit for libel, what could he offer? His witness had already spoken and her words substantiated the charge against him. Not a witness, not a scrap of paper, was to be had in his defense. A libel suit would be the rivet in his irons and he would face the public, perhaps for days, and be openly the subject of discussion. It was impossible, but he could fight.

The thought thrilled him to the heart. She should see that he was a man! He would not deal with slander suits, with newspapers; he would make the scoundrel eat his words or he would silence his mouth forever. The man soul was stirred; he no longer felt the humiliation that had rendered him incapable of thought. The truth of the story was not the issue; the injury was its use, false or true. He strode into Gerald's room and broke into the experiments of the scientists, already close friends.

"You have weapons here. Lend me one; the American uses the revolver, I believe?"

Gerald looked at him in astonishment, but he was interested.

"Here is one; can you shoot?"

"Badly; the small sword is my weapon."

"Then let me teach you." Gerald was a boy now; weapons had been his hobby years before.

"Wait, let me fix you a target!" He brushed a chalk drawing from a blackboard at the end of the room and stood, crayon in hand. "What would you prefer to shoot at, a tree, a figure——"

"A figure!"

Gerald rapidly sketched the outlines of a man with white shirt front and stepped aside. Five times the man with the weapon sighted and fired. The figure was not touched. Gerald was delighted. He ran up, took the pistol and reloaded it and fired twice in quick succession. Two spots appeared upon the shirt front; they were just where the lower and center shirt studs would have been.

"You are an artist, I believe," he said to Edward.

The latter bowed his head. "Now, professor, I will show you one of the most curious experiments in physics, the one that explains the chance stroke of billiards done upon the spur of the moment; the one rifle shot of a man's life, and the accurately thrown stone. Stand here," he said to Edward, "and follow my directions closely. Remember, you are a draftsman and are going to outline that figure on the board. Draw it quickly with your pistol for a pen, and just as if you were touching the board. Say when you have finished and don't lower the pistol. Edward drew as directed.

"It is done," he said.

"You have not added the upper stud. Fire!"

An explosion followed; a spot appeared just over the heart.

"See!" shouted Gerald; "a perfect aim; the pistol was on the stud when he fired, but beginners always pull the muzzle to the right, and let the barrel fly up. The secret is this, professor," he continued, taking a pencil and beginning to draw, "the concentration of attention is so perfect that the hand is a part of the eye. An artist who shoots will shoot as he draws, well or badly. Now, no man drawing that figure will measure to see where the stud should be; he would simply put the chalk spot in the right place."

Edward heard no more; loading the pistol he had departed. "If I meet the man!" he said to himself.

CHAPTER XVIII.

HOW THE CHALLENGE WAS WRITTEN.

The search for Royson was unavailing. His determined pursuer tried his office door; it was locked. He walked every business street, entered every restaurant and billiard saloon, every hotel lobby. The politician was not to be found. He himself attracted widespread attention wherever he went. Had he met Royson he would have killed him without a word, but as he walked he did a great deal of thinking. He had no friend in the city. The nature of this attack was such that few people would care to second him. The younger Montjoy was away and he was unwilling to set foot in the colonel's house again. Through him, Edward Morgan, however innocently it might be, had come the fatal blow.

He ran over the list of acquaintances he had formed among the younger men. They were not such as pleased him in this issue, for a strong, clear head, a man of good judgment and good balance, a determined man, was needed.

Then there came to his memory the face of one whom he had met at supper his first night in town—the quiet, dignified Barksdale. He sought this man's office. Barksdale was the organizer of a great railroad in process of construction. His reception of Edward was no more nor less than would have been accorded under ordinary circumstances. Had he come on the day before he would have been greeted as then.

"How do you do, Mr. Morgan? Be seated, sir." This with a wave of his hand. Then, "What can I do for you?" His manner affected Edward in the best way; he began to feel the business atmosphere.

"I have called, Mr. Barksdale, upon a personal matter and to ask your assistance. I suppose you have read to-day's extra?"

"I have."

"My first action, after fully weighing the intent and effect of that infamous publication," said Edward, "was to seek and kill the author. For this purpose I have searched the town. Royson is not to be found. I am so nearly a stranger here that I am forced to come to my acquaintances for assistance, and now I ask that you will advise me as to my next proceeding."

"Demand a retraction and apology at once!"

"And if it is refused?"

"Challenge him!"

"If he refuses to fight?"

"Publish him. That is all you can do."

"Will you make the demand for me—will you act for me?"

Barksdale reflected a moment and then said: "Do not misunderstand my hesitation; it is not based upon the publication, nor upon unwillingness to serve you. I am considering the complications which may involve others. I must, in fact, consult others before I can reply. In the meantime will you be guided by me?"

"I will."

"You are armed and contemplating a very unwise act. Leave your weapon here and take a hack home and remain there until I call. It is now 3:30 o'clock. I will be there at 8. If I do not act for you I will suggest a friend, for this matter should not lie over-night. But under no circumstances can I go upon the field; my position here involves interests covering many hundreds of thousands of invested funds, which I have induced. Dueling is clearly out of vogue in this country and clearly illegal. For the president of a railroad to go publicly into a duel and deliberately break the law would lessen public confidence in the north in both him and his business character and affect the future of his enterprise, the value of its stocks and bonds. You admit the reasonableness of this, do you not?"

"I do. There is my weapon! I will expect you at 8.
Good evening, Mr. Barksdale."

The hours wore away slowly at home. Edward studied
his features in the cheval glass; he could not find in them
the slightest resemblance to the woman in the picture.
He had not erred in that. The absence of any portrait
of John Morgan prevented his making a comparison
there. He knew from descriptions given by Eldridge
that he was not very like him in form or in any way that
he could imagine, but family likeness is an elusive fact.
Two people will resemble each other, although they may
differ in features taken in detail.

He went to Gerald's room, moved by a sudden impulse.
Gerald was demonstrating one of his theories concerning
mind pictures and found in the professor a smiling and
tolerant listener.

He was saying: "Now, let us suppose that from youth
up a child has looked into its mother's face, felt her touch,
heard her voice; that his senses carried to that forming
brain their sensations, each nerve touching the brain, and
with minute force setting up day by day, month by month,
and year by year a model. Yes, go back further and remember that this was going on before the child was a
distinct individual; we have the creative force in both
stages! Tell me, is it impossible then that this little brain
shall grow into the likeness it carries as its most serious
impression, and that forced to the effort would on canvas or in its posterity produce the picture it has made——"

"How can you distinguish the mind picture from the
memory picture? What is the difference?"

The question came from Morgan abruptly. Gerald
looked up.

"Not easily, but if I can produce a face which comes
to me in my dreams, which haunts my waking hours,
which is with me always, the face of one I have never
seen, it must come to me as a mind picture; and if that
picture is the feminine of my own, have I not reason to
believe that it stands for the creative power from which I
sprung? Such a picture as this."

He drew a little curtain aside and on the wall shone
the fair face of a woman; the face from the church sketch,

but robbed of its terror, the counterpart of the little painting upstairs. The professor looked grave, but Edward
gazed on it in awe.

"Now a simple brain picture," he said, almost in a
whisper; "draw me the face of John Morgan."

The artist made not more than twenty strokes of the
crayon upon the blackboard.

"Such is John Morgan, as I last saw him," said Gerald;
"a mere photograph; a brain picture!"

Edward gazed from one to the other; from the picture
to the artist astounded. The professor had put on his
glasses; it was he who broke the silence.

"That is Herr Abingdon," he said. Gerald smiled.

"That is John Morgan."

Without a word Edward left the room. Under an assumed name, deterred from open recognition by the sad
facts of the son's birth, his father had watched over and
cherished him. No wonder the letter had come back.
Abingdon was dead!

The front door was open. He plunged directly into
the arms of Barksdale as he sought the open air. Barksdale was one of those men who seem to be without sentiment, because they have been trained by circumstances
to look at facts from a business standpoint only. Yet the
basis of his whole life was sentiment.

In the difficulty that had arisen his quick mind grasped
at once the situation. He knew Royson and was sure
that he shielded himself behind some collateral fact, not
behind the main truth. In the first place he was hardly
in position to know anything of Morgan's history more
than the general public would have known. In the second, he would not have dared to use it under any circumstances if those circumstances did not protect him. What
were these? First there was Morgan's isolation; only one
family could be said to be intimate with him, and they
could not, on account of the younger Montjoy, act for
Edward. The single controlling idea that thrust itself
into Barksdale's mind was the proposition that Royson
did not intend to fight.

Then the position of the Montjoy family flashed upon
him. The blow had been delivered to crush the colonel

8

politically and upon a man who was his unselfish ally.
Owing to the nature of the attack Col. Montjoy could ask
no favors of Royson, and owing to the relationship, he
could not proceed against him in Morgan's interest. He
could neither act for nor advise, and in the absence of
Col. Montjoy, who else could be found?

Before replying to Edward, a plan of action occurred
to him. When he sent that excited individual home he
went direct to Royson's office. He found the door open
and that gentleman serenely engaged in writing. Even
at this point he was not deceived; he knew that his approach had been seen, as had Edward's, and preparations
made accordingly.

Royson had been city attorney and in reality the tool
of a ring. His ambition was boundless. Through friends
he had broached a subject very dear to him; he desired to
become counsel for the large corporations that Barksdale
represented, and there was a surprised satisfaction in his
tones as he welcomed the railroad president and gave
him a seat.

Barksdale opened the conversation on this line and
asked for a written opinion upon a claim of liability in a
recent accident. He went further and stated that perhaps later Royson might be relied upon frequently in
such cases. The town was talking of nothing else at that
time but the Royson card. It was natural that Barksdale
should refer to it.

"A very stiff communication, that of yours, about Mr.
Morgan," he said, carelessly; "it will probably be fortunate for you if your informant is not mistaken."

"There is no mistake," said Royson, leaning back in
his chair, glad that the subject had been brought up.
"It does seem a rough card to write, but I have reason to
think there was no better way out of a very ugly complication."

"The name of your informant will be demanded, of
course."

"Yes, but I shall not give it!"

"Then will come a challenge."

"Hardly!" Royson arose and closed the door. "If
you have a few moments and do not mind hearing this,

I will tell you in confidence the whole business. Who would be sought to make a demand upon me for the name of my informant?"

"One of the Montjoys naturally, but your relationship barring them they would perhaps find Mr. Morgan a second."

"But suppose that I prove conclusively that the information came from a member of the Montjoy family? What could they do? Under the circumstances which have arisen their hands are tied. As a matter of fact I am the only one that can protect them. If the matter came to that point, as a last resort I could refuse to fight, for the reason given in the letter."

Barksdale was silent. The whole devilish plot flashed upon him. He knew in advance the person described as a member of the Montjoy family, and he knew the base motives of the man who at that moment was dishonoring him with his confidence. His blood boiled within him. Cool and calm as he was by nature, his face showed emotion as he arose and said:

"I think I understand."

Royson stood by the door, his hand upon the knob, after his visitor had gone.

"It was a mistake; a great mistake," he said to himself in a whisper. "I have simply acted the fool!"

Barksdale went straight to a friend upon whose judgment he relied and laid the matter before him. Together they selected three of the most honorable and prominent men in the city, friends of the Montjoys, and submitted it to them.

The main interest was now centered in saving the Montjoy family. Edward had become secondary. An agreement was reached upon Barksdale's suggestion and all was now complete unless the aggrieved party should lose his case in the correspondence about to ensue.

Barksdale disguised his surprise when he assisted Edward at the door to recover his equilibrium.

"I am here, sir, as I promised," he said, "but the complications extend further than I knew. I now state that I cannot act for you in any capacity and ask that I be relieved of my promise." Edward bowed stiffly.

"You are released."

"There is but one man in this city who can serve you and bring about a meeting. Gerald Morgan must bear your note!" Edward repeated the name. He could not grasp the idea. "Gerald Morgan," said Barksdale again. "He will not need to go on the field. Good-night. And if that fails you here is your pistol; you are no longer under my guidance. But one word more—my telephone is 280; if during the night or at any time I can advise you, purely upon formal grounds, summon me. In the meantime see to it that your note does not demand the name of Royson's informant. Do not neglect that. The use he has made of his information must be made the basis of the quarrel; if you neglect this your case is lost. Good-night."

The thought flashed into Edward's mind then that the world was against him. This man was fearful of becoming responsible himself. He had named Gerald. It was a bruised and slender reed, but he would lean upon it, even if he crushed it in the use. He returned to the wing-room.

"Professor," he said, "you know that under no possible circumstances would I do you a discourtesy, so when I tell you, as now, that for to-night and possibly a day, we are obliged to leave you alone, you will understand that some vital matter lies at the bottom of it."

"My young friend," exclaimed that gentleman, "go as long as you please. I have a little world of my own, you know," he smiled cheerfully, "in which I am always amused. Gerald has enlarged it. Go and come when you can; here are books—what more does one need?" Edward bowed slightly.

"Gerald, follow me." Gerald, without a word, laid aside his crayon and obeyed. He stood in the library a moment later looking with tremulous excitement upon the man who had summoned him so abruptly. By reflection he was beginning to share the mental disturbance. His frail figure quivered and he could not keep erect.

"Read that!" said Edward, handing him the paper. He took the sheet and read. When he finished he was no longer trembling, but to the astonishment of Edward, very calm. A look of weariness rested upon his face.

"Have you killed him?" he asked, laying aside the paper, his mind at once connecting the incident of the pistol with this one.

"No, he is in hiding."

"Have you challenged him?"

"No! My God, can you not understand? I am without friends! The whole city believes the story." A strange expression came upon the face of Gerald.

"We must challenge him at once," he said. "I am, of course, the proper second. I must ask you in the first place to calm yourself. The records must be perfect." He seated himself at a desk and prepared to write. Edward was walking the room. He came and stood by his side.

"Do not demand the name of his informant," he said; "make the publication and circulation of the letter the cause of our grievance."

"Of course," was the reply. The letter was written rapidly. "Sign it if you please," said Gerald. Edward read the letter and noticed that it was written smoothly and without a break. He signed it. Gerald had already rung for the buggy and disappeared. "Wait here," he had said, "until I return. In the meantime do not converse with any one upon this subject." The thought that flashed upon the mind of the man left in the drawing-room was that the race courage had become dominant, and for the time being was superior to ill-health, mental trouble and environment. It was in itself a confirmation of the cruel letter. The manhood of Albert Evan had become a factor in the drama.

CHAPTER XIX.

BROUGHT TO BAY.

Col. Montjoy was apprised of the unexpected result in the backwoods at an early hour. He read the announcement quietly and went on his usual morning ride

undisturbed. Then through the family spread the news
as the other members made their appearance.

Mrs. Montjoy said, gently: "All happens for the best.
If Mr. Montjoy had been elected he would have been
exposed for years to the Washington climate, and he is
not very well at any time. He complained of his heart
several times last night."

But Mary went off and had a good cry. She could
not endure the thought of the slightest affront to her
stately father. She felt better after her cry and kissed
the old gentleman as he came in to breakfast.

"I see you have all heard the news," he said, cheerily.
"Well, it lifts a load from me. I spent four very trying
years up in the neighborhood of Washington, and I am
not well disposed toward the locality. I have done my
duty to the fullest extent in this matter. The people
who know me have given me an overwhelming indorse-
ment, and I have been beaten only by people who do
not know me! Swearingen will doubtless make a good
representative, after all. I am sorry for Evan," he
added, laughing. "It will be news to him to find out
that the old Fire-Eaters have been worsted at last." He
went to breakfast with his arms around wife and daughter. "All the honors of public life cannot compensate a
man for separation from his home," he said, "and Providence knows it."

Annie was silent and anxious. She made a feeble
effort to sympathize with the defeated, but with poor
success. During the morning she started at every sound
and went frequently to the front door. She knew her
cousin, and something assured her that his hand was in
this mischief. How would it affect her? In her room
she laughed triumphantly.

"Vain fools!" she exclaimed; "let them stay where
they belong!" In the afternoon there was the sound of
buggy wheels, and a servant brought to the veranda,
where they were sitting, a package. Adjusting his
glasses, the colonel opened it to find one of the extras.
At the head of this was written: "Thinking it probable
that it may be important for this to reach you to-day,
and fearing it might not otherwise, I send it by mes-

senger in buggy. Use him as you desire." To this was signed the name of a friend.

Annie, who watched the colonel as he read, saw his face settle into sternness, and then an expression of anxiety overspread it. "Anything serious, Norton?" It was the voice of his wife, who sat knitting.

"A matter connected with the election calls me to town," he said; "I hope it will be the last time. I will go in with the driver who brought the note." He went inside and made his few arrangements and departed hurriedly. After he was gone, Annie picked up the paper from the hall table, where he had placed it, and read the fatal announcement. Although frightened, she could scarcely conceal her exultation. Mary was passing; she thrust the paper before her eyes and said: "Read that! So much for entertaining strangers!"

Mary read. The scene whirled about her, and but for the knowledge that her suffering was bringing satisfaction to the woman before her she would have fallen to the floor. She saw in the gleeful eyes, gleaming upon her, something of the truth. With a desperate effort she restrained herself and the furious words that had rushed to her lips, and laid aside the paper with unutterable scorn and dignity.

"The lie was too cheap to pass anywhere except in the backwoods."

A smile curled the thin lips of the other as she witnessed the desperate struggle of the girl. The voice of Col. Montjoy, who had returned to the gate, was heard calling to Mary:

"Daughter, bring the paper from the hall table."

She carried it to him. Something in her pale face caused him to ask: "Have you read it, daughter?"

She nodded her head. He was instantly greatly concerned and began some rambling explanation about campaign lies and political methods. But he could not disguise the fact that he was shocked beyond expression. She detained him but a moment. Oh, wonderful power of womanly intuition!

"Father," she said faintly, "be careful what you do. The whole thing originated back yonder," nodding her

head toward the house. She had said it, and now her
eyes blazed defiance. He looked upon her in amazement, not comprehending, but the matter grew clearer
as he thought upon it.

Arriving in the city he was prepared for anything.
He went direct to Royson's office, and that gentleman
seeing him enter smiled. The visit was expected and
desired. He bowed formally, however, and moving a
chair forward locked the door. Darkness had just fallen,
but the electric light outside the window was sufficient for
an interview; neither seemed to care for more.

"Amos," said the old man, plunging into the heart of the
subject, "you have done a shameful and a cruel thing, and
I have come to tell you so and insist upon your righting
the wrong. You know me too well to suspect that personal reasons influence me in the least. As far as I am
concerned the wrong cannot be righted, and I would not
purchase nor ask a personal favor from you. The man
you have insulted so grievously is a stranger and has
acted the part of a generous friend to those who, although
you may not value the connection, are closely bound to
you. In the name of God, how could you do it?" He
was too full of indignation to proceed, and he had need
of coolness.

The other did not move nor give the slightest evidence
of feeling. He had this advantage; the part he was acting had been carefully planned and rehearsed. After a
moment's hesitation, he said:

"You should realize, Col. Montjoy, that I have acted
only after calm deliberation, and the matter is not one
to be discussed excitedly. I cannot refuse to talk with
you about it, but it is a cold-blooded matter of policy
only." The manner and tone of the speaker chilled the
elder to the heart. Royson continued: "As for myself
and you—well, it was an open, impersonal fight. You
know my ambition; it was as laudable as yours. I have
worked for years to keep in the line of succession; I could
not be expected to sit silent and while losing my whole
chance see my friend defeated. Your election meant the
eternal shelving of my hopes. All is fair in love and war
—and politics. I have used such weapons as came to

my hand, and the last I used only when defeat was certain."

Controlling himself with great effort, Col. Montjoy said:

"You certainly cannot expect the matter to end here!"

"How can it proceed?" A slight smile lighted the lawyer's face.

"A demand will be made upon you for your authority."

"Who will make it—you?"

A light dawned upon the elder. The cool insolence of the man was more than he could endure.

"Yes!" he exclaimed, rising. "As God is my judge, if he comes to me I will make the demand! Ingratitude was never charged against one of my name. This man has done me a lasting favor; he shall not suffer for need of a friend, if I have to sacrifice every connection in the world."

Again the lawyer smiled.

"I think it best to remember, colonel, that we can reach no sensible conclusion without cool consideration. Let me ask you, then, for information. If I should answer that the charges in my letter, so far as Morgan's parentage is concerned, were based upon statements made by a member of your immediate family, what would be your course?"

"I should denounce you as a liar and make the quarrel my own."

Royson grew pale, but made no reply. He walked to his desk, and taking from it a letter passed it to the angry man. He lighted the gas, while the colonel's trembling hands were arranging his glasses, and stood silent, waiting. The note was in a feminine hand. Col. Montjoy read:

"My Dear Amos: I have been thinking over the information I gave you touching the base parentage of the man Morgan, and I am not sure but that it should be suppressed so far as the public is concerned, and brought home here in another way. The facts cannot be easily proved, and the affair would create a great scandal, in which I, as a member of this absurd family, would be involved. You should not use it, at any rate, except as a desperate measure, and then only upon the understanding that you are to become responsible, and that I am in no way whatever to be brought into the matter.   Yours in haste,   Annie."

The reader let the paper fall and covered his face with his hands a moment.   Then he arose with dignity.

"I did not imagine, sir, that the human heart was capable of such villainy as yours has developed.   You have stabbed a defenseless stranger in the back; have broken faith with a poor, jealous, weak woman, and have outraged and humiliated me, to whom you are personally indebted financially and otherwise.   Unlock your door! I have but one honorable course left.   I shall publish a card in the morning's paper stating that your letter was based upon statements made by a member of my family; that they are untrue in every respect, and offer a public apology."

"Will you name the informant?"

"What is that to you, sir?"

"A great deal!   If you do name her, I shall reaffirm the truth of her statements, as in the absence of her husband I am her nearest relative.   If you do not name her, then the public may guess wrong.   I think you will not do so rash a thing, colonel.   Keep out of the matter. Circumstances give you a natural right to hands off!"

"And if I do!" exclaimed the old man, passionately, "who will act for him?"   The unpleasant smile returned to the young man's lips.

"No one, I apprehend!"

Montjoy could have killed him as he stood.   He felt the ground slipping from under him as he, too, realized the completeness and cowardliness of the plot.

"We shall see; we shall see!" he said, gasping and pressing his hand to his heart.   "We shall see, Mr. Royson!   There is a just God who looks down upon the acts of all men, and the right prevails!"

Royson bowed mockingly but profoundly.

"That is an old doctrine.   You are going, and there is just one thing left unsaid.   At the risk of offending you yet more, I am going to say it."

"I warn you, then, to be careful; there is a limit to human endurance and I have nearly reached mine."

"It is this: You have persistently ascribed to me the worst of motives in this matter, but I have as much pride in my family as you in yours. There are but few of us left. Will you concede that if there is danger, in her opinion, that she will become the sister-in-law of this man, and that she believed the information she has given to be true, will you concede that her action is natural, if not wise, and that a little more than selfishness may after all be mixed in mine?" Gradually his meaning dawned upon his hearer. For a second he was dumb. And all this was to be public property!

"I think," said Royson, coolly opening the door, "it will be well for you to confer with friends before you proceed, and perhaps leave to others the task of righting the wrongs of strangers who have taken advantage of your hospitality to offer the deadliest insult possible in this southern country. It may not be well to arm this man with the fact that you vouch for him; he may answer you in the future."

He drew back from the door suddenly, half in terror. A man, pale as death itself, with hair curling down upon his shoulders, and eyes that blazed under the yellow gaslight, stood before him.

"Mr. Amos Royson, I believe," the man was saying, in clear, musical tones. "I beg to hand you this note." Royson, his eyes riveted upon the face before him, whose eyes never for a moment left his, broke the seal. Then he read aloud:

"Mr. Amos Royson—Sir: I inclose for your inspection a clipping from an extra issued this day, and ask if you are the author of the letter it contains. If you answer yes, I hereby demand of you an unconditional retraction of and apology for the same, for publication in the paper which contained the original. This will be handed to you by my friend, Gerald Morgan.
                    "Edward Morgan."

Royson recovered himself with evident difficulty.

"This is not customary—he does not demand the name of my informant!" he said.

"We do not care a fig, sir, for your informant. The insult rests in the use you have made of a lie, and we propose to hold you responsible for it!"

Gerald spoke the words like a sweet-voiced girl and returned the stare of his opponent with insolent coolness. The colonel had paused, as he perceived the completeness of the lawyer's entrapping. Amos could not use his cousin's name before the public and the Montjoys were saved from interference. He was cornered. The colonel passed out hurriedly with an affectionate smile to Gerald, saying:

"Excuse me, gentlemen; these are matters which you will probably wish to discuss in private. Mr. Royson, I had friends wiser than myself at work upon this matter, and I did not know it."

CHAPTER XX.

IN THE HANDS OF THEIR FRIENDS.

It was not sunset when Col. Montjoy left home. Mary went to her room and threw herself upon her bed, sick at heart and anxious beyond the power of weeping. Unadvised, ignorant of the full significance of the information that had been conveyed to them, she conjured up a world of danger for her father and for Edward. Tragedy was in the air she breathed. At supper she was laboring under ill-concealed excitement. Fortunately for her, the little mother was not present. Sitting in her room, with the green glasses to which she had been reduced by the progress of her disease, she did not notice the expression of the daughter's face when she came as usual to look after the final arrangement of her mother's comfort.

By 8 o'clock the house was quiet. Throwing a light wrap over her shoulders and concealing in its folds her father's army pistol, Mary slipped into the outer darkness and whistled softly. A great shaggy dog came bounding around from the rear and leaped upon her.

She rested her hand on his collar, and together they
passed into the avenue.   Old Isam stood there and by
him the pony phaeton and mare.

"Stay up until I return, please, Uncle Isam, and be
sure to meet me here!"   The old man bowed.

"I'll be hyar, missy," he said.   "Don't you want me to
go, too?"

"No, thank you; I am going to Gen. Evan's and you
must stay and look after things.   Nero will go with me."
The dog had already leaped into the vehicle.   She sprang
in also, and almost noiselessly they rolled away over the
pine straw.

The old man listened; first he heard the dogs bark at
Rich's, then at Manuel's and then at black Henry's,
nearly a mile away.   He shook his head.

"Missy got somep'n on her mind!   She don't make no
hoss move in de night dat way for nothin'!   Too fast!
Too fast!"

He went off to his cabin and sat outside to smoke.
And in the night the little mare sped away.   On the
public roads the gait was comparatively safe, and she
responded to every call nobly.   The unbroken shadows
of the roadside glided like walls of gloom!   The little
vehicle rocked and swayed, and, underneath, the wheels
sang a monotonous warning rhyme.

Now and then the little structure fairly leaped from the
ground, for when Norton, a year previous, had bid in
that animal at a blooded-stock sale in Kentucky, she was
in her third summer and carried the blood of Wilkes and
Rysdyk's Hambletonian, and was proud of it, as her
every motion showed.

The little mare had the long route that night, but at last
she stood before the doorway of the Cedars.   The general was descending the steps as Mary gave Nero the
lines.

"What!   Mary—"

He feared to ask the question on his lips.   She was
full of excitement, and her first effort to speak was a
dismal failure.

"Come!   Come!   Come!" he said, in that descending
scale of voice which seems to have been made for sym-

pathy and encouragement. "Calm yourself first and talk later." He had his arms around her now and was ascending the steps. "Sit right down here in this big chair; there you are!"

"You have not heard, then?" she said, controlling herself with supreme effort.

"About your father's defeat? Oh, yes. But what of that? There are defeats more glorious than victories, my child. You will find that your father was taken advantage of. The Fire-Eaters were not whipped in a fair fight!" She buried her face in her hands.

"It is not about that, sir—the means they used!" And then, between sobs, she told him the whole story. He made no reply, no comment, but reaching over to the rail secured his corn-cob pipe and filled it. As he struck a match above the tobacco, she saw that his face was as calm as the candid skies of June. The sight gave her courage.

"Do you not think it awful?" she ventured.

"Awful? Yes! A man to descend to such depths of meanness must have suffered a great deal on the way. I am sorry for Royson—sorry, indeed!"

"But Mr. Morgan!" she exclaimed, excitedly.

"That must be attended to," he said, very gravely. "Mr. Morgan has placed us all under heavy obligations, and we must see him through."

"You must, general; you must, and right away! They have sent for poor papa, and he has gone to town, and I —I—just could not sleep, so I came to you." He laughed heartily.

"And in a hurry! Whew! I heard the mare's feet as she crossed the bridge a mile away. You did just right. And now of course the old general is expected to go to town and pull papa and Mr. Morgan out of the mud, and straighten out things. John!"

"Yes, sah!"

"Put the saddle on my horse at once. And now, how is the little mamma?" he asked, gently.

He held her on this subject until the horse was brought, and then they rode off down the avenue, the general following and rallying the girl upon her driving.

"Don't expect me to hold to that pace," he said. "I once crossed a bridge as fast, and faster, up in Virginia, but I was trying to beat the bluecoats. Too old now, too old."

"But you will get there in time?" she asked, anxiously.

"Oh, yes; they will be consulting and sending notes and raising points all night. I will get in somewhere along the line. When a man starts out to hunt up trouble he is rarely ever too late to find it." He saw her safely to where Isam was waiting, and then rode on to the city. He realized the complication, and now his whole thought was to keep his neighbor from doing anything rash. It did occur to him that there might be a street tragedy, but he shook his head over this when he remembered Royson. "He is too much of a schemer for that," he said. "He will get the matter into the hands of a board of honor." The old gentleman laughed softly to himself and touched up his horse.

In the meantime affairs were drawing to a focus in the city. After the abrupt departure of Gerald, Royson stood alone, holding the demand and thinking. An anxious expression had settled upon his face. He read and reread the curt note, but could find no flaw in it. He was to be held responsible for the publication; that was the injury. He was forced to confess that the idea was sound. There was now no way to involve the Montjoys and let them hush it up. He had expected to be forced to withdraw the card and apologize, but not until the whole city was informed that he did it to save a woman, and he would have been placed then in the position of one sacrificing himself. Now that such refuge was impossible he could not even escape by giving the name of his informant. He could not have given it had there been a demand.

He read between the lines that his authority was known; that he was dealing with some master mind and that he had been outgeneraled somewhere. To whom had he talked? To no one except Barksdale. He gave vent to a profane estimate of himself and left the office. There was no danger now of a street assault.

Amos Royson threw himself into a carriage and went to the residence of Marsden Thomas, dismissing the vehicle. The family of Marsden Thomas was an old one, and by reason of its early reputation in politics and at the bar had a sound and honorable footing. Marsden was himself a member of the legislature, a born politician, capable of anything that would advance his fortune, the limit only being the dead-line of disgrace.

He had tied to Royson, who was slightly his elder, because of his experience and influence.

He was noted for his scrupulous regard for the code as a basis of settlement between honorable men, and was generally consulted upon points of honor.

Secure in Thomas' room, Royson went over the events of the day, including Montjoy's and Gerald's visits, and then produced the demand that had been served upon him.

Thomas had heard him through without interruption. When Royson described the entrance of Gerald, with the unlooked-for note, a slight smile drew his lips; he put aside the note, and said:

"You are in a very serious scrape, Amos; I do not see how you can avoid a fight." His visitor studied him intently.

"You must help me out! I do not propose to fight." Thomas gravely studied the note again.

"Of course, you know the object of the publication," continued Royson; "it was political. Without it we would have been beaten. It was a desperate move; I had the information and used it."

"You had information, then? I thought the whole thing was hatched up. Who gave you the information?" Royson frowned.

"My cousin, Mrs. Montjoy; you see the complication now. I supposed that no one but the Montjoys knew this man intimately, and that their hands would be tied!"

"Ah!" The exclamation was eloquent. "And the young man had another friend, the morphine-eater; you had forgotten him!" Thomas could not restrain a laugh. Royson was furious. He seized his hat and made a feint to depart. Thomas kindly asked him to remain. It

would have been cruel had he failed, for he knew that
Royson had not the slightest intention of leaving.

"Come back and sit down, Amos. You do us all an
injustice. You played for the credit of this victory, contrary to our advice, and now you have the hot end of
the iron."

"Tell me," said Royson, reverting to the note, "is there
anything in that communication that we can take advantage of?"

"Nothing! Morgan might have asked in one note if
you were the author of the published letter and then in
another have demanded a retraction. His joining the
two is not material; you do not deny the authorship."

After a few moments of silence he continued: "There
is one point I am not satisfied upon. I am not sure but
that you can refuse to fight upon the ground you alleged
—in brief, because he is not a gentleman. Whether or
not the burden of proof would be upon you is an open
question; I am inclined to think it would be; a man is
not called upon in the south to prove his title to gentility.
All southerners with whom we associate are supposed to
be gentlemen," and then he added, lazily smiling, "except
the ladies; and it is a pity they are exempt. Mrs. Montjoy would otherwise be obliged to hold her tongue!"

Royson was white with rage, but he did not speak.
Secretly he was afraid of Thomas, and it had occurred
to him that in the event of his humiliation or death
Thomas would take his place.

This unpleasant reflection was interrupted by the voice
of his companion.

"Suppose we call in some of our friends and settle this
point." The affair was getting in the shape desired by
Royson, and he eagerly consented. Notes were at once
dispatched to several well-known gentlemen, and a short
time afterward they were assembled and in earnest conversation. It was evident that they disagreed.

While this consultation was going on there was a
knock at the door; a servant brought a card. Gen.
Evan had called to see Mr. Thomas, but, learning that
he was engaged and how, had left the note.

Thomas read it silently, and then aloud:

9

"Marsden Thomas, Esq.—Dear Sir: I have read in to-day's paper the painful announcement signed by Mr. Royson, and have come into the city hoping that a serious difficulty might thereby be averted. To assist in the settlement of this matter, I hereby state over my own signature that the announcement concerning Edward Morgan is erroneous, and I vouch for his right to the title and privileges of a gentleman. Respectfully,

"Albert Evan."

The silence that followed this was broken by one of the older gentlemen present.

"This simplifies matters very greatly," he said. "Without the clearest and most positive proof to the contrary, Evan's word will carry public opinion with it. He can be mistaken, but never false! Without such proof, Mr. Royson must retract or fight."

They took their departure at length, leaving Royson alone to gaze upon the open note. Thomas, returning, found him in the act of drawing on his gloves.

"I am going," said Royson, "to send a message to Annie. She must, she shall give me something to go on. I will not sit quietly by and be made a sacrifice!"

"Write your note; I will send it."

"I prefer to attend to it myself!" Thomas shook his head.

"If you leave this room to-night it is with the understanding that I am no longer your adviser. Arrest by the police must not, shall not—"

"Do you mean to insinuate—"

"Nothing! But I will take no chances with the name of Thomas!" said the other proudly. "You are excited; a word let fall—a suspicion—and we would be disgraced! Write your note; I will send it. We have no time to lose!" Royson threw himself down in front of a desk and wrote hurriedly:

"Annie: I am cornered. For God's sake give me proofs of your statements or tell me where to get them. It is life or death; don't fail me.   A. R."

He sealed and addressed this. Thomas rung the bell and to the boy he said: "How far is it to Col. Montjoy's?"

"Seven miles, sah!"

"How quickly can you go there and back?"

"On Pet?"

"Yes."

"One hour an' a half, sah."

"Take this note, say you must see Mrs. Norton Montjoy, Jr., in person, on important matters, and deliver it to her. Here is a $5 bill; if you are back in two hours, you need not return it. Go!"

There was a gleam of ivory teeth and the boy hurried away. It was a wretched wait, that hour and a half. The answer to the demand must go into the paper that night!

One hour and thirty-two minutes passed. They heard the horse in the street, then the boy upon the stairway. He dashed to the door.

"Miss Mary was up and at de gate when I got deir! Reck'n she hear Pet's hoof hit de hard groun' an' hit skeered her. I tole her what you say, and she sen' word dat Mrs. Montjoy done gone to sleep. I tell her you all mighty anxious for her to get dat note; dat Mr. Royson up here, waitin', an' gentlemen been comin' an' goin' all night. She took de note in den and putty soon she bring back the answer!"

He was searching his pockets as he rambled over his experience, and presently the note was found. It was the same one that had been sent by Royson, and across the back was written:

"Mr. Thomas: I think it best not to awaken Annie. Papa is in town; if the matter is of great importance call upon him. I am so certain this is the proper course that it will be useless to write again or call in person to-night. Respectfully,   M. M."

He passed the note to Royson in silence and saw the look of rage upon his face as he tore it into a thousand pieces.

"Even your little Montjoy girl seems to be against you," he said.

"She is!" exclaimed Royson; "she knew that my note to Annie was not in the interest of Edward Morgan, and she is fighting for him. She will follow him to the altar or the grave!"

"Ah," said Thomas, aside, drawing a long breath; "'tis the old story, and I thought I had found a new plot! Well," he continued aloud, "what next?"

"It shall not be the altar! Conclude the arrangements; I am at your service!"

"He will stick," said Thomas to himself; "love and jealousy are stronger than fear and ambition!"

CHAPTER XXI.

"THE WITNESS IS DEAD."

In his room at the hotel Col. Montjoy awaited the return of his friend Evan, who had gone to find out how, as he expressed it, the boys were getting on with their fight.

"I will strike the trail somewhere," he said, lightly. But he was greatly disturbed over Col. Montjoy's concern, and noticed at once the bad physical effect it had on him. His policy was to make light of the matter, but he knew it was serious.

To force Royson to back down was now his object; in the event of that failing, to see that Morgan had a fair show.

The colonel had removed his shoes and coat and was lying on the bed when Evan returned. "I think I have given them a basis of settlement," said the general. "I have vouched for the fact that the statements in Royson's letter are erroneous. Upon my declaration he can retract and apologize, or he must fight. I found him consulting with Thomas and others, and I took it for granted he was looking for some way to dodge."

The colonel looked at him in surprise. "But how could you?"

"Upon my faith in John Morgan! He was a man of honor! He would never have left his property to this man and put him upon the community if there had been a cloud upon his title to gentility," and then he added, with emotion: "A man who was willing to give his daughter to a friend can risk a great deal to honor that friend's memory."

"There is but one Albert Evan in the world," said Montjoy, after a long silence.

The general was getting himself a glass of wine. "Well, there is but one such Montjoy, for that matter, but we two old fellows lose time sitting up to pay each other compliments! There is much to be done. I am going out to see Morgan; he is so new here he may need help! You stay and keep quiet. The town is full of excitement over this affair, and people watch me as if I were a curiosity. You can study on politics if you will; consider the proposition that if Royson retracts we are entitled to another trial over yonder in the lost county; that or we will threaten them with an independent race."

"No! I am too glad to have a chance to stay out honorably. I know now that my candidacy was a mistake. It has weakened me here fatally."

Col. Montjoy placed his hand over his heart wearily. The general brought him the glass of wine he held.

"Nonsense! Too many cigars! Here's to long life, old friend, and to the gallant Fire-Eaters!" He laughed lightly over his remembrance of the checkmate he had accomplished, buttoned the blue coat over his broad chest and started. "I am going now to look in upon my outpost and see what arrangements have been made for the night. So far we hold the strong positions. Look for me about daylight!" And, lying there alone, his friend drifted back in thought to Mary. He was not satisfied.

The door stood open at Ilexhurst when the general alighted. There was no answer to his summons; he entered the lighted hall and went to the library. Edward was sleeping quietly upon a lounge.

"What!" exclaimed the general, cheerily, "asleep on guard!" Edward sprang to his feet.

"Gen. Evan!"

"Exactly; and as no one answered my summons to surrender I took possession." Apologizing, Edward drew a chair, and they became seated.

"Seriously, my young friend," began the old soldier. "I was in the city to-night and have learned from Col. Montjoy of the infamy perpetrated upon you. My days of warfare are over, but I could not sit by and see one to whom we all owe so much imposed upon. Let me add, also, that I was very much charmed with you, Mr. Morgan. If there is anything I can do for you in the way of advice and guidance in this matter kindly command me. I might say the same thing for Montjoy, who is at the hotel, but unfortunately, as you may not know, his daughter-in-law is Mr. Royson's cousin, and acting upon my advice he is silent until the necessity for action arises. I know him well enough to add that you can rely upon his sympathy, and if needed, his aid. I have advised him to take no action, as in the first place he is not needed, and in the second it may bring about an estrangement between his son and himself."

Edward was very grateful and expressed himself earnestly, but his head was in a whirl. He was thinking of the woman's story, and of Gerald.

"Such a piece of infamy as is embraced in that publication," said the general, when finally the conversation went direct to the heart of the trouble, "was never equaled in this state. Have they replied to your note?"

"Not yet. I am waiting for the answer!"

"And your—cousin—is he here to receive it?"

"Gerald? Yes, he is here—that is, excuse me, I will see!"

Somewhat alarmed over the possibility of Gerald's absence, he hurried through the house to the wing, and then into the glass-room. Gerald was asleep. The inevitable little box of pellets upon his table told the sad story. Edward could not awaken him.

"It is unfortunate, very," he said, re-entering the library hurriedly, "but Gerald is asleep and cannot be aroused. The truth is, he is a victim of opium. The poor fellow is now beyond cure, I am afraid; he is frail, nervous,

excitable, and cannot live without the drug. The day
has been a very trying one for him, and this is the first
time he has been out in years!"

"He must be awakened," said the general. "Of course
he cannot, in the event that these fellows want to fight,
go on the field, and then his relationship! But to-night!
To-night he must be aroused! Let me go with you."
Edward started almost in terror.

"It might not be well, general—it is not necessary—"

"On the contrary, a strange voice may have more
effect than yours—no ladies about? Of course not!
Lead on, I follow." Greatly confused, Edward led the
way. As they reached the wing he explained the fact
of the glass-room, the whim, the fancy of an imaginative
mind, and then they entered.

Gerald was sleeping, as was his habit, with one arm
extended, the other under his head; his long hair clustering about his face. The light was burning brightly,
and the general approached. Thrilled to the heart, Edward steeled himself for a shock. It was well he did.
The general bent forward and laid his hand on the
sleeper's shoulder. Then he stepped quickly back, seized
Edward with the strength of a giant and stood there
trembling, his eyes riveted upon the pale face on the
pillow.

"Am I dreaming?" he asked, in a changed voice. "Is
this—the young man—you spoke of?"

"It is Gerald Morgan."

"Strange! Strange! That likeness! The likeness of
one who will never wake again, my friend, never! Excuse me; I was startled, overwhelmed! I would have
sworn I looked upon that face as I did in the olden
times, when I used to go and stand in the moonlight
and dream above it!"

"Ah," said Edward, his heart turning to ice within him,
"whose was it?" The answer came in a whisper.

"It was my wife's face first, and then it was the face
of my daughter!" He drew himself up proudly, and,
looking long upon the sleeper, said, gently: "They shall
not waken you, poor child. Albert Evan will take your
place!" With infinite tenderness he brushed back a lock

of hair that fell across the white brow and stood watching
him.

Edward turned from the scene with a feeling that it
was too sacred for intrusion. Over the sleeping form
stood the old man. A generation of loneliness, of silence,
of dignified, uncomplaining manhood lay between them.
What right had he, an alien, to be dumb when a word
might bring hope and interest back to that saddened life?
Was he less noble than the man himself—than the frail
being locked in the deathlike slumber?

He glanced once more at Gerald. How he had risen
to the issue, and in the face of every instinct of a shrinking nature had done his part until the delicate machinery
gave way! Suppose their positions were reversed; that
he lay upon the bed, and Gerald stood gazing into the
night through the dew-gemmed glass, possessed of such
a secret. Would he hesitate? No! The answer formed
itself instantly—not unless he had base blood in his veins.

It was that taint that now held back him, Edward
Morgan; he was a coward. And yet, what would be the
effect if he should burst out in that strange place with
his fearful secret? There would be an outcry; Rita
would be dragged in, her story poured forth, and on him
the old man's eyes would be turned in horror and pity.
Then the published card would stand a sentence of social
degradation, and he in a foreign land would nurse the
memory of a woman and his disgrace. And Royson!
He ground his teeth.

"I will settle that first," he said in a hoarse whisper,
"and then if it is true I will prove, God helping me, that
His spirit can animate even the child of a slave!" He
bowed his head upon his breast and wept.

Presently there came to him a consciousness that the
black shadow pressing against the glass almost at his
feet was more than a shadow. It took the form of a
human being and moved; then the glass gave way and
through the shivered fragments as it fell, he saw the face
of Rita sink from view. With a loud cry he dashed at
the door and sprang into the darkness! Her tall form
lay double in the grass. He drew her into the path of
light that streamed out and bent above her. The woman

struggled to speak, moving her head from side to side and lifting it. A groan burst from her as if she realized that the end had come and her effort would be useless. He, too, realized it. He pointed upward quickly.

"There is your God," he said, earnestly, "waiting! Tell me in His name, am I your child? You know! A mother never forgets! Answer—close your eyes—give me a sign if they have lied to you!"

She half-rose in a frantic struggle. Her eyes seemed bursting from their sockets, and her lips framed her last sentence in almost a shriek.

"They lied!"

Edward was on his feet in an instant; his lips echoing her words. "They lied!" The gaslight from within illumined his features, now bright with triumph, as he looked upward.

The old general rushed out. He saw the prostrate form and fixed eyes of the corpse.

"What is it?" he asked, horrified. Edward turned to him, dizzily; his gaze followed the old man's.

"Ah!" he said, "the nurse! She has died of anxiety and watching!" A loud summons from the ponderous knocker echoed in the house. Edward, excited, had already begun to move away.

"Hold!" exclaimed the general, "where now?"

"I go to meet the slanderer of my race! God have mercy upon him now, when we come face to face!" His manner alarmed the general. He caught him by the arm.

"Easy now, my young friend; this poor woman's fate has unnerved you; not a step further." He led Edward to the wing-room and forced him down to the divan. "Stay until I return!" The summons without had been renewed; the general responded in person and found Marsden Thomas at the door, who gazed in amazement upon the stately form before him, and after a moment's hesitation said, stiffly:

"I have a communication to deliver to Gerald Morgan. Will you kindly summon him, general?"

"I know your errand," said Evan, blandly, "and you need waste no ceremony on me. Gerald is too ill to act longer for Edward Morgan.   I take his place to-night."

"You! Gen. Evan!"

"Why not? Did you ever hear that Albert Evan left a friend upon the field? Come in, come in, Thomas; we are mixed up in this matter, but it is not our quarrel. I want to talk with you."

Thomas smiled; the matter was to end in a farce.

Without realizing it, these two men were probably the last in the world to whom should have fallen an affair of honor that might have been settled by concessions. The bluff old general defeated Thomas' efforts to stand on formal ground, got him into a seat, and went directly at the matter.

"It must strike you, Thomas, as absurd that in these days men cannot settle their quarrels peacefully. There is obliged to be a right and a wrong side always, and sometimes the right side has some fault in it and the wrong side some justice. No man can hesitate, when this adjustment has been made, to align himself with one and repudiate the other. Now, we both represent friends, and neither of us can suffer them to come out of this matter smirched. I would not be willing for Royson to do so, and certainly not for Morgan. If we can bring both parties out safely, is it not our duty to do so? You will agree with me!" Thomas said without hesitation:

"I waive a great deal, general, on your account, when I discuss this matter at all; but I certainly cannot enter into the merits of the quarrel unless you withdraw your demand upon us. You have demanded a retraction of a charge made by us or satisfaction. You cannot expect me to discuss the advisability of a retraction when I have here a note—"

"Which you have not delivered, and which I, an old man sick of war and quarrels, beg that you will not deliver until we have talked over this matter fully. Why cannot Royson retract, when he has my assurance that he is in error?"

"For the reason, probably, general, that he does not believe your statements—although his friends do!" Evan arose and paced the room. Coming back he stood over the young man.

"Did he say so? By the eternal—"

"General, suppose we settle one affair at a time; I herewith hand you, as Royson's friend, his reply to the demand of Mr. Morgan. Now, give me your opinion as to the locality where this correspondence can be quietly and successfully concluded, in the event that your principal wishes to continue it." Trembling with rage the old man opened the message; it read:

"Mr. Edward Morgan—Sir: I have your communication of this date handed to me at 8 o'clock to-night by Mr. Gerald Morgan. I have no retraction or apology to make.   Amos Royson."

Gen. Evan looked upon the missive sadly and long. He placed it upon the table and resumed his seat, saying:

"Do you understand, Mr. Thomas, that what I have said is entirely upon my own responsibility and as a man who thinks his age and record have given him a privilege with his young friends?"

"Entirely, general. And I trust you understand that I am without the privilege of age and record, and cannot take the same liberties." The general made no reply, but was looking intently upon the face of the young man. Presently he said, earnestly:

"Your father and I were friends and stood together on many a bloody field. I bore him in my arms from Shiloh and gazed upon his dead face an hour later. No braver man ever lived than William Thomas. I believe you are the worthy son of a noble sire and incapable of any act that could reflect disgrace upon his name."

Thomas was deeply touched, and silent.

The general continued: "You cannot link yourself to an unjust cause and escape censure; such a course would put you at war with yourself and at war with those who hope to see you add new honors to a name already dear to your countrymen. When you aid and abet Amos Royson, in his attempt to put a stigma upon Edward Morgan, you aid and abet him in an effort to do that for which there is no excuse. Everything stated in Royson's letter, and especially the personal part of it, can be easily disproved." Thomas reflected a moment. Finally he said:

"I thank you, general, for your kind words. The matter is not one within my discretion, but give me the proofs you speak of, and I will make Royson withdraw, if possible, or abandon the quarrel myself!"

"I have given my word; is that not enough?"

"On that only, Mr. Royson's friends require him to give Mr. Morgan the recognition of a gentleman; without it he would not. The trouble is, you can be mistaken." Evan reflected and a look of trouble settled upon his face.

"Mr. Thomas, I am going to make a revelation involving the honor and reputation of a family very dear to me. I do it only to save bloodshed. Give me your word of honor that never in any way, so long as you may live, will you reveal it. I shall not offer my unsupported word; I will produce a witness."

"You have my word of honor that your communication will be kept sacred," said Thomas, greatly interested. The general bowed his head. Then he raised his hand above the little call bell; it did not descend. The martial figure for a moment seemed to shrink and age. When the general looked at length toward his visitor, he said in a whisper:

"The witness is dead!" Then he arose to his feet. "It is too late!" he added, with a slight gesture; "we will fight!"

CHAPTER XXII.

THE DUEL AT SUNRISE.

From that moment he discussed the arrangements formally. They were soon made and Thomas departed.

Edward, regaining his coolness in the wing-room, with the assistance of Virdow, who had been awakened by the disturbance, carried the body of Rita to her house in the yard and sent for a suburban physician near at hand.

The man of medicine pronounced the woman dead. Negroes from the quarters were summoned and took the body in charge. These arrangements completed, he met the general in the hall.

"A settlement is impossible," said the latter, sadly. "Get your buggy! Efforts may be made by arrests to stop this affair. You must go home with me to-night." Virdow was put in charge of the premises and an excuse made.

Alone, Edward returned to the side of the dead woman. Long and earnestly he studied her face, and at last said: "Farewell!" Then he went to Gerald's room and laid his lips upon the marble brow of the sleeper. Upstairs he put certain papers and the little picture in his pocket, closed the mother's room door and locked it. He turned and looked back upon the white-columned house as he rode away. Only eight weeks had passed since he first entered its doors.

Before leaving, the general had stabled his horse and telephoned Montjoy at the hotel. Taking a rear street he passed with Edward through the city and before daylight drew up in front of the Cedars.

Dueling at the time these events transpired was supposed to be dead in the south, and practically it was. The press and pulpit, the changed system of business and labor, state laws, but, above all these, occupation had rendered it obsolete; but there was still an element that resorted to the code for the settlement of personal grievances, and sometimes the result was a bloody meeting. The new order of things was so young that it really took more courage to refuse to fight than to fight a duel. The legal evasion was the invitation to conclude the correspondence outside the state.

The city was all excitement. The morning papers had columns and black head lines setting forth all the facts that could be obtained, and more besides. There was also a brief card from Edward Morgan, denouncing the author of the letter which had appeared in the extra and denying all charges brought against him, both personal and political.

At Mr. Royson's boarding place nothing had been seen

of him since the publication of the card, and his office was closed. Who it was that acted for Edward Morgan was a matter of surmise, but Col. Montjoy and Gen. Evan were in the city and quartered at the hotel. The latter had gone to Ilexhurst and had not returned.

Peace warrants for Morgan and Royson had been issued and placed in the hands of deputies, and two of them had watched outside a glass room at Ilexhurst waiting for a man who was asleep inside, and who had been pointed out to them by a German visitor as Mr. Morgan, to awaken. The sleeper, however, proved to be Gerald Morgan, an invalid.

At noon a bulletin was posted to the effect that Thomas and Royson had been seen on a South Carolina train; then another that Gen. Evan and Edward Morgan were recognized in Alabama; then came Tennessee rumors.

The truth was, so far as Edward Morgan was concerned, he was awakened before noon, given a room in a farmhouse, remote from the Evan dwelling, and there settled down to write important letters. One of these he signed in the presence of witnesses. The last one contained the picture, some papers and a short note to Gen. Evan; also Edward's surmises as to Gerald's identity. The other letters were for Virdow, Gerald and Mary. He had not signed the letter when Evan entered the room, but was sitting with his arms folded above it and his head resting on them.

"Letter writing!" said the general. "That is the worst feature of these difficulties." He busied himself with a case he carried, turning his back. Edward sealed his letter and completed his package.

"Well," he said, rising. "I am now at your service, Gen. Evan!"

"The horses are ready. We will start at once and I will give you instructions on the way."

The drive was thirty miles, to a remote station upon a branch road, where the horses were left.

Connection was made with the main line, yet more distant, and the next dawn found them at a station on the Florida border.

They had walked to the rendezvous and were waiting;

Edward stood in deep thought, his eyes fixed upon vacancy, his appearance suggesting profound melancholy. The general watched him furtively and finally with uneasiness. After all, the young man was a stranger to him. He had been drawn into the difficulty by his sympathies, and based his own safety upon his ability to read men. Experience upon the battle field, however, had taught him that men who have never been under fire sometimes fail at the last moment from a physical weakness unsuspected by even themselves. What if this man should fail? He went up to Edward and laid a hand upon his shoulder.

"My young friend, when you are as old as I you will realize that in cases like these the less a man thinks the better for his nerves. Circumstances have removed you from the realm of intellect and heart. You are now simply the highest type of an animal, bound to preserve self by a formula, and that is the blunt fact." Edward seemed to listen without hearing.

"General," he said, presently, "I do not want your services in this affair under a misapprehension. I have obeyed directions up to this moment, but before the matter goes further I must tell you what is in my mind. My quarrel with Amos Royson is because of his injury to me and his injury to my friends through me. He has made charges, and the customs of this country, its traditions, make those charges an injury. I believe that a man has a right to resent any injury and punish the spirit behind it." Gen. Evan was puzzled. He waited in silence.

"I did not make these fine distinctions at first, but the matter has been upon my mind and now I wish you to understand that if this poor woman were my mother I would not fight a duel even if I could, simply because some one told me so in print. If it were true, this story, there would be no shame to me in it; there would be no shame to me unless I deserted her. If it were true I would be her son in deed and truth. I would take her by the hand and seek her happiness in some other land. For, as God is my judge, to me the world holds nothing so sacred as a mother, and I would not exchange the affection of such were she the lowliest in the land, for all the privileges of any society. It is right that you should know the heart of the man you are seconding. If I fall my memory shall be clear of the charge of unmanliness."

Gen. Evan's appearance, under less tragic circumstances, would have been comical. For one instant, and for the first time in his life, he suffered from panic. His eyes, after a moment of wide-open amazement, turned helplessly toward the railroad and he began to feel for his glasses. When he got them adjusted he studied his companion critically. But the explosion that should have followed when the situation shaped itself in the old slaveholder's mind did not come. He saw before him the form of his companion grow and straighten, and the dark eyes, softened by emotion, shining fearlessly into his. It was the finest appeal that could have been made to the old soldier. He stretched out his hand impulsively.

"Unorthodox, but, by Georgia, I like it," he said.

The up train brought Royson and Thomas and a surgeon from a Florida town. Evan was obliged to rely upon a local doctor.

At sunrise the two parties stood in the shadow of live oaks, not far apart. Evan and Thomas advanced and saluted each other formally. Evan waited sadly for the other to speak; there was yet time for an honorable settlement. Men in the privacy of their own rooms think one way, and think another way in the solemn silence of a woodland sunrise.

And preceding it all in this instance there had been hours for reflection and hours of nervous apprehension. The latter told plainly upon Amos Royson. White and haggard, he moved restlessly about his station, watching the seconds and ever and anon stealing side-long glances at Morgan. Why, he asked himself, did the man stare at him with that fixed, changeless expression? Was he seeking to destroy his nerves, to overpower him with superior will? No. The gaze was simply contemplative; the gaze of one looking upon a landscape and considering its features. But it was a never-ending one to all appearances.

Hope died away from the general's heart at the first words of Thomas.

"We are here, Gen. Evan. What is your pleasure as to the arrangements? I would suggest that we proceed at once to end this affair. I notice that we are beginning to attract attention and people are gathering."

The general drew him aside and they conversed. The case of pistols was opened, the weapons examined and carefully loaded and then the ground was stepped off—fifteen paces upon a north and south line, with the low, spreading mass of live oaks behind each station. There were no perpendicular lines, no perspective, to influence the aim of either party. There was really no choice of positions, but one had to be chosen. A coin flashed in the sunlight as it rose and descended.

"We win," said Thomas, simply, "and choose the north stand. Take your place." The general smiled grimly.

"I have faced northward before," he said. He stood upon the point designated, and beckoned to Edward. Then the latter was forced to speak. He still gazed fixedly upon his antagonist. The general looked steadily into his pale face, and, pointing to his own track as he moved aside, said:

"Keep cool, now, my boy, and fire instantly. These pistols are heavier than revolvers; I chose them because the recoil of a revolver is destructive of an amateur's aim. These will shoot to the spot. Keep cool, keep cool, for God's sake, and remember the insult!"

"Have no fear for me," said Morgan. "I will prove that no blood of a slave is here!"

He took the weapon and stood in position. He had borne in mind all the morning the directions given by Gerald; he knew every detail of that figure facing him in the now bright sunlight; he had sketched it in detail to the mouth that uttered its charge against him. The hour might pass with no disaster to him; he might fall a corpse or a cripple for life; but so long as life lasted this picture would remain: A man with a hard, pale face, a white shirt front, dark trousers, hand clasping nervously a weapon, and behind all the deep green of the oaks, with their chiaroscuro. Only one thing would be missing; the picture in mind, clear cut and perfect in every other detail, lacked a mouth!

10

Some one is calling to them.

"Are you ready, gentlemen?" 'Twas the hundredth part of a second, but within it he answered "yes," ready to put the pencil to that last feature—to complete the picture for all time!

"Fire!" He raised his brush and touched the spot; there was a crash, a shock, and—what were they doing? His picture had fallen from its frame and they were lifting it. But it was complete; the carmine was spattered all over the lower face. He heard the general's voice:

"Are you hurt, Edward?" and the pistol was taken from his grasp.

"Hurt! No, indeed! But I seemed to have spoiled my painting, general. Look! My brush must have slipped; the paint was too thin."

The general hurried away.

"Keep your place; don't move an inch! Can I be of assistance, gentlemen?" he continued to the opposite party; "our surgeon can aid you, my principal being uninjured." He paused; an exclamation of horror escaped him. The mouth and nose of Royson seemed crushed in, and he was frantically spitting broken teeth from a bloody gap where his mouth had been. The surgeons worked rapidly to stay the flow of crimson. While thus busy the general in wonder picked up Royson's pistol. Its trigger and guard were gone. He looked at the young man's right hand; the forefinger was missing.

"An ugly wound, gentlemen," he said, "but not fatal, I think. The ball struck the guard, cut away a finger, and drove the weapon against the mouth and nose."

The surgeon looked up.

"You are right, I think. A bad disfigurement of those features, but not a dangerous wound." Thomas saluted.

"I have to announce my principal disabled, general."

"We are then satisfied."

Returning to Edward, who was quietly contemplating the scene with little apparent interest, he said, almost gayly:

"A fine shot, Edward; a fine shot! His pistol saved him! If he had raised it an instant later he would have been struck fairly in the mouth by your bullet! Let us be going."

"It is perhaps fortunate that my shot was fired when it was," said Edward. "I have a bullet hole through the left side of my shirt." The general looked at the spot and then at the calm face of the speaker.

He extended his hand again.

CHAPTER XXIII.

THE SHADOW OVER THE HALL.

Col. Montjoy returned home early. He rode into the yard and entered the house with as much unconcern as he could affect. Annie met him at the door with an unusual display of interest. Had he rested well? Was not the hotel warm, and—was there anything of interest stirring in the city? To all of these questions he responded guardedly and courteously. Mary's white face questioned him. He put his arm about her.

"And how is the little mamma to-day—have her eyes given her any more trouble?"

"She is staying in the darkened room to avoid the light," said the girl. He went to her and the two young women were left alone. Annie was smiling and bent upon aggravation.

"I think I will ride in," she said at length. "There is something afoot that is being kept from me. Amos Royson is my cousin and I have a right to know if he is in trouble." Mary did not reply for a moment. At last she said:

"A man having written such a letter must expect to find himself in trouble—and danger, too." The other woman laughed contemptuously.

"I did not say danger! Amos has little to fear from the smooth-faced, milk-and-water man he has exposed."

"Wait and see,". was the reply. "Amos Royson is a coward; he will not only find himself in danger, but if necessary to save himself from a cowhiding will involve other people—even a woman!"

"What do you mean? You have not always thought him a coward; you have accepted his attentions and would have married him if you had the chance." Mary looked up quickly.

"I treated him with politeness because he was your cousin; that is all. As for marriage with him, that is too absurd even to have occurred to me."

Annie ordered Isam to bring her pony carriage, and as she waited Mary watched her in silence and with a strange expression upon her face. When her father returned she said, resolutely:

"Annie, I was awake last night and heard a horse coming. Thinking it might be papa, although the pace was rather fast for him, I went out to the gate. There was a negro with a note for you from Mr. Royson. Mamma had just got to sleep and I was afraid of waking her, so I sent Mr. Royson word to see papa at the hotel."

The sister-in-law seized her by the shoulder.

"By what right, miss, do you meddle with my business! It may have been a question of a man's life! You have ruined everything!" She was trembling with rage. Mary faced her resolutely.

"And it may have been a question of a man's honor. In either case, my father is the one to consult!"

"Sit down, both of you! Annie—Mary, I desire this matter to end at once!" Col. Montjoy spoke calmly but firmly. He retained his clasp upon his daughter's hand and gradually as he talked drew her to his knees.

"There is a serious difficulty pending between Mr. Morgan and Amos Royson, as you both probably know," he said, quietly. "The matter is in good hands, however, and I think will be satisfactorily arranged. I do not know which were better, to have delivered Amos' note or not. It was a question Mary had to decide upon the spur of the moment. She took a safe course, at least. But it is unseemly, my children, to quarrel over it! Drop the matter now and let affairs shape themselves. We cannot take one side or the other." Annie made no reply, but her lips wore their ironical smile as she moved away.

Mary hid her face upon her father's breast and wept

softly. She knew that he did not blame her, and she knew by intuition that she had done right, but she was not satisfied. No shadow should come between her father and herself.

"I was certain," she said, "that there was something wrong in that note. You remember what I told you. And I was determined that those two people should not hatch up any more mischief in this house. Mr. Morgan's safety might have depended upon keeping them apart." The colonel laughed and shook his head. But he only said:

"If it will help clear up your skies a little, I don't mind telling you that I would not have had that note delivered last night for half this plantation." She was satisfied then.

"Who ordered the cart, Isam?" The negro was at the gate.

"Young mis', sah. She goin' to town."

"Well, you can put it back. It will not be necessary for her to go now. Annie," he said, turning to that lady, as she appeared in the door, "I have sent the cart back. I prefer that none of my family be seen upon the streets to-day." There was an unwonted tone in his voice which she did not dare disregard. With a furious look, which only Mary saw, she returned to her room. A negro upon a mule brought a note. It read:

"Dear Norton: All attempts at settlement have failed. I would like to see you, but think you had better maintain strict neutrality. Will wire you to-morrow.   A. E."

"There is no answer," he said to the boy. And then, greatly depressed, he went to his room. Mary, who read every thought correctly, knew that the matter was unsettled and that her father was hopeless. She went about her duties steadily, but with her heart breaking. The chickens, pigeons, the little kids, the calves—none of them felt the tragedy in their lives. Their mistress was grave and inappreciative; nothing more. But her eyes were not closed. She saw little Jerry armed with a note go out on the mare across the lower-creek bridge, and

the expectant face of Annie for two hours or more in
every part of the house that commanded a view of that
unused approach.

Then Jerry came back and went to the sister-in-law's
door. He had not reached his quarters before Mary called
him to help her catch a fractious hen. Then she got him
into the dining-room and cut an enormous slice of iced
cake.

"Jerry," she said, "how would you like that?" Jerry's
white eyes and teeth shone resplendent. He shifted himself to his left foot and laughed. "Tell me where you
have been and it is yours." Jerry looked abashed and
studied a silver quarter he held in his hand. Then he
glanced around cautiously.

"Honest, missy?"

"Honest! Quick, or I put the cake back." She made
a feint.

"Been to town."

"Of course.   Who was the note for?"

"Mr. Royson."

"Did he answer it?"

"No'm.   Couldn't find him. Er nigger tole me he gone
ter fight wid Mr. Morgan, and everybody waitin' ter hear
de news."

"You can—go—Jerry. There," she handed him the
cake, and, walking unsteadily, went to her room. She
did not come out until supper time and then her face was
proof that the "headache" was not feigned.

And so into the night. She heard the doors open and
shut, the sound of her father's footsteps on the porch as
he came and went. She went out and joined him, taking
his arm.

"Papa," she said, after awhile, "you need not keep it
from me. I know all. They did not settle it. Mr. Morgan and Mr. Royson have gone to fight." She could not
proceed. Her father laid his hand upon hers.

"It will all come out right, Mary; it will all come out
right." Presently he said: "Amos used to come here. I
hope you are not interested in him."

"No," she said bitterly, "I could never think much of
Annie's relatives. One in the family is enough."

"Hush, my child; everything must give way now on Norton's account. Don't forget him. But for Norton I would have settled this matter in another way."

"Yes, and but for him there would never have been a necessity. Amos depended upon his relationship to keep you out of it." Col. Montjoy had long unconsciously relied upon the clear mind of the girl, but he was not prepared for this demonstration of its wisdom. He wondered anew as he paced the floor in silence. She continued: "But Amos is only the tool, papa; all of us have an enemy here in the house. Annie——"

"Hush! Hush!" he whispered, "don't say it. It seems too awful to think of! Annie is foolish! She must never know, on Norton's account, that she is in any way suspected of complicity in this matter." And then in silence they waited for dawn.

At last the merciful sun rolled away the shadows. Breakfast was a sad affair. All escaped from it as soon as possible.

It was a fateful day—7, 8, 9 o'clock. The matter was ended; but how? Mary's haggard face questioned her father at every turn. He put his arm about her and went to see her pets and charges. But still no word between them. She would not admit her interest in Edward Morgan, nor would he admit to himself that she had an interest at stake.

And then toward noon there came a horseman, who placed a message in his hands. He read it and handed it to Mary. If he had not smiled she could not have read it. One word only was there:

"Safe!"

Her father was at the moment unfolding an "extra." She read it with him in breathless interest. Following an unusual display of head lines came an accurate account of the duel. Only a small part of the padded narrative is reproduced here:

"Royson was nervous and excited and showed the effects of unrest. But Morgan stood like a statue. For some reason he never moved his eyes from his adversary a moment after they reached the field. Both men fired at the command, their weapons making but one report.

Some think, however, that Morgan was first by the hundredth part of a second, and this is possible, as the single report sounded like a crash or a prolonged explosion. Royson fell, and it was supposed was certainly killed. He presented a frightful appearance instantly, being covered with blood. It was quickly ascertained, however, that he was not dangerously hurt, his opponent's shot having cut off a finger and the pistol guard, and had hurled the heavy weapon into his face. He escaped with a broken nose and the loss of his front teeth.

"Morgan, who had preserved his wonderful coolness from the first, received a bullet through a fold of his shirt that darkened the skin to the left of his heart. It was a narrow escape. Parties took the up train."

The extra went on to say that since the first reading of the original card the public mind had undergone a revulsion in Morgan's favor; a feeling greatly stimulated by the fact that Gen. Evan had come to the rescue of that gentleman; had vouched for him in every respect and was acting as his second. When the colonel had finished the thrilling news he noticed that Mary's head was in his lap, and felt tears upon his hand above which her own were clasped. Annie was looking on, cold and white.

"There has been a duel, my daughter," he said to her kindly, "and, fortunately, without alarming results. Mr. Royson lost a finger, I believe, and received a bruise in the face; that is all. Nothing serious. It might have been very much worse. Here is the paper," he concluded, "probably an exaggerated account." She took it in silence and returned to her room. She ran her eye through every sentence without reading and at last threw the sheet aside.

Only those who knew the whole character of Annie Montjoy would have understood. She was looking for her name; it was not there. Her smiling face was proof enough.

Long they sat, father and daughter, his hand still stroking lightly her bowed head. At last he said, very gently, the hand trembling a little:

"This has been a hard trial for us both—for us both! I am glad it is over! Morgan is too fine a fellow to have been sacrificed to this man's hatred and ambition." She looked up, her face wet and flushed.

"There was more than that, papa."

"More? How could there be?"

She hesitated, and then said, bravely: "Mr. Royson has more than once asked me to marry him." The colonel's face grew black with sudden rage.

"The scoundrel!"

"And he has imagined that because Mr. Morgan came here to help your election—oh, I cannot." She turned hastily and went away in confusion.

And still the colonel sat and thought with clouded face. "I must ask Evan," he said.

"Colonel, Mis' Calline says come deir, please." A servant stood by him. He arose and went into his wife's room. She was standing by the open window, its light flooding the apartment, her bandages removed.

"Why, Caroline, you are imprudent, don't you know? What is it, my dear? She was silent and rigid, a living statue bathed in the glory of the autumn sun. She waited until she felt his hand in hers.

"Norton," she said, simply, but with infinite pathos, "I am afraid that I have seen your loved face for the last time. I am blind!" He took her in his arms—the form that even age could not rob of its girlishness—and pressed her face to his breast. It had come at last. His tears fell for the first time since boyhood.

CHAPTER XXIV.

THE PROFILE ON THE MOON.

Virdow felt the responsibility of his position. He had come on a scientific errand and found himself plunged into a tragedy. And there were attendant responsibilities, the most serious of which was the revelation to Gerald of what had occurred.

The young man precipitated the crisis. The deputies

gone, he wanted his coffee; it had not failed him in a
lifetime. Again and again he rung his bell, and finally
from the door of his wing-room called loudly for Rita.
Then the professor saw that the time for action had come.
The watchers about the body were consulting. None
cared to face that singular being of whom they felt a
superstitious dread, but if they did not come to him he
would finally go to them. What would be the result of
his unexpected discovery of the tragedy? It might be dis-
astrous. He would make an effort to deaden the blow.

He drew Gerald gently into his room and closed the
door. As he spoke, he removed his glasses from time to
time, carefully wiping and replacing them, his faded
eyes beaming in sympathy and anxiety upon his young
acquaintance.

"Herr Gerald," he began, "you know the human
heart?" Gerald frowned and surveyed him with impatience.

"Well?" he said, waiting. The little man nodded his
head.

"Sometimes at last the little valve, as you call it—
sometimes the little valve grows weak, and when the
blood leaps out too quickly and can't run on quickly
enough—you understand—it comes back suddenly again
and drives the valve lid back the wrong way."

"Then it is a ruined piece of machinery."

"So," said the professor, sadly; "you have stated it
correctly. So, Rita—she had an old heart—and it is
ruined!"

Gerald gazed upon him in doubt, but fearful.

"You mean Rita is dead?"

"Yes," said Virdow. "Poor Rita!" Gerald studied the
face before him curiously, passed his hand across his
brow, as if to clear away a cloud, and then went out across
the yard. The watchers fled at his approach. In the little
room he came upon the body. The woman, dressed in
her best but homely attire, lay with her hands crossed
upon her bosom, her face calm and peaceful. Upon her
lips was that strange smile which sometimes comes back
over a gulf of time from a forgotten youth. He touched
her wrist and watched her.

Virdow was right; she was dead.

As if to converse with a friend, he took a seat upon the couch and lifting one cold hand held it while he remained. This was Rita, who had always come to wake him when he slept too late; had brought his meals, had answered whenever he called, and found him when he wandered too long under the stars and guided him back to his room. Rita, who, when his moods distracted him, had only to fix her eyes on his and speak his name, and all was peace again.

This was Rita. Dead!

How could it be? How could anything be wrong with Rita? It was impossible! He put his hand above the heart; it was silent. He spoke her name. She did not reply.

Gradually, as he concentrated his attention upon the facts, his mind emerged from its shadows. Yes, Rita, his friend, was dead. And then slowly, his life, with its haunting thoughts, its loneliness, came back, and the significance of these facts overwhelmed him.

He knew now who Rita was; it was an old, old story. He knelt and laid his cheek upon that yellow chilled hand, the only hand that had ever lovingly touched him.

She had been a mother indeed; humoring his every whim. She had never scolded; not Rita!

The doctors had said he could sleep without his opium; they shut him up and he suffered torments. Rita came in the night. Her little store of money had been drawn on. They, together, deceived the doctors. For years they deceived them, he and Rita, until all her little savings were gone. And then she had worked for the gentlemen down-town; had schemed and plotted and brought him comfort, until the doctors gave up the struggle.

Now she was gone—forever! Strange, but this contingency had never once occurred to him. How egotistical he must have been; how much a child—a spoiled child!

He looked about him. Rita had years ago told him a secret. In the night she had bent over him and called him fond names; had wept upon his pillow. She had told him to speak the word just once, never again but that

one time, and then to forget it. Wondering he said it—
"Mother." He could not forget how she fell upon him
then and tearfully embraced him; he the heir and nephew
of John Morgan. But it pleased good Rita and he was
happy.

Dead! Rita! Would it waken her if he spoke that
name again? He bent to her cheek to say it, but first he
looked about him cautiously. Rita would not like for any
one to share the secret. He bent until his lips were touching hers and whispered it again:

"Mother!" She did not move. He spoke louder and
louder.

"Mother." How strange sounded that one word in the
deserted room. A fear seized him; would she never
speak again? He dropped on his knees in agony; and,
with his hand upon her forehead, almost screamed the
word again. It echoed for the last time—"Mother!" Just
then the face of Virdow appeared at the door, to be withdrawn instantly.

Then Gerald grew cool. "She is dead," he said, sadly
to himself. "She would have answered that!"

A change came over him! He seemed to emerge from
a dream; Virdow stood by him now. Drawing himself
up proudly he gazed upon the dead face.

"She was a good nurse—a better no child ever had.
Were my uncle living he would build her a great monu-
ment. I will speak to Edward about it. It is not seemly
that people who have served the Morgans so long and
faithfully should sleep in unmarked graves. Farewell,
Rita; you have been good and true to me." He went to
his room. An hour later Virdow found him there, crying
as a child.

With a tenderness that rose superior to the difficulties
of language and the differences of race and customs, Virdow comforted and consoled him. And then occurred
one of those changes familiar to the students of nature
but marvelous to the unobservant. To Virdow, who had
seen the vine of his garden torn from the supporting rod
about which it had tied itself with tendrils, attach itself
again by the gluey points of new ones to the smooth face
of the wall itself, coiling them into springs to resist the

winds, the change that came upon Gerald was natural. The broken tendrils of his life touched with quick intelligence the sympathetic old German and linked the simple being of the child-man to him. By an intuition, womanly in its swift comprehension, Virdow knew at once that he had become in some ways necessary to the life of the frail being, and he was pleased. He gave himself up to the mission without effort, disturbing in no way the new process. Watching Gerald, he appeared not to watch; present at all times, he seemed to keep himself aloof.

Virdow called up an undertaker from the city in accordance with the directions left with him and had the body of Rita prepared for the burial, which was to take place upon the estate, and then left all to the care of the watchers. During the day from time to time Gerald went to the little room, and on such visits those in attendance withdrew.

There was little excitement among the negroes. The singing, shouting and violent ecstasies which distinguished the burials of the race were wanting; Rita had been one of those rare servants who keep aloof from her color. Gradually withdrawn from all contact with the world, her life had shrunk into a little round of duties and the care of the Morgan home.

It was only natural that the young master should find himself alone with the nurse on each return to her coffin. During one of these visits Virdow at a distance beheld a curious thing. Gerald had gazed long and thoughtfully into the silent face and returning to his room had secured paper and crayon. Kneeling, he drew carefully the profile of his dead friend and went away to his studio. Standing in his place a moment later, Virdow was surprised to note the change that had come over the face; the relaxing power of death seemed to have rolled back the curtain of age and restored for the hour a glimpse of youth. A woman of 25 seemed lying there, her face noble and serene, a glorified glimpse of what had been. The brow was smooth and serene, the facial angle high, the hair, now no longer under the inevitable turban, smooth and black, with just a suspicion of frost above the temples. The lips were curved and smiling.

Why had the young man drawn her profile? What real position did this woman occupy in that strange family? As to the latter he could not determine; he would not try. He had nothing to do with the domestic facts of life. There had been a deep significance in the first scene at the bedside. And yet "Mother" under the circumstances might after all mean nothing. He had heard that southern children were taught this, or something like it, by all black nurses. But as to the profile, there was a phenomenon possibly, and science was his life. The young man had drawn the profile because it was the first time he had within his recollections ever seen it. In the analysis of his dreams that profile might be of momentous importance.

The little group that had gathered followed the coffin to a clump of trees not far removed. The men who bore it lowered it at once to the open grave. An old negro preacher lifted his voice in a homely prayer, the women sung a weird hymn, and then they filled up the cavity. The face and form of Rita were removed from human vision, but only the face and form. For one of that concourse, the young white man who had come bareheaded to stand calm and silent at the foot of the grave, she lived clear and distinct upon the hidden film of memory.

Virdow was not deceived by that calmness; he knew and feared the reaction which was inevitable. From time to time during the evening he had gone silently to the wing-room and to the outer yard to gaze in upon his charge. Always he found him calm and rational. He could not understand it.

Then, disturbed by the suspense of Edward's absence, and the uncertainty of his fate, he would forget himself and surroundings in contemplation of the possible disasters of an American duel—exaggerated accounts of which dwelt in his memory. He resolved to remain up until the crisis came.

It was midnight when, for the twentieth time, probably, he went to look in upon Gerald. The wing-room, the glass-room, the little house deprived by death of its occupant, the outer premises—he searched them all in vain. Greatly troubled, he stood revolving the new perplexity in his mind when his eye caught in the faint glow of the east, where the moon was beginning to show its approach, the outline of the cemetery clump of trees. It flashed upon him then that, drawn by the power of association, the young man might have wandered off to pay a visit to the grave of his friend. He turned his own feet in the same direction, and approached the spot. The grave had been dug under the widespread limbs of a cedar, and there he found the object of his quest.

Slowly the moon rose above the level field beyond, outlining a form. In his dressing gown stood Gerald, with folded arms, his long hair falling upon his shoulders, lost in deep thought.

Thrilled by the scene, Virdow was about to speak, when, in the twinkling of an eye, there was flashed upon him a vision that sent his blood back to his heart and left him speechless with emotion. For in that moment the half-moon was at the level of the head, and outlined against its silver surface he saw the profile of the face he had studied in the coffin. Appalled by the discovery, he turned silently and sought his room.

CHAPTER XXV.

THE MIDNIGHT SEARCH.

It was late in the day when Virdow awoke. The excitement, the unwonted hours which circumstances forced him to keep, brought at last unbroken rest and restored his physical structure to its normal condition.

He dressed himself and descended to find a brief telegram announcing the safety of Edward. It was a joyful addition to the conditions that had restored him. The telegram had not been opened. He went quickly to Gerald's room and found that young man at work upon a painting of Rita as he had seen her last—the profile sketch. His emotional nature had already thrown off its gloom, and with absorbed interest he was pushing his work. Already the face had been sketched in and the priming completed. Under his rapid and skillful hands the tints and contours were growing, and Virdow, accustomed as he was to art in all its completeness and technical perfection, marveled to see the changed face of the woman glide back into view, the counterpart he knew of the vivid likeness clear cut in the sensitive brain that held it. He let him work undisturbed. A word might affect its correctness. Only when the artist ceased and laid aside his brush for a brief rest did he speak.

Gerald turned to him as to a co-laborer, and took the yellow slip of paper, so potent with intelligent lettering. He read it in silence; then putting it aside went on with his painting. Virdow rubbed his brow and studied him furtively. Such lack of interest was inconceivable under the conditions. He went to work seriously to account for it and this he did to his own satisfaction. In one of his published lectures on memory, years after, occurred this sentence, based upon that silent reverie:

"Impressions and forgetfulness are measurable by each other; indeed, the power of the mind to remember vividly seems to be measured by its power to forget."

But afterward Gerald picked up the telegram, read it intently and seemed to reflect over the information it contained. Later in the day the postman brought the mail and with it one of the "extras." Virdow read it aloud in the wing-room. Gerald came and stood before him, his eyes revealing excitement. When Virdow reached the part wherein Edward was described as never removing his eyes from his antagonist, his hearer exclaimed:

"Good! He will kill him!"

"No," said Virdow, smiling; "fortunately he did not. Listen."

"Fortunately!" cried Gerald; "fortunately! Why? What right has such a man to live? He must have killed him!" Virdow read on. A cry broke from Gerald's lips as the explanation appeared.

"I was right! The hand becomes a part of the eye when the mind wills it; or, rather, eye and hand become mind. The will is everything. But why he should have struck the guard——" He went to the wall and took down two pistols. Handing one to Virdow and stepping back he said: "You will please sight at my face a moment; I cannot understand how the accident could have happened." Virdow held the weapon gingerly.

"But, Herr Gerald, it may be loaded."

"They are empty," said Gerald, breeching his own and exposing the cylinder chambers, with the light shining through. "Now aim!" Virdow obeyed; the two men stood at ten paces, aiming at each other's faces. "Your hand," said the young man, "covers your mouth. Edward aimed for the mouth."

There was a quick, sharp explosion; Virdow staggered back, dropping his smoking pistol. Gerald turned his head in mild surprise and looked upon a hole in the plastering behind.

"I have no recollection of loading that pistol," he said. And then: "If your mind had been concentrated upon your aim I would have lost a finger and had my weapon driven into my face." Virdow was shocked at the narrow escape and pale as death.

"It is nothing," said Gerald, replacing the weapon; "you would not hit me in a dozen trials, shooting as you do."

At 10 o'clock that night Edward, pale and weary, entered. He returned with emotion the professor's enthusiastic embrace, and thanked him for his care of and attention of Gerald and the household and for his services to the dead. Gerald studied him keenly as he spoke, and once went to one side and looked upon him with new and curious interest. The professor saw that he was examining the profile of the speaker by the aid of the powerful lamp on a table beyond. The discovery set his mind to working in the same direction, and soon he saw the profiles of both. Edward's did not closely resemble the other. That this was true, for some reason, the expression that had settled upon Gerald's face attested. The portrait had been covered and removed.

Edward, after concluding some domestic arrangements, went directly to his room and, dressed as he was, threw himself upon his bed and slept.

And as he slept there took place about him a drama that would have set his heart beating with excitement

11

could he have witnessed it. The house was silent; the
city clock had tolled the midnight hour, when Gerald
came into the room, bearing a shaded lamp. The sleeper
lay on his back, locked in the slumber of exhaustion.
The visitor, moving with the noiselessness of a shadow,
glided to the opposite side of the bed, and, placing the
lamp on a chair, slowly turned up the flame and tilted
the shade. In an instant the strong profile of the sleeper
flashed upon the wall. With suppressed excitement
Gerald unwrapped a sheet of cardboard, and standing
it on the mantel received upon it the shadow. As if by
a supreme effort, he controlled himself and traced the
profile on his paper. Lifting it from the mantel he
studied it for a moment intently and then replaced it.
The shadow filled the tracing. Taking it slowly from its
position he passed from the room. Fortunately his dis-
traction was too great for him to notice the face of
Virdow, or to perceive it in the deep gloom of the little
room as he passed out.

The German waited a few moments; no sound came
back from the broad carpeted stair; taking the forgotten
lamp, he followed him silently. Passing out into the
shrubbery, he made his way to the side of the conservatory and looked in. Gerald had placed the two profiles,
one on each side of the mirror, and with a duplex glass
was studying his own in connection with them. He stood
musing, and then, as if forgetting his occupation, he let
the hand-glass crash upon the floor, tossed his arms in
an abandonment of emotion, and, covering his face with
his hands, suddenly threw himself across the bed.

Virdow was distressed and perplexed. He read the
story in the pantomime, but what could he do? No
human sympathy could comfort such a grief, nor could
he betray his knowledge of the secret he had surrep-
titiously obtained. He paced up and down outside until
presently the moving shadow of the occupant of the
room fell upon his path. He saw him then take from a
box a little pill and put it in his mouth, and he knew
that the troubles of life, its doubts, distress and loneliness,
would be forgotten for hours.

Forgotten? Who knows? Oh, mystery of creation;

that invisible intelligence that vanishes in sleep and in death; gone on its voyage of discovery, appalling in its possibilities; but yet how useless, since it must return with no memory of its experience!

And he, Virdow, what a dreamer! For in that German brain of subtleties lived, with the clearness of an incandescent light in the depths of a coal mine, one mighty purpose; one so vast, so potent in its possibilities, as to shake the throne of reason, a resolution to follow upon the path of mind and wake a memory never touched in the history of science. It was not an ambition; it was a leap toward the gates of heaven! For what cared he that his name might shine forever in the annals of history if he could claim of his own mind the record of its wanderings? The future was not his thought. What he sought was the memory of the past!

He went in now, secure of the possibility of disturbing the sleeper, and stood looking down into the white face and whiter brow. His eyes roved to the room's appointments; there were the two profiles on either side of the mirror; upon the floor the shivered fragments of the hand-glass.

Virdow returned to his room, but before leaving he took from the little box one of the pellets and swallowed it. If he was to know that mind, he must acquaint himself with its conditions. He had never before swallowed the drug; he took this as the Frenchman received the attenuated virus of hydrophobia from the hands of Pasteur—in the interest of science and the human race.

As he lay upon his bed he felt a languor steal upon him, saw in far dreams cool meadows and flowery slopes, felt the solace of perfect repose envelop him. And then he stood beside a stream of running water under the shade of the trees, with the familiar hills of youth along the horizon. A young woman came and stood above the stream and looked intently upon its glassy surface. Her features were indistinct. Drawing near he, too, looked into the water, and there at his feet was the sad, sweet face of—Marion Evan. He turned and then looked closer at the woman; he saw in her arms the figure of an infant, over whose face she had drawn a fold of her

gown. She shook her head as he extended his hand
to remove this and pointed behind her. There the grass
ran out and only white sand appeared, with no break to
the horizon.

Toiling on through this, with a bowed head, was a
female figure. He knew her; she was Rita, and the
burden she, too, carried in her arms was the form of a
child. The figures disappeared and a leaf floated down
the stream; twenty-six in succession followed, and then
he saw a man descending the mountains and coming forward, his eyes fixed on something beyond him. It was
Edward. He looked in the same direction; there was a
frail man toiling toward him through the deep sands in
the hot sunlight. It was Gerald. And then the figures
faded away. There memory ceased to record.

Whatever else was the experience of that eager mind
as it wandered on through the night is kept secret. No
opium was to unlock the mystery, and phantasmagoria
has no place in science. He remembered in the morning
up to one point only.

It was his last experience with the drug.

CHAPTER XXVI.

GATHERING THE CLEWS.

Edward drifted for several days upon the tide of the
thoughts that came over him. He felt a singular dis-
inclination to face the world again. He knew that as
life goes he had acquitted himself manfully and that
nothing remained undone that had been his duty to per-
form. He was sensible of a feeling of deep gratitude
to the old general for his active and invaluable backing;
without it he realized then that he would have been
drawn into a pitfall and the opportunity for defense gone.
He did not realize, however, how complete the public
reaction had been until card after card had been left at
Ilexhurst and the postman had deposited congratulatory

missives by the score.   One of these contained notice of
his election to the club.

Satisfactory as was all this he put aside the social and
public life into which he had been drawn, conscious that,
while the affront to him had been resented and rendered
harmless, he himself was as much in the dark as ever;
that as a matter of fact he was without name and family,
without right to avail himself of the generous offers laid
at his door.   Despite his splendid residence, his future,
his talents and his prestige as a man of honor, he was—
nobody; an accident of fate; a whim of an eccentric
old man.

He would not involve any one else in the possibility
of ruin.   He would not let another share his danger.
There could be no happiness with this mystery hanging
over him.

Soon after his return, while his heart was yet sore and
disturbed, he had received a note from Mary.   She wrote:

"We suffer greatly on your account.   Poor papa was
bound down by circumstances with which you are familiar, though he would have gone to you at any cost had
it been necessary.   In addition his health is very delicate
and he has been facing a heavy sorrow—now realized at
last!   Poor little mamma's eyesight is gone—forever,
probably.   We are in deep distress, as you may imagine,
for, unused as yet to her misfortune, she is quite helpless
and needs our constant care, and it is pitiful to see her
efforts to bear up and be cheerful.

"I need not tell you how I have sorrowed over the
insult and wrongs inflicted upon you by a cowardly connection of our family, nor how anxious I was until the
welcome news of your safety reached us.   We owe you
much, and more now since you were made the innocent
victim of a plot aimed to destroy papa's chances.

"It is unbearable to think of your having to stand up
and be shot at in our behalf; but oh, how glad I am that
you had the old general with you.   Is he not noble and
good?   He is quite carried away with you and never
tires of talking of your coolness and courage.   He says
everything has ended beautifully but the election, and

he could remedy that if papa would consent, but nothing
in the world could take papa away from us now, and if
he had been elected his resignation would have speedily
followed.

"I know you are yet weary and bitter, and do not
even care to see your friends, but that will pass and
none will give you a more earnest welcome when you
do come than   Mary."

He read this many times, and each time found in it a
new charm. Its simplicity and earnestness impressed
him at one reading and its personal interest at another;
its quick discerning sympathy in another.

It grew upon him, that letter. It was the only letter
ever penned by a woman to him. Notes he had had by
the score; rich young men in the gay capitals of Europe
do not escape nor seek to escape these, but this was
straight from the heart of an earnest, self-reliant, sympathetic woman; one of those that have made the south
a fame as far as her sons have traveled. It was a new
experience and destined to be a lasting one.

Its effect was in the end striking and happy. Gradually he roused himself from the cynical lethargy into
which he was sinking and began to look about him.
After all he had much to live for, much with reason to
hope for! Peace came upon him, and with peace came
new manhood. He would fight for the woman who had
faith in him—such a fight as no man ever dared before.
He looked up to find Virdow smiling on him through
his tears.

He stood up. "I am going to make a statement now
that will surprise and shock you, but the reason will be
sufficient. First I ask that you promise me, as though
we stood before our Creator, a witness, that never in
this life nor the next, if consciousness of this goes with
you, will you betray by word or deed anything of what
you hear from my lips to-night. I do not feel any uneasiness, but promise."

"I promise," said Virdow, simply, "but if it distresses
you, if you feel bound to me—"

"On the contrary, the reason is selfish entirely. I tell

you because the possession of this matter is destroying my ability to judge fairly; because I want help and believe you are the only being in the world who can give it." He spoke earnestly and pathetically. "Without it, I shall become—a wreck." The keen eyes of the professor studied him anxiously. Then he seized the speaker's hand.

"Go on, Edward. All the help that Virdow can give is yours in advance."

Edward related to him the causes that led up to the duel—the political campaign, the publication of Royson's card, and the history of the challenge.

"You call me Edward," he said; "the world knows me and I know myself as Edward Morgan. I have no evidence whatever to believe myself entitled to bear the name. All the evidence I have points to the fact that it was bestowed upon me as was my fortune itself—in pity. The mystery that overspreads me envelops Gerald also. But fate has left him superior to misfortune."

"It has already done for him what you fear for yourself—it has wrecked his life, if not his mind!" The professor spoke the words sadly and gently, looking into the night through the open window.

Edward turned toward him in wonder.

"You think, then, he knows something of this—"

"I am sure. Listen and I will tell you why. To me it seems fatal to him, but for you there is consolation." Graphically he described then the events that had transpired during the few days of his stay at Ilexhurst; his quick perception that the mind of Gerald was working feverishly, furiously, and upon defined lines to some end; that something haunted and depressed him. His secret was revealed in his conduct upon the death of Rita.

He described the drawing and comparison of the profiles, and the scene over the grave of Rita.

"It is plain," said Virdow finally, "that this thought —this uncertainty—which has haunted you for weeks, has been wearing upon him since childhood. Of the events that preceded it I have little or no information."

Edward, thrilled to the heart by this recital and the fact to which it seemed to point, walked the floor greatly agitated. Presently he said:

"Of these you shall judge also." He took from the desk in the adjoining room the fragmentary story and read it. "This," he said, as he saw the face of the old man beam with intelligence, "is confirmed as an incident in the life of Gerald or myself; in fact, the beginning of life." He gave the history of the fragmentary story and of Rita's confession.

"By this evidence," he went on, "I was led to believe that the woman erred in the recognition of her own child; that I am in fact that child and that Gerald is the son of Marion. This in her last breath she seemed to deny, for when I begged her to testify upon it, as before her God, and asked the question direct, she cried out: 'They lied!' In this it seems to me that her heart went back to its secret belief and that in the supreme moment she affirmed forever his nativity. Were this all I confess I would be satisfied, but there is a fatal fact to come!" He took from his pocket the package he had prepared for Gen. Evan, and tore from it the picture of Marion.

"Now," he exclaimed excitedly, "as between the two of us, how can this woman be other than the mother of Gerald Morgan? And, if I could be mistaken as to the resemblance, how could her father fall into my error? For I swear to you that on the night he bent over the sleeping man he saw upon the pillow the face of his wife and daughter blended in those features!" Virdow was looking intently upon the picture.

"Softly, softly," he said, shaking his head; "it is a true likeness, but it does not prove anything. Family likeness descends only surely by profiles. If we could see her profile, but this! There is no reason why the child of Rita should not resemble another. It would depend upon the impression, the interest, the circumstances of birth, of associations—" He paused. "Describe to me again the mind picture which Gerald under the spell of music sketched—give it exactly." Edward gave it in detail.

"That," said Virdow, "was the scene flashed upon the woman who gazed from under the arch. It seems impossible for it to have descended to Gerald, except by one of the two women there—the one to whom the man's back was turned. Had this mental impression come from the other source it seems to me he would have seen the face of that man, and if the impression was vivid enough to descend from mother to child it would have had the church for a background, in place of the open arch, with storm-lashed trees beyond. This is reasonable only when we suppose it possible that brain pictures can be transmitted. As a man I am convinced. As a scientist I say that it is not proved."

Edward, every nerve strained to its utmost tension, every faculty of mind engaged, devoured this brief analysis and conclusion. But more proof was given! Over his face swept a shadow.

"Poor Gerald! Poor Gerald!" he muttered. But he became conscious presently that the face of Virdow wore a concerned look; there was something to come. He could not resist the temptation to clear up the last vestige of doubt if doubt could remain.

"Tell me," he said, "what do you require to satisfy you that between the two I am the son of Marion Evan?"

"Two things," said Virdow, quickly. "First, proof that Rita was in no way akin to the Evan family, for if she was in the remotest degree, the similarity of profiles could be accounted for. Second, that your own and the profile of Marion Evan were of the same angle. Satisfy me upon these two points and you have nothing to fear."

A feeling of weakness overwhelmed Edward. The general had not seen in his face any likeness to impress him. And yet, why his marked interest? The whole subject lay open again.

And Marion Evan! Where was he to obtain such proof?

Virdow saw the struggle in his mind.

"Leave nothing unturned," said Edward, "that one of us may live free of doubt, and just now, God help me, it seems my duty to strive for him first."

"And these efforts—when—"

"To-night! Let us descend."

"We go first to the room of the nurse," said Virdow. "We will begin there."

Edward led the way and with a lighted lamp they en-

tered the room.   The search there was brief and uneventful.   On the wall in a simple frame was a portrait
of John Morgan, drawn years before from memory by
Gerald.   It was the face of the man known only to the
two searchers as Abingdon, but its presence there might
be significant.

Her furniture and possessions were simple.   In her little
box of trinkets were found several envelopes addressed
to her from Paris, one of them in the handwriting of a
man, the style German.   All were empty, the letters
having in all probability been destroyed.   They, however, constituted a clew, and Edward placed them in his
pocket.   In another envelope was a child's golden curl,
tied with a narrow black ribbon; and there was a drawer
full of broken toys.   And that was all.

CHAPTER XXVII.

THE FACE THAT CAME IN DREAMS.

Virdow was not a scientist in the strict sense of the
term.   He had been a fairly good musician in youth and
had advanced somewhat in art.   He was one of those
modern scientists, who are not walled in by past conclusions, but who, like Morse, leap forward from a vantage
point and build back to connect with old results.   Early
in life he had studied the laws of vibration, until it seemed
revealed to him that all forms, all fancies, were born of it.
Gradually as his beautiful demonstrations were made and
all art co-ordinated upon this law, he saw in dreams a
fulfillment of his hopes that in his age, in his life, might
bloom the fairest flower of science, a mind memory opened
to mortal consciousness.

Dreaming further along the lines of Wagner, it had
come to him that the key to this hidden, dumb and sleeping record of the mind was vibration; that the strains of
music which summon beautiful dreams to the minds of
men were magic wands lifting the vision of this past;

not its immediate past, but the past of ages; for in the
brain of the subtle German was firmly fixed the belief
that the minds of men were in their last analysis one and
indivisible, and older than the molecules of physical creation.

He held triumphantly that "then shall you see clearly,"
was but one way of saying "then shall you remember."

To this man the mind picture which Gerald had drawn,
the church, with its tragic figures, came as a reward of a
generation of labor. He had followed many a false
trail and failed in hospital and asylum. In Gerald he
hoped for a sound, active brain, combined with the faculty
of expression in many languages and the finer power of
art; an organism sufficiently delicate to carry into that
viewless vinculum between body and soul; vibration,
rhythms and co-ordinations delicate enough to touch a
new consciousness and return its reply through organized
form. He had found these conditions perfect, and he
felt that if failure was the result, while still firmly fixed in
his belief, never again would an opportunity of equal
merit present itself. If in Gerald his theory failed of
demonstration, the mind's past would be, in his lifetime,
locked to his mortal consciousness.

Much of this he stated as they sat in the wing-room.
Gerald lay upon the divan when he began talking, lost
in abstraction, but as the theory of the German was gradually unfolded Edward saw him fix his bright eye upon
the speaker, saw him becoming restless and excited.
When the explanation ended he was walking the floor.

"Experiments with frogs," he said, abruptly; "acci-
dents to the human brain and vivisection have proved
the separateness of memory and consciousness. But I
shall do better; I shall give to the world a complete
picture descended from parent to child—an inherited
brain picture of which the mind is thoroughly conscious."
His listeners waited in breathless suspense; both knew
to what he referred. "But," he added, shaking his head,
"that does not carry us out of the material world."

His ready knowledge of this subject and his quick
grasp of the proposition astonished Virdow beyond expression.

"Go on," he said, simply.

"When that fusion of mind and matter occurs," said Gerald, positively; "when the consciousness is put in touch with the mind's unconscious memory there will be no pictures seen, no records read; we shall simply broaden out, comprehend, understand, grasp, know! That is all! It will not come to the world, but to individuals, and, lastly, it has already come! Every original thought that dawns upon a human, every intuitive conception of the truth, marks the point where a mind yielded something of a memory to human consciousness."

The professor moved uneasily in his seat; both he and Edward were overwhelmed with the surprise of the demonstration that behind the sad environment of this being dwelt a keen, logical mind. The speaker paused and smiled; his attention was not upon his company.

"So," he said, softly, "come the songs into the mind of the poet, so the harmonies to the singer and so the combination of colors to the artist; so the rounded periods of oratory and so the conception that makes invention possible. No facts appear, because facts are the results of laws, the proofs of truths. The mind-memory carries none of these; it carries laws and the truth which interprets it all; and when men can hold their consciousness to the touch of mind without a falling apart, they will stand upon the plane of their Creator, because they will then be fully conscious of the eternal laws and in harmony with them."

"And you," said Virdow, greatly affected, "have you ever felt the union of consciousness and mind memory?"

"Yes," he replied; "what I have said is the truth; for it came from an inner consciousness without previous determination and intention. I am right, and you know I am right!" Virdow shook his head.

"I had hoped," he said, gently, "that in this mind-memory dwelt pictures. We shall see, we shall see." Gerald turned away impatiently and threw himself upon his couch. Presently in the silence which ensued rose the solemn measure of Mendelssohn's heart-beat march. The strange, sad, depressing harmony filled the room; even Virdow felt its wonderful power and sat mute and disturbed. Suddenly he happened to gaze toward Gerald. He lay with ashen face and rigid eyes fixed upon the ceiling, to all appearances a corpse. Virdow bounded forward and snatched the bow from Edward's hand.

"Stop!" he cried; "for his sake stop, or you will kill him!"

They dragged the inanimate form to the window and bathed the face. A low moan escaped the young man, and then a gleam of intelligence came into his eyes. He tried to speak, but without success; an expression of surprise and distress came upon his face as he rose to his feet. For a moment he stood gasping, but presently his breath came normally.

"Temporary aphasia," he said, in a low tone. Going to the easel he drew rapidly the picture of a woman kneeling above the prostrate form of another, and stood contemplating it in silence. Edward and Virdow came to his side, the latter pale with excitement. Gerald did not notice them. Only the back of the kneeling woman was shown, but the face of the other was distinct, calm and beautiful. It was the girl in the small picture.

"That face—that face," he whispered. "Alas! I see it only as my ancestors saw it." He resumed his lounge dejectedly.

"You have seen it before, then?" said Virdow, earnestly.

"Before! In my dreams from childhood! It is a face associated with me always. In the night, when the wind blows, I hear a voice calling Gerald, and this vision comes. Shall I tell you a secret—" His voice had become lower and now was inaudible. Placing his hand upon the white wrist, Virdow said:

"He sleeps; it is well. Come away, my young friend; I have learned much, but the experience might have been dearly bought. Sometime I will explain." Noiselessly they withdrew to Edward's room. Edward was depressed.

"You have gained, but not I," he said. The back of the kneeling woman was toward him.

"Wait," said Virdow; "all things cannot be learned in a night. We do not know who witnessed that scene."

CHAPTER XXVIII.

THE THREE PICTURES.

Virdow had arisen and been to town when Edward made his appearance late in the morning. After tossing on his pillow all night, at daylight he had fallen into a long, dreamless sleep.

Gerald was looking on, and the professor was arranging an experimental apparatus of some kind. He had suspended a metal drum from the arch of the glass-room by steel wires, and over the upper end of the drum had drawn tightly a sheet of rubber obtained from a toy balloon manufacturer. In the base of this drum he inserted a hollow stem of tin, one end of which was flared like a trumpet. The whole machine when completed presented the appearance of a gigantic pipe; the mouthpiece enlarged. When Edward came in the German was spreading upon the rubber surface of the drum an almost impalpable powder, taken from one of the iron nodules which lay about on the surrounding hills and slightly moistened.

"I have been explaining to Gerald," said Virdow, cheerily, "some of my bases for hopes that vibration is the medium through which to effect that ether wherein floats what men call the mind, and am getting ready to show the co-ordinations of forms with certain measures of vibration. Edward, you have a trained voice; I want you to sing now a note into the mouth of this eidophone, beginning with medium force and increasing steadily and evenly. Try what you Americans call 'A' in the middle register and remember that you have before you a detective that will catch your slightest error." He was closing doors and openings as he spoke.

Edward obeyed. Placing his mouth near the trumpet opening he began. The simple note, prolonged, rang out in the silent room, increasing in strength to a certain point and ending abruptly. Then was seen a marvelous thing; animated, the composition upon the disk rushed to the exact center and then tremulously began to take definite shape. A little medallion appeared, surrounded by minute dots, and from these little tongues ran outward. The note died away, and only the breathing of the eager watchers was heard. Before them in bas-relief was a red daisy, as perfect, aye, more nearly perfect, than art could supply. Gerald after a moment turned his head and seemed lost in thought.

"From that we might infer," said Virdow, "that the daisy is the 'A' note of the world; that of it is born all the daisy class of flowers, from the sunflower down—all vibrations of a standard."

Again and again the experiment was repeated, with the same result.

"Now try 'C,'" said the German, and Edward obeyed. Again the mass rushed together, but this time it spread into the form of a pansy. And then with other notes came fern shapes, trees and figures that resembled the scale armor of fish. And finally, from a softly sounded and prolonged note, a perfect serpent in coils appeared, with every ring distinctly marked. This form was varied by repetition to shells and cornucopias.

So through the musical scale went the experiments, each yielding a new and distinct form where the notes differed. Virdow enjoyed the wonder of Edward and the calm concentration of Gerald. He continued:

"Thus runs the scale in colors; each of the seven— red, orange, yellow, green, blue, indigo and violet—is a note, and as there are notes in music that harmonize, so in colors there are the same notes, the hues of which blend harmoniously. What have they to do with the mind memory? This: As a certain number of vibrations called to life in music the shell, in light the color, and in music the note, so once found will certain notes, or more likely their co-ordinations, awaken the memories of the mind, since infallibly by vibrations were they first born.

"This is the border land of speculation, you think, and you are partly correct. What vibration could have fixed the form of the daisy and the shape we have found in nature is uncertain, but remember that the earth swings in a hollow drum of air as resonant and infinitely more sensitive than the rubber; and the brain—there is a philosophic necessity for the shape of a man's head."

"If," said Gerald, "you had said these vibrations awakened the memories of the brain instead of mind, I could have agreed with you. Yours are on the order of the London experiments. I am familiar with them, but only through reading." Again Virdow wondered, but he continued:

"The powers of vibration are not understood—in fact, only dreamed of. Only one man in the world, your Keely, has appreciated its possibilities, and he is involved in the herculean effort to harness it to modern machinery. It was vibration simply that affected Gerald so deeply last night; a rhythm co-ordinating with his heart. I have seen vast audiences—and you have, too, Edward—painfully depressed by that dangerous experiment of Mendelssohn; for the heart, like a clock, will seek to adjust itself to rhythms. Your tempo was less than seventy-two to the minute; Gerald's delicate heart caught time and the brain lacked blood. A quick march would have sent the blood faster and brought exhilaration. Under the influence of march time men cheer and do deeds of valor that they would not otherwise attempt, though the measure is sounded only upon a drum; but when to this time is added a second, a third and a fourth rhythm, and the harmonies of tone against tone, color against color, in perfect co-ordination, they are no longer creatures of reason, but heroes. The whole matter is subject to scientific demonstration.

"But back to this 'heart-beat march.' The whole nerve system of man since the infancy of the race has been subject to the rhythm of the heart, every atom of the human body is attuned to it; for while length of life, breadth of shoulders, chest measure and stature have changed since the days of Adam we have no evidence that the solemn measure of the heart, sending its seventy-two waves against all the minute divisions of the human machine, has ever varied in the normal man. Lessen it, as on last night, and the result is distressing. And as you increase it, or substitute for it vibrations more rapid against those myriad nerves, you exhilarate or intoxicate.

"But has any one ever sent the vibration into that 'viewless vinculum' and awakened the hidden mind? As our young friend testifies, yes! There have been times when these lower co-ordinations of song and melodies have made by a momentary link mind and matter one, and of these times are born the world's greatest treasures —jewels wrested from the hills of eternity! What has been done by chance, science should do by rule."

Gerald had listened, with an attention not hoped for, but the conclusion was anticipated in his quick mind. Busy with his portfolio, he did not attend, but upon the professor's conclusion he turned with a picture in his hand. It was the drawing of the previous night.

"What is it?" he asked.

"A mind picture, possibly," said Virdow.

"You mean by that a picture never impressed upon the brain, but living within the past experience of the mind?"

"Exactly."

"And I say it is simply a brain picture transmitted to me by heredity."

"I deny nothing; all things are possible.. But by whom? One of those women?" Gerald started violently and looked suspiciously upon his questioner. Virdow's face betrayed nothing.

"I do not know," said Gerald; "you have gaps in your theory, and this is the gap in mine. Neither of these women could have seen this picture; there must have been a third person." Virdow smiled and nodded his head.

"And if there was a third person he is my missing witness. From him comes your vision—a true mind picture."

"And this?" Gerald drew from the folio a woman's face—the face that Edward had shown, but idealized and etherealized. "From whom comes this?" cried the young man with growing excitement. "For I swear to you that I have never, except in dreams, beheld it, no tongue has described it! It is mine by memory alone, not plucked from subtle ether by a wandering mind, but from the walls of memory alone. Tell me." Virdow shook his head; he was silent for fear of the excitement. But

Gerald came and stood by him with the two pictures; his voice was strained and impassioned, and his tones just audible:

"The face in this and the sleeper's face in this are the same; if you were on the stand to answer for a friend's life would you say of me, this man descends from the kneeling woman?" Virdow looked upon him unflinchingly.

"I would answer, as by my belief in God's creation, that by this testimony you descend from neither, for the brain that held those pictures could belong to neither woman. One could not hold an etheralized picture of her own face, nor one a true likeness of her own back." Gerald replaced the sheets.

"You have told me what I knew," he said; "and yet —from one of them I am descended, and the pictures are true!" He took his hat and boat paddle and left them abruptly. The portfolio stood open. Virdow went to close it, but there was a third drawing dimly visible. Idly he drew it forth.

It was the picture of a white seagull and above it was an arch; beyond were the bending trees of the first picture. Both men studied it curiously, but with varying emotions.

CHAPTER XXIX.

"HOME, SWEET HOME."

Edward approached the hall that afternoon with misgivings. A charge had been brought against him, denied, and the denial defended with his life; but the charge was not disproved. And in this was the defect of the "code of honor." It died not because of its bloodiness but of inadequacy. A correct aim could not be a satisfactory substitute for good character nor good morals.

Was it his duty to furnish proof to his title to the name of gentleman? Or could he afford to look the world in the face with disdain and hold himself above suspicion?

The latter course was really his only choice. He had no proofs.

This would do for the world at large, but among intimates would it suffice? He knew that nowhere in the world is the hearthstone more sacred than in the south, and how long would his welcome last, even at the hall, with his past unexplained? He would see! The first hesitancy of host or hostess, and he would be self-banished!

There was really no reason why he should remain in America; agents could transact what little business was his and look after Gerald's affairs. Nothing had changed within him; he was the same Edward Morgan, with the same capacities for enjoyment.

But something had changed. He felt it with the mere thought of absence. What was it? As in answer to his mental question, there came behind him the quick breath of a horse and turning he beheld Mary. She smiled in response to his bow. The next instant he had descended from his buggy and was waiting.

"May I ride with you?" Again the face of the girl lighted with pleasure.

"Of course. Get down, Jerry, and change places with Mr. Morgan." Jerry made haste to obey. "Now, drop behind," she said to him, as Edward seated himself by her side.

"You see I have accepted your invitation," he began; "only I did not come as soon as I wished to, or I would have answered your kind note at once in person. All are well, I trust?" Her face clouded.

"No. Mamma has become entirely blind—probably for all time. I have just been in to telegraph Dr. Campbell to come to us. We will know to-morrow." He was greatly distressed.

"My visit is inopportune—I will turn back. No, I was going from the hall to the general's; I can keep straight on."

"Indeed, you shall not, Mr. Morgan. Mamma is bearing up bravely, and you can help so much to divert her mind if you tell her of your travels." He assented readily. It was a novel sensation to find himself useful.

"To-morrow morning," she continued, "perhaps I can find time to go to the general's—if you really want to go—"

"I do," he said. "My German friend, Virdow, has a theory he wishes to demonstrate and has asked me to find the dominant tones in a waterfall; I remembered the general's little cascade, and owing him a visit am going to discharge both duties. What a grand old man the general is!"

"Oh, indeed, yes. You do not know him, Mr. Morgan. If you could have seen how he entered into your quarrel—" she blushed and hesitated. "Oh, what an outrage was that affair!"

"It is past, Miss Montjoy; think no more upon it. It was I who cost your father his seat in congress. That is the lamentable feature."

"That is nothing," said the young girl, "compared with the mortification and peril forced upon you. But you had friends—more than you dreamed of. The general says that the form of your note to Mr. Royson saved you a grave complication."

"You mean that I am indebted to Mr. Barksdale for that?"

"Yes. I love Mr. Barksdale; he is so manly and noble." Edward smiled upon her; he was not jealous of that kind of love.

"He is certainly a fine character—the best product of the new south, I take it. I have neglected to thank him for his good offices. I shall call upon him when I return."

"And," she said in a low tone, "of course you will assure the general of your gratitude to-morrow. You owe him more than you suspect. I would not have you fail there."

"And why would you dislike to have me fail?" She blushed furiously when she realized how she had become involved, but she met his questioning gaze bravely.

"You forget that I introduced you as my friend, and one does not like for friends to show up in a bad light."

He fell into moody silence, from which with difficulty only he could bring himself to reply to questions as she led the way from personal grounds. The hall saved him from absolute disgrace.

In the darkened sitting-room was Mrs. Montjoy when the girl and the young man entered. She lifted her patient face where she sat knitting and turned her bandaged eyes to the door as she heard their voices in the hall.

"Mamma, here is Mr. Morgan," said Mary. The family had instinctively agreed upon a cheerful tone; the great oculist was coming; it was but a question of time when blessed sight would return again. The colonel raised himself from the lounge where he had been dozing and came forward. Edward could not detect in his grave courtesy the slightest deviation of manner. He welcomed him smilingly and inquired of Gerald. And then, continuing into the room, the young man took the soft hand of the elder woman. She placed the other on his and said with that singular disregard of words peculiar to the blind:

"I am glad to see you, Mr. Morgan. We have been so distressed about you. I spent a wretched day and night thinking of your worry and danger."

"They are all over now, madam; but it is pleasant to know that my friends were holding me up all the time. Naturally I was somewhat lonesome," he said, forcing a smile, "until the general came to my rescue." Then recollecting himself, he added with feeling: "But those hours were as nothing to this, madam. You cannot understand how distressed I was to learn, as I have just now, of your illness." She patted his hand affectionately, after the manner of old ladies.

"Oh, yes, I can. Mary has told us of your offer to take us to Paris on that account. I am sure sometimes that one's misfortunes fall heaviest upon friends."

"It is not too late," he said, earnestly. "If the colonel will keep house and trust you two with me, it is not too late. Really, I am almost obliged to visit Paris soon, and if—" he turned to the colonel at a loss for words. That gentleman had passed his hand over his forehead and was looking away.

"You are more than kind, my young friend," he said,

sadly; "more than kind. We will see Campbell. If it is necessary Mrs. Montjoy will go to Paris."

Mary had been a silent witness of the little scene. She turned away to hide her emotion, fearful that her voice, if she spoke, would betray her. The Duchess came in and climbed onto grandma's lap and wound her arms around the little woman. The colonel had resumed his seat when Mary brought in from the hall the precious violin and laid it upon the piano, waiting there until the conversation lagged.

"Mamma," she said, then, "Mr. Morgan has his violin; he was on his way through here to the general's when I intercepted him. I know you can rely upon him to play for us."

"As much and as often as desired," said Edward heartily. "I have a friend at home, an old professor with whom I studied in Germany, who is engaged in some experiments with vibration, and he has assigned me rather a novel task—that is, I am to go over to the general's and determine the tone of a waterfall, for everything has its tone—your window glass, your walking stick, even—and these will respond to the vibrations which make that tone. Your memories are born of vibration, and old airs bring back old thoughts." He arose and took the violin as he talked.

If the presence of the silent sufferer was not sufficient to touch his heart, there were the brown, smiling eyes of the girl whose fingers met his as he took the instrument. He played as seldom if ever before. Something went from him into the ripe, resonant instrument, something that even Virdow could not have explained, and through the simple melodies he chose, affected his hearers deeply. Was it the loneliness of the man speaking to the loneliness of the silent woman, whose bandaged forehead rested upon one blue-veined hand? Or was it a new spring opened up by the breath, the floating hair, the smooth contour of cheeks, the melting depths of brown eyes, the divine sympathy of the girl who played his accompaniments?

All the old music of the blind woman's girlhood had been carefully bound and preserved, as should all old mu-

sic be when it has become a part of our lives; and as this
man with his subtle power awoke upon that marvelous
instrument the older melodies he gave life to the dreams
of her girlish heart. Just so had she played them—if not
so true, yet feelingly. By her side had stood a gallant
black-haired youth, looking down into her face, reading
more in her upturned eyes than her tongue had ever uttered; eyes then liquid and dark with the light of love
beaming from their depths; alas, to beam now no more
forever! Love must find another speech. She reached
out her hand and in eloquent silence it was taken.

Silence drew them all back to earth. But behind the
players an old man's face was bent upon the smooth
soft hand of the woman, and eyes that must some day see
for both of them, left their tender tribute.

Edward Morgan linked himself to others in that hour
with strands stronger than steel. Even the little Duchess
felt the charm and power of that violin in the hands of
the artist. Wondering, she came to him and stretched
up her little hands. He took her upon his knee then, and,
holding the instrument under her chin and her hands in
his, awoke a little lullaby that had impressed him. As
he sung the words, the girl smiled into the faces of the
company.

"Look, gamma," she said gleefully; "look!" And she,
lifting her face, said gently:

"Yes, dear; grandma is looking." Mary's face was
quickly averted; the hands of the colonel tightened upon
the hand he held.

The Duchess had learned to sing "Rockaby Baby" and
now she lifted her thin, piping voice, the player readily
following, and sung sweetly all the verses she could remember. Mary took her in her arms when tired, and
Edward let the strains run on slower and softer. The
eyes of the little one drooped wearily, and then as the
player, his gaze fixed upon the little scene, drifted away
into "Home, Sweet Home," they closed in sleep. The
blind woman still sat with her hand in her husband's, his
head bent forward until his forehead rested upon it.

CHAPTER XXX.

THE RAINBOW IN THE MIST.

Mary had lighted him to his room and handed him the lamp; "sweet sleep and pleasant dreams," she had said, gravely bowing to him as she withdrew—a family custom, as he had afterward learned. But the sleep was not sweet nor the dreams pleasant. Excited and disturbed he dozed away the hours and was glad when the plantation bell rung its early summons. He dressed and made his way to the veranda, whence he wandered over the flower garden, intercepting the colonel, who was about to take his morning look about. Courteously leaving his horse at the gate that gentleman went on foot with him. It was Edward's first experience on a plantation and he viewed with lively interest the beginning of the day's labor. Cotton was opening and numbers of negroes, old and young, were assembling with baskets and sacks or moving out with a show of industry, for, as it was explained to him, it is easy to get them early started in cotton-picking time, as the work is done by the hundred pounds and the morning dew counts for a great deal. "Many people deduct for that," said Montjoy, "but I prefer not to. Lazy as he is, the negro is but poorly paid."

"But," said Edward, laughing, "you do not sell the dew, I suppose?"

"No. Generally it evaporates, but if it does not the warehouse deducts for it."

"You seem to have a great many old negroes."

"Too many; too many," he said, sadly; "but what can be done? These people have been with me all my life and I can't turn them adrift in their old age. And the men seem bent upon keeping married," he added, good-naturedly. "When the old wives die they get new and young ones, and then comes extravagant living again."

"And you have them all to support?"

"Of course. The men do a little chopping and cotton-picking, but not enough to pay for the living of themselves and families. What is it, Nancy?"

"Pa says please send him some meal and meat. He ain't had er mouthful in four days." The speaker was a little negro girl. "Go, see your young mistress. That is a specimen," said the old gentleman, half-laughing, half-frowning. "Four days! He would have been dead the second! Our system does not suit the new order of things. It seems to me the main trouble is in the currency. Our values have all been upset by legislation. Silver ought never have been demonetized; it was fatal, sir. And then the tariff."

"Is not overproduction a factor, colonel? I read that your last crops of cotton were enormous."

"Possibly so, but the world has to have cotton, and a little organization would make it buy at our own prices. These are enormous variations, of course, we can't figure in advance, and whenever a low price rules, the country is broke. The result is the loan associations and cotton factors are about to own us."

The two men returned to find Mary with the pigeons upon her shoulders and a flock of poultry begging at her feet.

"You are going with me to the general's," he said, pleadingly, as he stood by her. She shook her head.

"I suppose not this time; mamma needs me." But at the breakfast table, when he renewed the subject, that lady from her little side table said promptly: "Yes." Mary needed the exercise and diversion, and then there was a little mending to be done for the old general. He always saved it for her. It was his whim.

So they started in Edward's buggy, riding in silence until he said abruptly:

"I am persevering, Miss Montjoy, as you will some day find out, and I am counting upon your help."

"In what?" She was puzzled by his manner.

"In getting Moreau in Paris to look into the little mamma's eyes." She reflected a moment.

"But Dr. Campbell is coming."

"It is through him I was going to accomplish my purpose; he must send her to Paris."

"But," she said, sadly, "we can't afford it. Norton could arrange it, but papa would not be willing to incur such a debt for him."

"His son—her son!" Edward showed his surprise very plainly.

"You do not understand. Norton has a family; neither papa nor mamma would borrow from him, although he would be glad to do anything in the world he could. And there is Annie——" she stopped. Edward saw the difficulty.

"Would your father accept a loan from me?" She flushed painfully.

"I think not, Mr. Morgan. He could hardly borrow money of his guest."

"But I will not be his guest, and it will be a simple business transaction. Will you help me?" She was silent.

"It is very hard, very hard," she said, and tears stood in her eyes. "Hard to have mamma's chances hang upon such a necessity."

"Supposing I go to your father and say: 'This thing is necessary and must be done. I have money to invest at 5 per cent and am going to Paris. If you will secure me with a mortgage upon this place for the necessary amount I will pay all expenses and take charge of your wife and daughter.' Would it offend him?"

"He could not be offended by such generosity, but it would distress him—the necessity."

"That would not count in the matter," he said, gravely. "He is already distressed. And what is all this to a woman's eyesight?"

"How am I to help?" she asked after a while.

"The objection will be chiefly upon your account, I am afraid," he said, after reflection. "You will have to waive everything and second my efforts. That will settle it." She did not promise, but seemed lost in thought. When she spoke again it was upon other things.

"Ah, truant!" cried the general, seeing her ascending the steps and coming forward, "here you are at last. How are you, Morgan? Sit down, both of you. Mary," he said, looking at her sternly, "if you neglect me this way again I shall go off and marry a grass widow. Do you hear me, miss? Look at this collar." He pointed dramatically to the offending article; one of the Byronic affairs, to which the old south clings affectionately, and which as affectionately clings to the garment it is supposed to adorn, since it is a part of it. "I have buttoned that not less than a dozen times to-day." She laughed and, going in, presently returned with thread and needle and sitting upon his knee restored the buttonhole to its proper size. Then she surveyed him a moment.

"Why haven't you been over to see us?"

"Because——"

"You will have to give the grass widow a better excuse than that. 'Tis a woman's answer. But here is Mr. Morgan, come to see if he can catch the tune your waterfall plays—if you have no objection." Edward explained the situation.

"Go with him, Mary. I think the waterfall plays a better tune to a man when there is a pretty girl around." She playfully stopped his mouth and then darted into the house.

"General," said Edward, earnestly, "I have not written to you. I preferred to come in person to express anew my thanks and appreciation of your kindness in my recent trial. The time may come——"

"Nonsense, my boy; we take these things for granted here in the south. If you are indebted to anybody it is to the messenger who brought me the news of your predicament, put me on horseback and sent me hurrying off in the night to town for the first time in twenty years."

"And who could have done that?" he asked. Evan's keen glance read that he was genuinely surprised.

"Well," he said, enjoying the other's interest, "if I wasn't afraid she would overhear me I would tell you."

"And was she the messenger?" Edward asked, overwhelmed with emotion. "From whom?"

"From nobody. She summed up the situation, got behind the little mare and came over here in the night. Morgan, that is the rarest girl in Georgia. Take care, sir; take care, sir." He was getting himself indignant over some contingency when the object of his eulogium appeared.

"Now, general, you are telling tales on me."

"Am I? Ask Morgan. I'd swear on a stack of bibles as high as yonder pine I have not mentioned your name."

"Well, it is a wonder. Come on, Mr. Morgan."

The old man watched them as they picked their way through the hedge and concluded his interrupted remark: "If you break that loyal heart—if you bring a tear to those brown eyes, you will meet a different man than Royson." But he drove the thought away while he looked affectionately after the pair.

Down came the little stream, with an emphasis and noise disproportioned to its size, the cause being, as Edward guessed, the distance of the fall and the fact that the rock on which it struck was not a solid foundation, but rested above a cavity. Mary waited while he listened, turning away to pluck a flower and to catch in the falling mist the colors of the rainbow. But as Edward stood, over him came a flood of thoughts; for the air was full of a weird melody, the overtone of one great chord that thrilled him to the heart. As in a dream he saw her standing there, the blue skies and towering trees above her, a bit of light in a desert of solitude. Near, but separated from him by an infinite gulf. "Forever" was the one word that seemed to roll up and mock him from the depths, and in that strange sad tone. "Forever! Forever!" all else was blotted out.

She saw on his face the white desperation she had noticed once before.

"You have found it," she said. "What is the tone?"

"Despair," he answered, sadly. "It can mean nothing else."

"And yet," she said, a new thought animating her mobile face, as she pointed into the mist above, "over it hangs the rainbow."

CHAPTER XXXI.

THE HAND OF SCIENCE.

A feeling of apprehension and solemnity pervaded the hall when at last the old family coach deposited its single occupant, Dr. Campbell, at the gate. The colonel stood at the top of the steps to welcome him. Edward and Mary were waiting in the sitting-room.

The famous practitioner, a tall, shapely figure, entered, and as he removed his glasses he brought sunshine into the room, with his cheery voice and confident manner. To Mrs. Montjoy he said:

"I came as soon as the telegram was received. Anxiety and loss of rest in cases like yours are exceedingly undesirable. It is better to be informed—even of the worst. Before we discuss this matter, come to the window and let me examine the eye, please." He was assisting her as he spoke. He carefully studied the condition of the now inflamed and sightless organ, and then replaced the bandage.

"It is glaucoma," he said, briefly. "You will remember that I feared it when we fitted the glasses some years ago. The slowness of its advance is due to the care you have taken. If you are willing I would prefer to operate at once." All were waiting in painful silence. The brave woman replied: "Whenever you are ready I am," and resumed her knitting. He had been deliberate in every word and action, but the occasion was already robbed of half its terrors, so potent are confidence, decision and action. Edward was introduced and would have taken his leave, but the oculist detained him.

"I shall probably need you," he said, "and will be obliged if you remain. The operation is very simple."

The room was soon prepared; a window was thrown open, a lounge drawn under it and bandages prepared. Mary, pale with emotion, when the slender form of her mother was stretched upon the lounge hurriedly withdrew. The colonel seated himself and turned away his face. There was no chloroform, no lecture. With the simplicity of a child at play, the great man went to work. Turning up the eyelid, he dropped upon the cornea a little cocaine, and selecting a minute scalpel from his case, with two swift, even motions cut downward from the center of the eye and then from the same starting point at right angles. The incisions extended no deeper than the transparent epidermis of the organ. Skillfully turning up the angle of this, he exposed a thin, white growth—a minute cloud it seemed to Edward.

"Another drop of cocaine, please," the pleasant voice

of the oculist recalled him, and upon the exposed point he let fall from the dropper the liquid. Lifting the little cloud with keen pinchers, the operator removed it, restored the thin epidermis to its place, touched it again with cocaine, and replaced the bandage. The strain of long hours was ended; he had not been in the house thirty minutes.

"I felt but the scratch of a needle," said the patient; "it is indeed ended?"

"All over," he said, cheerfully. He then wrote out a prescription and directions for dressing, to be given to the family physician. Mary was already by her mother's side, holding and patting her hand.

The famous man was an old friend of the family, and now entered into a cheerful discussion of former times and mutual acquaintances. The little boy had entered, and somehow had got into his lap, where all children usually got who came under his spell. While talking on other subjects he turned down the little fellow's lids.

"I see granulation here, colonel. Attend to it at once. I will leave a prescription." And then with a few words of encouragement, he went off to the porch to smoke.

After dinner the conversation came back to the patient. "She will regain her vision this time," said Dr. Campbell, "but the disease can only be arrested; it will return. The next time it will do no good to operate. It is better to know these things and prepare for them." The silence was broken by Edward.

"Are you so sure of this, doctor, that you would advise against further consultation? In Paris, for instance, is Moreau. In your opinion, is there the slightest grounds for his disagreeing with you?"

"In my opinion, no. But my opinion never extends to the point of neglecting any means open to us. Were I afflicted with this disease I would consult everybody within reach who had had experience." Edward glanced in triumph at Mary. Dr. Campbell continued:

"I would be very glad if it were possible for Mrs. Montjoy to see Moreau about the left eye. You will remember that I expressed a doubt as to the hopelessness of restoring that one when it was lost. It was not affected with glaucoma; there is a bare possibility that something might be done for it with success. If the disease returns upon the right eye, the question of operating upon the other might then come up again." Edward waited a moment and then continued his questions:

"Do you not think a sea voyage would be beneficial, doctor?"

"Undoubtedly, if she is protected from the glare and dust while ashore. We can only look to building up her general health now." Edward turned away, with throbbing pulses.

"But," continued the doctor, "of course nothing of this sort should be attempted until the eye is perfectly well again; say in ten days or two weeks." Mary sat with bowed head. She did not see why Dr. Campbell arose presently and walked to where Edward was standing. She looked upon them there. Edward was talking with eager face and the other studying him through his glasses. But somehow she connected his parting words with that short interview.

"And about the sea voyage and Moreau, colonel; I do not know that I ought to advise you, but I shall be glad if you find it convenient to arrange that, and will look to you to have Moreau send me a written report. Good-by." But Edward stopped him.

"I am going back directly, doctor, and can take you and the carriage need not return again. I will keep you waiting a few moments only." He drew Col. Montjoy aside and they walked to the rear veranda.

"Colonel," he said, earnestly, "I want to make you an offer, and I do it with hesitancy only because I am afraid you cannot understand me thoroughly upon such short acquaintance. I believe firmly in this trip and want you to let me help you bring it about. Without having interested myself in your affairs, I am assured that you stand upon the footing of the majority of southerners whose fortunes were staked upon the confederacy, and that just now it would inconvenience you greatly to meet the expense of this experiment. I want you to let me take the place of John Morgan and do just as he would have done in this situation—advance you the necessary money

upon your own terms." As he entered upon the subject
the old gentleman looked away from him, and as he proceeded Edward could see that he was deeply affected. He
extended his hand impulsively to the young man at last
and shook it warmly. Tears had gathered in his eyes.
Edward continued:

"I appreciate what you would say, colonel; you think
it too much for a comparative stranger to offer, or for
you to accept, but the matter is not one of your choosing.
The fortunes of war have brought about the difficulty,
and that is all. You have risked your all on that issue
and have lost. You cannot risk the welfare of your wife
upon an issue of pride. You must accept. Go to Gen.
Evan; he will tell you so."

"I cannot consider the offer, my young friend, in any
other than a business way. Your generosity has already
put us under obligation we can never pay and has only
brought you mortification."

"Not so," was the reply. "In your house I have known
the first home feeling I ever experienced. Colonel, don't
oppose me in this. If you wish to call it business, give it
that term."

"Yours will be the fourth mortgage on this place; I
hesitate to offer it. The hall is already pledged for $15,-
000."

"It is amply sufficient."

"I will consider the matter, Mr. Morgan," he said after
a long silence; "I will consider it and consult Evan. I do
not see my way clear to accept your offer, but whether
or not, my young friend"—putting his arm over the other's shoulder, his voice trembling—"whether I do or not
you have in making it done me an honor and a favor that
I will remember for life. It is worth something to meet
a man now and then who is worthy to have lived in nobler
times. God bless you—and now you must excuse me."
He turned away abruptly. Thrilled by his tone and
words, Edward went to the front. As he shook hands
with Mary he said:

"I cannot tell yet. But he cannot refuse. There is no
escape for him."

At the depot in the city the doctor said: "Do not count

too hopefully upon Paris, my young friend. There is a chance, but in my opinion the greatest good that can be achieved is for the patient to store in memory scenes upon which in other days she may dwell with pleasure. Keep this in mind and be governed accordingly." He climbed aboard the train and waved an adieu.

Edward was leaving the depot when he overtook Barksdale. Putting his buggy in the care of a boy, he walked on with the railroader at his request to the club. Barksdale took him into a private room and over a choice cigar Edward gave him all the particulars of the duel and then expressed his grateful acknowledgments for the friendly services rendered him.

"I am assured by Gen. Evan," he said, "that had my demand been made in a different form I might have been seriously embarrassed."

"Royson depended upon the Montjoys to get him out of the affair; he had no idea of fighting."

"But how could the Montjoys have helped him?"

"They could have appealed to him to withdraw the charges he had made, and he would have done so because the information came really from a member of the Montjoy family. I do not think you will need to ask her name. I mention it to you because you should be informed." Edward comprehended his meaning at once. Greatly agitated, he exclaimed:

"But what object could she have had in putting out such slander? I do not know her nor she me." Barksdale waved his hand deprecatingly:

"You do not know much of women."

"No. I have certainly not met this kind before."

Barksdale reflected a few moments, and then said, slowly: "Slander is a curious thing, Mr. Morgan. People who do not believe it will repeat it. I think if I were you I would clear up all these matters by submitting to an interview with a reporter. In that you can place your own and family history before the public and end all talk." Edward was pale, but this was the suggestion that he had considered more than once. He shook his head quickly.

"I disagree with you. I think it beneath the dignity

13

of a gentleman to answer slander by the publication of his family history. If the people of this city require such statements from those who come among them, then I shall sell out my interest here and go abroad, where I am known. This I am, however, loath to do; I have a few warm friends here." Barksdale extended his hand.

"You will, I hope, count me among them. I spoke only from a desire to see you fairly treated."

"I have reason to number you among them. I am going to Paris shortly, I think, with Mrs. Montjoy. Her eyesight is failing. I will be glad to see you again before then."

"With Mrs. Montjoy?" exclaimed Barksdale.

"Yes; the matter is not entirely settled yet, but I do not doubt that she will make the trip. Miss Montjoy will go with us."

Barksdale did not lift his eyes, but was silent, his hand toying with his glass.

"I will probably call upon you before your departure," he said, as he arose.

CHAPTER XXXII.

THE FLASHLIGHT PHOTOGRAPH.

Twilight was deepening over the hills and already the valleys were in shadow when Edward reached Ilexhurst. He stood for a moment looking back on the city and the hills beyond. He seemed to be laying aside a sweeter life for something less fair, and the old weight descended upon him. After all was it wise to go forth, when the return to the solitude of a clouded life was inevitable? There was no escape from fate.

In the east the hills were darkening, but memory flashed on him a scene—a fair-faced girl, as he had seen her, as he would always see her, floating upon an amethyst stream, smiling upon him, one hand laving the waters and over them the wonders of a southern sunset.

In the wing-room Virdow and Gerald were getting

ready for an experiment with flashlight photography. Refusing to be hurried in his scientific investigations, Gerald had insisted that until it had been proved that a living substance could hold a photographic imprint he should not advance to the consideration of Virdow's theory. There must be brain pictures before there could be mind pictures. At least, so he reasoned. None of them knew exactly what his experiment was to be, except that he was going to test the substance that envelops the body of the bass, the micopterus salmoides of southern waters. That sensitive plate, thinner than art could make it, was not only spoiled by exposure to light, but by light and air combined was absolutely destroyed. And the difficulty of controlling the movements of this fish seemed absolutely insuperable. They could only watch the experimenter.

Into a thin glass jar Gerald poured a quantity of powder, which he had carefully compounded during the day. Virdow saw in it the silvery glimmer of magnesium. What the combined element was could not be determined. This compound reached only a third of the distance up the side of the glass. The jar was then stopped with cork pierced by a copper wire that touched the powder, and hermetically sealed with wax. With this under one arm, and a small galvanic battery under the other, and restless with suppressed excitement, Gerald, pointing to a small hooded lantern, whose powerful reflector was lighting one end of the room, bade them follow him.

Virdow and Edward obeyed. With a rapid stride Gerald set out across fields, through strips of woodlands and down precipitous slopes until they stood all breathless upon the shore of the little lake. There they found the flat-bottom bateau, and although by this time both Edward and Virdow had begun seriously to doubt the wisdom of blindly following such a character, they resigned themselves to fate and entered.

Gerald propelled the little craft carefully to a stump that stood up distinct against the gloom under the searchlight in the bow, and reaching it took out his pocket compass. Turning the boat's head northeast, he fol-

lowed the course about forty yards until at the left the
reflector showed him two stakes in line. Here he brought
the little craft to a standstill, and in silence, which he
invoked by lifting his hand warningly, turned the lantern
downward over the stern of the boat, and with a tube,
whose lower end was stubbed with a bit of glass and
inserted in the water, examined the bottom of the lake
twenty feet below. Long and patient was the search,
but at last the others saw him lay aside his glass and
let the boat drift a few moments. Then very gently, only
a ripple of the surface marking the action, he lowered
the weighted jar until the slackening wire indicated that
it was upon the bottom. He reached out his hand
quickly and drew the battery to him, firmly grasping the
cross-handle lever. The next instant there was a rumbling, roaring sound, accompanied by a fierce, white light,
and the end of the boat was in the air. In a brief moment
Edward saw the slender form of the enthusiast bathed
in the flash, his face as white as chalk, his eyes afire
with excitement—the incarnation of insanity, it seemed
to him. Then there was a deluge of spray, a violent
rocking of the boat and the water in it went over their
shoetops. Instantly all was inky blackness, except
where in the hands of the fearless man in the stern the
lantern, its slide changed, was now casting a stream of
red light upon the surface of the lake. Suddenly Gerald
uttered a loud cry.

"Look! Look! There he is!" And floating in that
crimson path, with small fishes rising around him, was
the dead body of a gigantic bass. Lifting him carefully
by the gills, Gerald laid him in a box drawn from under
the rear seat.

"What is it?" broke from Virdow, whose anxiety was
glad to find expression. "We have risked our lives and
ruined our clothes—for what?"

"For a photograph upon a living substance! On the
side of this fish, which was exposed to the flashlight,
you will find the outlines of the grasses in this lake, or
the whole film destroyed. If the outlines are there then
there is no reason why the human brain, infinitely more
sensitive and forever excluded from light, cannot contain

the pictures of those twin cameras—the human eyes."
He turned the boat shoreward and seizing his box disappeared in the darkness, his enlarged pupils giving him
the visual powers of a night animal. Virdow and Edward, even aided by the lantern, found their way back
with difficulty.

The two men entered the wing-room to find it vacant.
Virdow, however, pointed silently to the red light gleaming through the glass of the little door to the cabinet.
The sound of trickling water was heard.

At that instant a smothered half-human cry came from
within, and, holding the fish at arm's length, ghastly
pale and trembling violently, Gerald staggered into the
room. They took hold of him, fearing he would fall.
Straining their eyes, they both saw for an instant only
the half-developed outlines of a human profile extended
along the broad side of the fish. As they watched, the
surface grew into one tone and the carcass fell to the
floor.

Gazing into their faces as he struggled for freedom,
Gerald cast off their hands. The lithe, sinewy form
seemed to be imbued at the moment with the strength
of a giant. Before they could speak he had seized the
lantern and was out into the night. Without a moment's
hesitation, Edward, bareheaded, plunged after him. Well
trained to college athletics though he was, yet unfamiliar
with the grounds, it taxed his best efforts to keep him in
sight. He divined that the wild race would end at the
lake, and the thought that on a few seconds might hang
the life of that strange being was all that held him to the
prolonged and dangerous strain. He reached the shore
just in time, by plunging waist deep into the water, to
throw himself into the boat. His own momentum thrust
it far out upon the surface.

With unerring skill and incredible swiftness, the young
man carried the boat over its former course and turned
the glare of the lamp downward. Suddenly he uttered
a loud cry, and, dropping the lantern in the boat, stood
up and leaped into the water. The light was now out
and all was as black as midnight.

Edward slipped off his shoes, seized the paddle and

waited for a sound to guide him. It seemed as though nothing human could survive that prolonged submergence; minutes appeared to pass; with a groan of despair he gave up hope.

But at that moment, with a gasp, the white face of Gerald burst from the waters ten feet away, and the efforts he made showed that he was swimming with difficulty. With one mighty stroke Edward sent the boat to the swimmer and caught the floating hair. Then with great difficulty he drew him over the side.

"Home!" The word escaped from Gerald between his gasps, but when he reached the shore, with a return of energy and a total disregard of his companion, he plunged into the darkness toward the house, Edward this time keeping him within view with less difficulty.

They reached the door of the wing-room almost simultaneously and rushed in side by side, Gerald dripping with water and exhausted. He leaned heavily against the table. For the first time Edward was conscious that he carried a burden in his arms. In breathless silence, he with Virdow approached, and then upon the table Gerald placed an object and drew shuddering back. It was a half life-size bust of darkened and discolored marble, and for them, though trembling with excitement, it seemed to have no especial significance until they were startled by a cry so loud, so piercing, so heartrending, that they felt the flesh creep upon their bones.

Looking from the marble to the face of the young man they saw that the whiteness of death was upon every feature. Following the direction of his gaze, they beheld a silhouette upon the wall; the clear-cut profile of a woman, cast by the carved face before them. To Edward it was an outline vaguely familiar; to Virdow a revelation, for it was Edward's own profile. Had the latter recognized it there would have been a tragedy, for, without a word after that strange, sad, despairing cry, Gerald wrenched a dagger from the decorated panel, and struck at his own heart. It was Edward's quickness that saved him; the blade made but a trifling flesh wound. Seizing him as he did from the rear he was enabled to disturb his equilibrium in time.

"Morphine," he said to Virdow. The latter hurried away to secure the drug. He found with the pellets a little pocket case containing morphine powders and a hypodermic injector. Without a struggle, Gerald lay breathing heavily. In a few minutes the drug was administered, and then came peace for the sufferer. Edward released his hold and looked about him. Virdow had moved the bust and was seated lost in thought.

"What does it mean?" he asked, approaching, awed and saddened by his experience. Virdow held up the little bust.

"Have you ever seen that face before?"

"It is the face of the young woman in the picture!"

"And now," said Virdow, again placing the marble so as to cast its outlines upon the wall, "you do not recognize it, but the profile is your own!"

CHAPTER XXXIII.

THE TRADE WITH SLIPPERY DICK.

Amos Royson, in the solitude of his room, had full time for reflection upon the events of the week and upon his position. His face, always sinister, had not improved under its contact with the heavy dueling pistol driven so savagely against it. The front teeth would be replaced and the defect concealed under the heavy mustache he wore, and the cut and swollen lips were resuming their normal condition. The missing finger, even, would inconvenience him only until he had trained the middle one to discharge its duties—but the nose! He trembled with rage when for the hundredth time he studied his face in the glass and realized that the best skill of the surgeon had not been able to restore its lines.

But this was not the worst. He had carefully scanned the state press during his seclusion and awoke from his personal estimate to find that public opinion was overwhelmingly against him. He had slandered a man for political purposes and forced a fight upon a stranger to whom, by every right of hospitality, the city owed a welcome. The general public could not understand why he had entered upon the duel if his charges were true, and if not true why he had not had the manliness to withdraw them.

Moreover, he had incurred the deadly enmity of the people who had been deceived in the lost county. One paper alluded to the unpleasant fact that Edward Morgan was defending and aiding Mr. Royson's connections at the time of the insult.

He had heard no word from Swearingen, who evidently felt that the matter was too hot at both ends for him to handle safely. That gentleman had, on the contrary, in a brief card to one of the papers, disclaimed any knowledge of the unfortunate letter and declined all responsibility for it. This was sufficient, it would seem, to render almost any man unhappy, but the climax was reached when he received a letter from Annie, scoring him unmercifully for his clumsiness and informing him that Edward Morgan, so far from being destroyed in a certain quarter, was being received in the house as a friend to whom all were indebted, and was petted and made much of.

"So far as I can judge," she added, maliciously, "it seems settled that Mary is to marry him. He is much with Col. Montjoy and is now upon a confidential footing with every one here. Practically he is already a member of the family." It contained a request for him to inform her when he would be at his office.

He had not replied to this; he felt that the letter was aimed at his peace of mind and the only satisfaction he could get out of this affair was the recollection that he had informed her father-in-law of her perfidy.

"I would be glad to see the old gentleman's mind at work with Annie purring around him," he said to himself, and the idea brought the first smile his face had known for many a day. But a glimpse of that face in the glass, with the smile upon it, startled him again.

What next? Surrender? There was no surrender in the make-up of the man. His legal success had

hinged less upon ability than upon dogged pertinacity.
In this way he had saved the life of more than one criminal and won a reputation that brought him practice.
He had made a charge, had been challenged and had
fought.   With almost any other man the issue would
have been at an end as honorably settled, but his habit
of mind was opposed to accepting anything as settled
which was clearly unsettled.   The duel did not give
Morgan the rights of a gentleman if the main charge were
true, and Royson had convinced himself that it was true.
He wrote to Annie, assured that her visit would develop
his next move.

So it was that one morning Royson found himself face
to face with his cousin, in the office.   There was no word
of sympathy for him.   He had not expected one, but he
was hardly prepared for the half-smile which came over
her face when he greeted her, and which, during their
interview, returned from time to time.   This enraged him
beyond endurance, and nothing but the remembrance that
she alone held the key to the situation prevented his
coming to an open breach with her.   She saw and read
his struggle aright, and the display put her in the best
of humor.

"When shall we see you at the hall again?" she asked,
coolly.

"Never," he said, passionately, "until this man Morgan
is exposed and driven out."   She arched her brows.

"Never, then, would have been sufficient."

"Annie, this man must be exposed; you have the
proofs—you have information; give it to me."   She
shook her head, smiling.

"I have changed my mind, Amos; I do not want to
be on bad terms with my brother-in-law of the future;
the fact is, I am getting fond of him.   He is very kind
to everybody.   Mother is to go to Paris to have her eyes
attended to, and Mary is to accompany her.   Mr. Morgan has been accepted as their escort."

The face of the man grew crimson with suppressed
rage.   By a supreme effort Royson recovered and returned the blow.

"What a pity, Annie, it could not have been you!

Paris has been your hobby for years. When Mary returns she can tell you how to dress in the best form and
correct your French." It was a successful counter. She
was afraid to trust herself to reply. Royson drew his
chair nearer.

"Annie," he said, "I would give ten years of life to
establish the truth of what you have told me. So far
as Mary is concerned, we will leave that out, but I am
determined to crush this fellow Morgan at any cost.
Something tells me we have a common cause in this
matter. Give me a starting point—you owe me something. I could have involved you; I fought it out alone."
She reflected a moment.

"I cannot help you, now, as much as you may think.
I am convinced of what I told you, but the direct proof is
wanting. You can imagine how difficult such proof is.
The man is 30 years old, probably, and witnesses of his
mother's times are old or dead."

"And what witnesses could there have been?"

"Few. John Morgan is gone. The next witness would
be Rita. Rita is the woman who kept Morgan's house
for the last thirty years. She owned a little house in the
neighborhood of the hall and was until she went to
Morgan's a professional nurse. There may be old negroes who can give you points."

"And Rita—where is she?"

"Dead!"

A shade of disappointment swept over his face. He
caught her eyes fixed upon him with the most peculiar
expression. "She is the witness on whom I relied," she
said, slowly. "She was, I believe, the only human being
in the world who could have furnished conclusive testimony as to the origin of Edward Morgan. She died
suddenly the day your letter was published!" She did
not look away as she concluded, but continued with her
eyes fixed upon his; and gradually, as he watched her,
the brows contracted slightly and the lids tightened under
them. A gleam of intelligence passed to him. His face
grew white and his hands closed convulsively upon the
arms of his chair.

"But that would be beyond belief," he said, at last, in a

whisper. "If what you think true is true, he was her
son!" She raised her brows as she replied:
"There was no tie of association! With him everything was at stake. You can probably understand that
when a man is in love he will risk a great deal."
Royson arose and walked the room. No man knew
better than he the worst side of the human heart. There
is nothing so true in the history of crime as that reputation is held higher than conscience. And in this case
there was the terrible passion of love. He did not reply
to her insinuation.
"You think, then," he said, stopping in front of the
woman, "that, reading my letter, he rushed home, and
in this you are correct since I saw him across the street
reading the paper, and a few minutes later throw himself into a hack and take that direction; that he rushed
into the presence of this woman, demanded the truth,
and, receiving it, in a fit of desperation, killed her!"
"What I may think, Amos, is my right to keep to
myself. The only witness died that day! There was no
inquest! You asked me for a starting point." She drew
her gloves a little tighter, shook out her parasol and rose.
"But I am giving you too much of my time. I have
some commissions from Mary, who is getting ready for
Paris, and must leave you."
He neither heard her last remark nor saw her go.
Standing in the middle of the room, with his chin upon
his chest, he was lost to all consciousness of the moment.
When he looked to the chair she had occupied it was
vacant. He passed his hand over his brow. The scene
seemed to have been a dream.
But Amos Royson knew it was real. He had asked
for a starting point, and the woman had given it.
As he considered it, he unconsciously betrayed how
closely akin he was to the woman, for every fact that
came to him was in that legal mind, trained to building
theories, adjusted in support of the hypothesis of crime.
He was again the prosecuting attorney. How natural
at least was such a crime, supposing Morgan capable of it.
And no man knew his history!
With one blow he had swept away the witness. That
had been done a thousand times in the annals of crime.

Poison, the ambush, the street encounter, the midnight shot through the open window, the fusillade at the form outlined in its own front door; the press had recorded it since the beginning of newspapers. Morgan had added one more instance. And if he had not, the suspicion, the investigation, the doubt would remain!

At this point by a perfectly natural process the mind of the man reached its conclusion. Why need there be any suspicion, any doubt? Why might not an inquest develop evidences of a crime? This idea involved action and decision upon his part, and some risk.

At last he arose from the desk, where, with his head upon his hand, he had studied so long, and prepared for action. At the lavatory he caught sight of his own countenance in the glass. It told him that his mind was made up. It was war to the knife, and that livid scar upon the pallor of his face was but the record of the first failure. The next battle would not be in the open, with the skies blue above him and no shelter at hand. His victim would never see the knife descend, but it would descend nevertheless, and this time there would be no trembling hand nor failure of nerve.

From his office he went direct to the coroner's and examined the records. The last inquest was of the day previous; the next in line more than a month before. There was no woman's name upon the list. So far Annie was right.

Outside of cities in the south no burial permits are required. Who was the undertaker? Inquiry would easily develop the fact, but this time he was to remain in the dark. If this crime was fastened upon Morgan, the motive would be self-evident and a reaction of public opinion would re-establish Royson high in favor. His experience would rank as martyrdom.

But a new failure would destroy him forever, and there was not a great deal left to destroy, he felt.

In the community, somewhere, was a negro whose only title was "Slippery Dick" won in many a hotly contested criminal trial. It had been said of this man that the entire penal code was exhausted in efforts to convict him, and always without success. He had been prosecuted for nearly every offense proscribed by state laws. Royson's first experience with the man was as prosecuting attorney. Afterward and within the preceding year he had defended him in a trial for body-snatching and had secured a verdict by getting upon the jury one man who was closely kin to the person who purchased the awful merchandise. This negro, plausible and cunning, hesitated at nothing short of open murder —or such was his reputation. It was to find him that Royson went abroad. Nor was it long before he succeeded.

That night, in a lonely cabin on the outskirts of the city, a trade was made. Ten dollars in hand was paid. If upon an inquest by the coroner it was found that there was a small wound on the back of the head of the woman and the skull fractured, Slippery Dick was to receive $100 more.

This was the only risk Royson would permit himself to take, and there were no witnesses to the trade. Dick's word was worth nothing. Discovery could not affect the plot seriously, and Dick never confessed. The next day he met Annie upon the road, having seen her in the city, and posted himself to intercept her.

"I have investigated the death of Rita," he said, "and am satisfied that there are no grounds for suspecting murder. We will wait!" The woman looked him in the face.

"Amos," she said, "if you were not my cousin, I would say that you are an accomplished liar!" Before he replied there was heard the sound of a horse's feet. Edward Morgan drove by, gravely lifting his hat.

CHAPTER XXXIV.

THE FACE OF THE BODY-SNATCHER.

The methods of Royson's emissary were simple and direct. One day he wandered in among the negroes at Ilexhurst in search of a lost hound puppy, for Dick was a mighty hunter, especially of the midnight 'possum.

No one had seen the puppy, but all were ready to talk, and the death of Rita had been the latest sensation. From them he obtained every detail from the time Edward had carried the body in his arms to the little house, until it had been buried under the crooked cedar in the plantation burying-ground.

The body had been dressed by two of the women. There had been a little blood on her head, from a small wound in the left temple, where she had cut herself against the glass when she was "taken with a fit."

The coffin was a heavy metal one and the top screwed on. That was all.

When Royson received the report of the cut in the head and the blood, his breath almost forsook him. Morgan might have been innocent, but what a chain of circumstantial evidence! If Dick should return to tell him some morning that the false wound he was to make was already on the spot selected, he would not be surprised. So far he could show a motive for the crime, and every circumstance necessary to convict his enemy with it. All he needed was a cause of death.

Dick's precautions in this venture were novel, from the Caucasian standpoint. His superstition was the strongest feature of his depraved mind. The negro has an instinctive dread of dead bodies, but a dead and buried cadaver is to him a horror.

In this instance, however, Dick's superstition made his sacrilege possible; for while he believed firmly in the reappearance and power of departed spirits, he believed equally in the powers of the voodoo to control or baffle them. Before undertaking his commission, he went to one of these voodoo "doctors," who had befriended him in more than one peril, and by the gift of a fat 'possum secured a charm to protect him.

The dark hour came, and at midnight to the little clump of trees came also Slippery Dick. His first act was to bore a hole with an auger in the cedar, insert the voodoo charm and plug the hole firmly. This chained the spirit of the dead. Then with a spade and working rapidly, he threw the mound aside and began to toss out the earth from above the coffin. In half an hour his spade laid the wooden case bare. Some difficulty was experienced in removing the screws, but down in that cavity, the danger from using matches was reduced to a minimum, and by the aid of these he soon loosened the lid and removed it. To lift this out, and take off the metal top of the burial case, was the work of but a few minutes longer, and the remains of poor Rita were exposed to view.

In less than an hour after his arrival Slippery Dick had executed his commission and was filling up the grave. With the utmost care he pressed down the earth and drew up the loosened soil.

There had been a bunch of faded flowers upon the mound; he restored these and with a sigh of relief shouldered his spade and auger and took his departure, glad to leave the grewsome spot.

But a dramatic pantomime had been enacted near him which he never saw. While he was engaged in marking the head of the lifeless body, the slender form of a man appeared above him and shrank back in horror at the discovery. This man turned and picked up the heavy spade and swung it in air. If it had descended the negro would have been brained. But thought is a monarch! Slowly the arm descended, the spade was laid upon the ground, and the form a moment before animated with an overwhelming passion stood silent and motionless behind the cedar.

When the negro withdrew, this man followed, gliding from cover to cover, or following boldly in the open, but at all times with a tread as soft as a panther's. Down they went, the criminal and his shadow, down into the suburbs, then into the streets and then into the heart of the city. Near the office of Amos Royson the man in front uttered a peculiar whistle and passed on. At the next corner under the electric lamp he turned and found himself confronted by a slender man, whose face shone white under the ghastly light of the lamp, whose hair hung upon his shoulders, and whose eyes were distended with excitement. Uttering a cry of fright, the negro sprang from the sidewalk into the gutter, but the other passed on without turning except to cross the street,

where in a friendly shadow he stopped.   And as he stood
there the negro retraced his steps and paused at the door
of the lawyer's office.   A dimly outlined form was at the
window above.   They had no more than time to exchange a word when the negro went on and the street
was bare, except that a square away a heavy-footed policeman was approaching.

The man in the shadow leaned his head against a tree
and thought.   In his brain, standing out as distinct as
if cut from black marble, was the face of the man he had
followed.

Gerald possessed the reasoning faculty to an eminent
degree, but it had been trained altogether upon abstract
propositions.   The small affairs of life were strange and
remote to him, and the passions that animate the human
breast were forces and agencies beyond his knowledge
and calculations.

Annie Montjoy, with the facts in his possession, would
have reached a correct conclusion as to their meaning
instantly.   He could not handle them.   His mind was
absolutely free of suspicion.   He had wandered to the
little graveyard, as he had before when sleepless and
harassed, and discovered that some one was disfiguring
the body of his lifelong friend.   To seize the spade and
wreak vengeance upon the intruder was his first impulse,
but at the moment that it should have fallen he saw that
the head of the woman was being carefully replaced in
position and the clothing arranged.   He paused in wonder.   The habitual opium-eater develops generally a cunning that is incomprehensible to the normal mind, and
curiosity now controlled Gerald.   The moment for action
had passed.   He withdrew behind the tree to witness
the conclusion of the drama.

His following the retreating figure was but the con-
tinuance of his new mood.   He would see the affair out
and behold the face of the man.   Succeeding in this he
went home, revolving in mind the strange experience he
had gained.

But the excitement would not pass away from him,
and in the solitude of his studio, with marvelous skill he
drew in charcoal the scene as it shone in memory—the

man in the grave, the sad, dead face of the woman, shrinking into dissolution, and then its every detail perfect, upon a separate sheet the face of the man under the lamp. The memories no longer haunted him. They were transferred to paper.

Then Gerald underwent the common struggle of his existence; he lay down and tossed upon his pillow; he arose and read and returned again. At last came the surrender, opium and—oblivion.

Standing by the easel next morning, Virdow said to Edward: "The brain cannot survive this many years. When dreams of memories such as these, vivid enough to be remembered and drawn, come upon it, when the waking mind holds them vivid, it is in a critical condition." He looked sadly upon the sleeper and felt the white wrist that overlay the counterpane. The flesh was cold, the pulse slow and feeble. "Vitality small," he said. "It will be sudden when it comes; sleep will simply extend into eternity."

Edward's mind reverted to the old general. What was his own duty? He would decide. It might be that he would return no more, and if he did not, and Gerald was left, he should have a protector.

Virdow had been silent and thoughtful. Now he turned with sudden decision.

"My experiments will probably end with the next," he said. "The truth is, I am so thoroughly convinced that the cultivation of this singular power which Gerald possesses is destructive of the nervous system I cannot go on with them. In some way the young man has wound himself about me. I will care for him as I would a son. He is all gold." The old man passed out abruptly, ashamed of the feeling which shook his voice.

But Edward sat upon the bed and taking the white hand in his own, smoothed it gently, and gave himself up to thought. What did it all mean? And how would it end? The sleeper stirred slightly. "Mother," he said, and a childish smile dwelt for a moment upon his lips. Edward replaced the hand upon the counterpane and withdrew.

14

CHAPTER XXXV.

THE GRAVE IN THE PAST.

When Col. Montjoy rode over to Gen. Evan's, a few mornings after the operation upon his wife's eyes, it was with but ill-defined notions of what he would say or what would be the result of the interview. Circumstances had placed him in a strange and unpleasant position.

Col. Montjoy felt that the Paris trip could not be well avoided. He realized that the chances of accomplishing any real good for his wife were very small, but Dr. Campbell had distinctly favored it, and the hesitancy had evidently only been on account of the cost.

But could he accept the generous offer made by Morgan? That was the embarrassing question. He was not mentally blind; he felt assured that the real question for him to decide then was what he should answer when a demand for the hand of his daughter was made. For in accepting the loan and escort of Edward Morgan, he accepted him. Could he do this?

So far as the rumors about the young man were concerned, he never entertained them seriously. He regarded them only as a desperate political move, and so did the public generally. But a shadow ought not to hang over the life of his daughter.

The old general was at home and partially read his visitor's predicament in his face as he approached the veranda.

"Come in, Norton," he said without moving from his great rocker; "what is troubling you?" And he laughed maliciously. "But by the way," he added, " how is the madam to-day? Mary told me yesterday she was getting along finely."

"Well, we can't tell, Evan," said his visitor, drawing his chair next to the rail; "we can't tell. In fact, nothing will be known until the bandages are removed. I came off without my tobacco—" He was holding his pipe. The general passed him his box.

"Oh, well, she can't but come through all right; Campbell is never mistaken."

"That is true, and that is what troubles me. Campbell predicts a return of the trouble and thinks in the near future her only chance for vision will lie in the eye which has been blind for several years. He is willing to admit that Moreau in Paris is better authority and would be glad for Caroline to see him and have his opinion."

"Ah, indeed!" It was expressive. The colonel knew that Evan comprehended the situation, if not the whole of it. If there had been any doubt, it would have been dispelled. "A great expense, Norton, in these days, but it must be attended to." Col. Montjoy ran his hand through his hair and passed it over his brow nervously.

"The trouble is, Evan, the matter has been attended to, and too easily. Edward Morgan was present during the operation and has offered to lend me all the money necessary for the trip with or without security and with or without interest." The general shook with silent laughter and succeeded in getting enough smoke down his throat to induce a disguising cough.

"That is the trouble, Norton, that hasn't afflicted us old fellows much of late—extra ease in money matters. Edward is rich and will not be in any way embarrassed by a small matter like this. I think you will do well to make it a business transaction and accept."

"You do not understand. I have noticed marked attentions to Mary on the part of the young man, and Mary," he said, sadly, "is, I am afraid, interested in him."

"That is different," said the general, with resolute gravity. "Very different. Before you decide on accepting this offer, you feel that you must decide on the young man himself, I see. What do you think?"

"I haven't been able to think intelligently, I am afraid, upon that point. What do you think, Evan? Mary is about as much your property as mine."

"I think," said the general, throwing off his disguise, "that in Edward Morgan she will get the only man I ever saw to whom I would be willing to give her up. He is as straight and as brave as any man that ever followed me into battle." Montjoy was silent awhile.

"You know," he said, presently, "I value your opinion more than any man's and I do not wish to express or to intimate a doubt of Mr. Morgan, who, I see, has impressed you. I believe the letter of Royson's was infamous and untrue in every respect, but it has been published—and it is my daughter. Why in the name of common sense hasn't he come to me and given me something to go upon?"

"It has occurred to me," said the general, dryly, "that he will do so when he comes for Mary. In the meantime, a man isn't called upon to travel with a family tree under his arm and show it to every one who questions him. Morgan is a gentleman, sans peur et sans reproche. If he is not, I do not know the breed.

"So far as the charge of Royson is concerned," continued the general, "let me calm your mind on that point. I have never entered upon this matter with you because the mistakes of a man's kindred are things he has no right to gossip about, even among friends. The woman, Rita Morgan, has always been free; she was given her freedom in infancy by John Morgan's father. Her mother's history is an unfortunate one. It is enough to say that she was sent out from Virginia with John Morgan's mother, who was, as you know, a blood relative of mine; and I know that this woman was sent away with an object. She looked confoundedly like some of the family. Well, John Morgan's father was wild; you can guess the result.

"Rita lived in her own house, and when her husband died John took her to his home. He told me once in so many words that his father left instructions outside his will to that effect, and that Rita's claims upon the old man, as far as blood was concerned, were about the same as his. You see from this that the Royson story is an absurdity. I knew it when I went in and vouched for our young friend, and I would have proved it to Thomas the night he called, but Rita dropped dead that day."

Montjoy drew a long breath."

"You astonish me," he said, "and relieve me greatly. I had never heard this. I did not really doubt, but you have cleared up all possibility of error."

"Nor has any other man heard the story. My conversation with John Morgan grew out of his offer to buy of me Alec, a very handsome mulatto man I owned, to whom Rita had taken a fancy. He wanted to buy him and free him, but I had never bought or sold a slave, and could not bring myself to accept money for Alec. I freed him myself. John was not willing for her to marry a slave. They were married and he died in less than a year. That is Rita's history. When Alec died Rita went to John Morgan and kept house for him.

"When it was that Gerald came in I do not know," pursued the general musingly. "The boy was nearly grown before I heard of him. He and Edward are children of distant relatives, I am told. John never saw the latter at all, probably, but educated him and, finding Gerald incapacitated, very wisely left his property to the other, with Gerald in his charge.

"No, I have taken the greatest fancy to these two young fellows, although I only have known one a few weeks and the other by sight and reputation." He paused a moment, as though his careless tones had desecrated a sacred scene; the face of the sleeper rose to his mind. "But they are game and thoroughbreds. Accept the proposition and shut your eyes to the future. It will all work out rightly." Montjoy shook his head sadly.

"I will accept it," he said, "but only because it means a chance for Caroline which otherwise she would not have. Of course you know that Mary is going with her, and Morgan is to be their escort?"

The general uttered a prolonged whistle and then laughed. "Well, confound the little darling, to think she should come over here and tell me all the arrangements and leave herself out; Montjoy, that is the only one of your family born without grit; tell her so. She is afraid of one old man's tongue."

"Here she comes, with Morgan," said Montjoy, smiling. "Tell her yourself."

Edward's buggy was approaching rapidly and the flushed and happy face of the girl could be seen within.

"Plotting against me," she called out, as she descended, "and I dare you to own it." The general said:

"On the contrary, I was about telling your father what a brave little woman you are. Come in, Mr. Morgan," he added, seeing from her blushes that she understood him.

"Mr. Morgan was coming over to see the general," said Mary, "and I came with him to ride back with papa."

"Then," said the colonel, "we will start right away." And, despite the protests of all the others, he presently got Mary into the buggy and carried her off. "You will stop as you come by, Mr. Morgan," he called out. "I will be glad to see you on a matter of business."

The buggy was yet in sight when Edward turned to his old friend and said:

"Gen. Evan, I have come to make a statement to you, based upon long reflection and a sense of justice. I am about to leave the state for France, and may never return. There are matters connected with my family which I feel you should know, and I prefer to speak rather than write them." He paused to collect his thoughts, the general looking straight ahead and recalling the conversation just had with Col. Montjoy. "If I seem to trespass on forbidden grounds or stir unpleasant memories, I trust you will hear me through before condemning me. Many years ago you lost a daughter——"

"Go on," said the general as Edward paused and looked doubtfully toward him.

"She was to have married my uncle, I am informed, but she did not. On the contrary, she married a foreigner—her music teacher. Is this not true?"

"Go on."

"She went abroad, but unknown to you she came back and her child was born."

"Ah." The sound that came from the old man's lips was almost a gasp. For the first time since the recital was begun he turned his eyes upon his companion.

"At this birth, which took place probably at Ilexhurst, possibly in the house of Rita Morgan, whose death you know of, occurred the birth of Rita's child also. Your daughter disappeared. Rita was delirious, and when she recovered could not be convinced that this child was not her own; and she thought him her son until the day of her death."

"Where is this child?" Why was I not informed?" The old general's voice was hoarse and his words scarcely audible. Edward, looking him full in the face, replied :

"At Ilexhurst! His name, as we know it, is Gerald Morgan."

Evan, who had half-risen, sunk back in his chair.

"And this is your belief, Mr. Morgan?"

"That is the fact, as the weight of evidence declares. The woman in health did not claim Gerald for her son. In the moment of her death she cried out: 'They lied!' This is what you heard in the yard and I repeated it at that time. I was, as you know, laboring under great excitement. There is a picture of your daughter at Ilexhurst and the resemblance is strong. You yourself were struck with the family resemblance.

"I felt it my duty to speak, even at the risk of appearing to trespass upon your best feelings. You were my friend when I needed friends, and had I concealed this I would have been ungrateful." Edward rose, but the general, without looking up, laid his hand upon his arm.

"Sit down, Mr. Morgan. I thank you. You could not have done less. But give me time to realize what this means. If you are correct, I have a grandson at Ilexhurst"—Edward bowed slightly—"whom my daughter abandoned to the care of a servant." Again Morgan bowed, but by the faintest motion of his head.

"I did not say abandoned," he corrected.

"It cannot be true," said the old man; "it cannot be true. She was a good girl and even infatuation would not have changed her character. She would have come back to me."

"If she could," said Edward. He told him the story of the unfinished manuscript and the picture drawn by Gerald. He was determined to tell him all, except as related to himself. That was his own and Virdow's secret. "If that story is true, she may not have been able to get to you; and then the war came on; you must know all before you can judge." The old soldier was silent.

He got up with apparent difficulty and said formally: "Mr. Morgan, I will be glad to have you join me in a glass of wine. I am not as vigorous as I may appear, and this

is my time o' day. Come in." Edward noticed that, as
he followed, the general's form had lost something of its
martial air.

No words were exchanged over the little southern ceremony. The general merely lifted his glass slightly and
bowed.

The room was cool and dark. He motioned Edward
to a rocker and sunk into his leather-covered easy-chair.
There was a minute's silence broken by the elder man.

"What is your belief, Mr. Morgan, as to Gerald?"

"The facts as stated are all——"

"Nevertheless, as man to man—your belief."

"Then, in my opinion, the evidence points to Gerald as
the child of this woman Rita. I am sure also that it is
his own belief. The only disturbing evidence is the likeness, but Virdow says that the children of servants very
frequently bear likeness to a mistress. It is a delicate
question, but all of our ancestors were not immaculate.
Is there anything in the ancestry of Rita Morgan—is
there any reason why her child should bear a likeness to
—to——"

The general lifted his hand in warning. But he said:
"What became of the other child?" The question did not
disturb or surprise the young man. He expected that it
would be asked. It was natural. Yet, prepared as he
was, his voice was unsteady when he replied:

"That I do not know."

"You do not know!" The general's tone of voice was
peculiar. Did he doubt?

"I had two objects in view when I brought up this subject," said Edward, when the silence grew embarrassing;
"one was to acquaint you with the possibilities out at Ilexhurst, and to ask your good offices for Gerald in the
event my absence is prolonged or any necessity for assistance should arise. The other is to find the second child
if it is living and determine Gerald's status; and, with this
as my main object, I venture to ask you if, since her disappearance, you have ever heard of Marion Evan?"

"God help me," said Evan, brokenly; "yes. But it was
too soon; too soon; I could not forgive her."

"And since then?" The old man moved his hand slowly
and let it fall.

"Silence—oblivion."

"Can you give me the name of her husband?" Without reply the veteran went to the secretary and took from a pigeonhole a well-worn letter.

"No eye but mine has ever read these lines," he said, simply. "I do not fear to trust them to you! Read! I cannot now!"

Edward's hand trembled as he received the papers. If Rita Morgan spoke the truth he was about to look upon lines traced by his mother's hand. It was like a message from the dead.

CHAPTER XXXVI.

THE PLEDGE THAT WAS GIVEN.

Edward opened the letter with deep emotion. The handwriting was small and unformed, the writing of a schoolgirl. It read:

"Jan 3, 18—. My Darling Papa: When you read this I will be far away upon the ocean and separated from you by circumstances compared with which leagues are but trifles. You probably know them by telegram before now, but I cannot leave you and my native land without a farewell. Papa, I am now the wife of an honorable, loving man, and happy as I could be while remembering you and your loneliness. Why I have done this, why I have taken this step without coming to you first and letting you decide, I cannot tell, nor do I know. I only know that I love my husband as I have never loved before; that I have his whole affection; that he wanted me to go with him blindly, and that I have obeyed. That is all. There is no ingratitude in my heart, no lessening of affection for you; you still are to me the one man in my old world; but my husband had come in and made a new world of it all. and I am his. You will blame me, I am afraid, and perhaps disown me. If so, God is merciful to women who suffer for those they love. I would lay down my life for

Gaspard; I have laid down everything dear to life. We go to his childhood's home in Silesia, where with the money he has saved and with his divine art, we hope to be happy and face the world without fear. Oh, papa, if you could forgive me; if you could remember your own love for that beautiful mamma of whom you never tired telling, and who, I am sure, is near me now; if you could remember and forgive me, the world would hold nothing that I would exchange a thought for. Gaspard is noble and manly. You would admire him and he would adore you, as do I, your only child. Papa, you will write to me; a father can never forsake his child. If I am wrong, you cannot forsake me; if I am right, you cannot. There is no arrangement in all God's providence for such a contingency, and Christ did not turn even from the woman whom others would stone. Can you turn from me, when if I have erred it is through the divine instinct that God has given me? No! You cannot, you will not! If you could, you would not have been the noble, patient, brave man whom all men love. Write at once and forgive and bless your child. Marion."

On a separate slip, pinned to the letter, was:

"My address will be Mrs. Gaspard Levigne, Breslau, Silesia. If we change soon, I will write to you. God bless and care for you. M."

Edward gently replaced the faded letter upon the table; his eyes were wet and his voice changed and unnatural.

"You did not write?"

The general shook his head.

"You did not write?" Edward repeated the question; this time his voice almost agonized in the weight of emotion. Again the old general shook his head, fearing to trust his voice. The young man gazed upon him long and curiously and was silent.

"I wrote five years later," said Evan, presently. "It was the best I could do. You cannot judge the antebellum southern planter by him of to-day. I was a king in those times! I had ambition. I looked to the future of my child and my family! All was lost; all perished in the act of a foolish girl, infatuated with a music master. I can forgive now, but over me have rolled waves enough in thirty years to wear away stone. The war came on; I carried that letter from Manassas to Appomattox and then I wrote. I set inquiries afoot through consuls abroad. No voice has ever risen from the silence. My child is dead."

"Perhaps not," said Edward, gently; "perhaps not. If there is any genius in European detective bureaus that money can command, we will know—we will know."

"If she lived she would have written. I cannot get round that. I know my child. It was the trueness of her heart that led her off. It could not remain silent nearly thirty years."

"Unless silenced by circumstances over which she had no control." The old man searched for a hidden meaning in the word.

"I have been thinking much during my stay in this country," continued Edward, "and every side of this matter has presented itself to me. Your daughter had one firm, unchanging friend—my uncle, John Morgan. He has kept her secret—perhaps her child. Is it not possible that he has known of her existence somewhere; that she has been all along informed of the condition and welfare of the child—and of you?" Evan did not reply; he was intently studying the young man.

"John offered to find her a year after she was gone. He came and pleaded for her, but I gave him conditions and he came no more."

"It is not only possible that she lives," said Edward, "but probable. And it is certain that if John Morgan knew of her existence and then that she had passed away, that all pledges would have been suspended in the presence of a father's right to know that his child was dead. I go to unravel the mystery. I begin to feel that I will succeed, for now, for the first time, I have a starting point. I have name and address." He took down the information in his memorandum book.

Edward prepared to take his departure, when Evan, throwing off his mood, stood before him thoughtful and distressed.

"Say it," said Edward, bravely, reading a change in the frank face.

"One moment, and I will bid you farewell and godspeed." He laid his hand upon Edward's shoulder and fixed a penetrating gaze upon him. "Young man, my affairs can wait, but yours cannot. I have no questions to ask of yourself; you came among us and earned our gratitude. In time of trouble I stood by you. It was upon my vouching personally for your gentility that your challenge was accepted. We went upon the field together; your cause became mine. Now this; I have yet a daughter, the young woman whom you love—not a word now—she is the pride and idol of two old men. She is well disposed toward you, and you are on the point of going upon a journey in her company under circumstances that place her somewhat at a disadvantage. I charge you that it is not honorable to take advantage of this to win from her a declaration or a promise of any kind. Man to man, is it not true?"

"It is true," said Edward, turning pale, but meeting his gaze fearlessly. "It is so true that I may tell you now that from my lips no word of love has ever passed to her; that if ever I do speak to her upon that subject it will be while she is here among her own people and free from influences that would bias her decision unfairly." The hands of the two men met impulsively. A new light shone in the face of the old soldier.

"I vouched for you, and if I erred then there is no more faith to be put in manhood, for if you be not a true man I never have seen one. Go and do your best for Gerald—and for me. I must reflect upon these matters —I must reflect! As yet their full import has failed me. You must send me the manuscript."

Deeply impressed and touched, Edward withdrew The task was finished. It had been a delicate and trying one for him.

At the hall Edward went with Mary into the darkened room and took the little mother's hand in his and sat beside her to tell of the proposed journey. He pictured vividly the scenes to be enjoyed and life in the gay capital, and all as a certainty for her. She did not doubt; Dr.

Campbell had promised sight; it would return. But this journey, the expense, they could not afford it.

But Mary came to the rescue there; her father had told her he was entirely able to bear the expense, and she was satisfied. This, however, did not deceive the mother, who was perfectly familiar with the family finances. She knitted away in discreet silence, biding her time.

The business to which Col. Montjoy had referred was soon finished. He formally accepted the very opportune offer and wished to know when they should meet in the city to arrange papers. To this Edward objected, suggesting that he would keep an accurate account of expenses incurred and arrange papers upon his return; and to this, the only reasonable arrangement possible, Col. Montjoy acceded.

One more incident closed the day. Edward had nearly reached the city, when he came upon a buggy by the roadside, drawn up in the shade of a tree. His own animal, somewhat jaded, was leisurely walking. Their approach was practically noiseless, and he was alongside the vehicle before either of the two occupants looked up. He saw them both start violently and the face of the man flush quickly, a scar upon the nose becoming at once crimson. They were Royson and his cousin.

Greatly pained and embarrassed, Edward was at a loss how to act, but unconsciously he lifted his hat, with ceremonious politeness. Royson did not respond, but Annie, with more presence of mind, smiled sweetly and bowed. This surprised him. She had studiously avoided meeting him at the hall.

The message of Mary, "Royson is your enemy," flashed upon him. He had felt intuitively the enmity of the woman. Why this clandestine interview and to what did it tend? He knew in after days.

Arriving at home he found Virdow writing in the library and forbore to disturb him. Gerald was slumbering in the glass-room, his deep breathing betraying the cause. Edward went to the little room upstairs to secure the manuscript and prepare it for sending to Gen. Evan. Opening the desk he was surprised to see that the document was not where he placed it. A search developed it under all the fragmentary manuscript, and he was about to inclose it in an envelope when he noticed that the pages were reversed. The last reader had not slipped the pages one under another in handling, but had placed them one on another, probably upon the desk, thus bringing the last page on top.

Edward remembered at that moment that in reading the manuscript he had carefully replaced each page in its proper position and had left the package on top of all others. Who could have disturbed them? Not Virdow, and there was none else but Gerald!

He laid aside the package and reflected. Of what use could this unexplained manuscript be to Gerald? None that he could imagine; and yet only Gerald could have moved it. Greatly annoyed, he restored the leaves and placed them in an envelope.

He was still thinking of the singular discovery he had made, and idly glancing over the other fragments, when from one of them fell a newspaper clipping. He would not in all probability have read it through, but the name "Gaspard," so recently impressed upon his mind, caught his eye. The clipping was printed in French and was headed "From our Vienna correspondent." Translated, it read as follows:

"To-day began the trial of Leon Gaspard for the murder of Otto Schwartz in this city on the 18th ult. The case attracts considerable attention, because of the fact that Gaspard has been for a week playing first violin in the orchestra of the Imperial theater, where he has won many admirers and because of the peculiar circumstances of the case. Schwartz was a stranger and came to this city only upon the day of his death. It seems that Gaspard, so it is charged, some years previously had deserted a sister of Schwartz after a mock marriage, but this he denies. The men met in a cafe and a scuffle ensued, during which Schwartz was stabbed to the heart and instantly killed. Gaspard claims that he had been repeatedly threatened by letter, and that Schwartz came to Vienna to kill him, and that he (Schwartz) struck the first blow. He had upon his face a slight cut, inflicted, he claims, by a seal ring worn by Schwartz. Bystanders did not see

the blow, and Schwartz had no weapons upon his body.
Gaspard declares that he saw a knife in the dead man's
hand and that it was picked up and concealed by a
stranger who accompanied him into the cafe. Unless he
can produce the threatening letters, and find witnesses to
prove the knife incident, the trial will go hard with him."

Another clew! And the husband of Marion Evan was
a murderer! Who sent that clipping to John Morgan?
Probably a detective bureau. Edward folded it sadly,
and gave it place by the memoranda he had written in
his notebook.

CHAPTER XXXVII.

"WHICH OF THE TWO WAS MY MOTHER?"

The sleeper lay tranquilly forgetful of the morning
hours redolent of perfumes and vocal with the songs of
birds. The sunlight was gone, a deep-gray cloud having
crept up to shadow the scene. All was still in the glass-
room. Virdow shook his head.

"This," he said, "strange, as it may seem, is his real life.
Waking brings the dreams. We will not disturb him."

Edward would have returned his violin to its case, but
as he sat looking upon the face of the sleeper and revolving in mind the complications which had enslaved him,
there came upon the roof of glass the unheralded fall of
the rain. As it rose and fell in fine cadences under the
fitful discharge of moisture from the uneven cloud drifting past, a note wild but familiar caught his ear; it was the
note of the waterfall. Unconsciously he lifted his bow,
and blending with that strange minor chord, he filled the
room with low, sweet melody.

And there as the song grew into rapture from its sadness under the spell of a new-found hope, under the memory of that last scene, when the rainbow overhung the waters and the face of the girl had become radiant with the
thought she expressed, Gerald arose from his couch and
stood before the easel. All the care lines were gone from

his face. For the first time in the knowledge of the two men he stood a cool, rational being. The strains ran on. The artist drew, lingering over a touch of beauty, a shade of expression, a wave of fine hair upon the brow. Then he stood silent and gazed upon his work. It was finished. The song of the violin trembled—died away.

He did not for the moment note his companions; he was looking upward thoughtfully. The sun had burst open the clouds and was filling the outer world with yellow light, through the water-steeped air. Far away, arching the mellow depths of a cloud abyss, its colors repeated upon the wet grass around him, was a rainbow. Then he saw that Virdow and Edward were watching him. The spell was broken. He smiled a little and beckoned to Edward.

"Here is a new face," he said. "It is the first time it has come to me. It is a face that rests me." Edward approached and gazed upon the face of Mary! Speechless with the rush of feeling that came over him, he turned and left the room.

To Virdow it meant nothing except a fine ideal, but, impressed with the manner of the musician, he followed to the great hall. The girl of the picture stood in the doorway. Before he had time to speak, he saw the martial figure of Evan overshadow hers and heard the strong, manly voice asking for Edward.

Edward came forward. Confused by his recent experience, and the sudden appearance of the original of the picture, he with difficulty managed to welcome his guests and introduce his friend.

"I thought best to come," said Evan when Virdow, with easy courtesy, was engaging the attention of the lady. "I have passed a sleepless night. Where can we speak privately?" Edward motioned to the stairway, but hesitated.

"Never mind Mary," said the general, divining his embarrassment. "I took her away from the colonel on the road; she and the professor will take care of themselves." She heard the remark and smiled, replying gayly:

"But don't stay too long. I am afraid I shall weary your friend."

Virdow made his courtliest bow.

"Impossible," he said. "I have been an untiring admirer of the beautiful since childhood."

"Bravo!" cried Evan. "You will do!" Virdow bowed again.

"I would be glad to have you answer a question," he said, rather abruptly, gazing earnestly into her eyes. She was astonished, but managed to reply assuringly. "It is this: Have you ever met Gerald Morgan?"

"Never. I have heard so much of him lately, I would be glad to see him."

"Has he ever seen you?"

"Not that I am aware of——"

"Certainly not face to face—long enough for him to remember your every feature—your expression?"

"Why, no." The old man looked troubled and began to walk up and down the hall, his head bent forward. The girl watched him nonplused and with some little uneasiness.

"Pardon me—pardon me," he said, finally, recalling the situation. "But it is strange, strange!"

"May I inquire what troubles you, sir?" she asked, timidly.

"Yes, certainly, yes." He started, with sudden resolution, and disappeared for a few moments. When he returned, he was holding a large sheet of cardboard. "It is this," he said. "How could a man who has never seen you face to face have drawn this likeness?" He held Gerald's picture before her. She uttered an exclamation of surprise.

"And did he draw it—did Mr. Gerald——"

"In my presence."

"He has never seen me."

"Yes," said a musical voice; "as you were then, I have seen you." She started with fright. Gerald, with pallid face and hair upon his shoulders, stood before her. "So will I see you—forever." She drew nearer to Virdow.

"This, my young friend, is Mary." It was all he could remember. And then to her: "This is Gerald."

"Mary," he said, musingly, "Mary? What a pretty name! It suits you. None other would." She had ex-

15

tended her hand shyly. He took it and lifted it to his lips.
It was the first time a girl's hand had rested in his. He
did not release it; she drew away at last. Something in
his voice had touched her; it was the note of suffering, of
unrest, which a woman feels first. She knew something
of his history. He had been Edward's friend. Her father
had pictured the scene wherein he had cornered and de-
fied Royson.

"I am sure we shall be friends, Mr. Gerald. Mr. Morgan is so fond of you."

"We shall be more than friends," he said, gently; "more
than friends." She misunderstood him. Had he divined
her secret and did Edward promise him that?"

"Never less," she said. He had not removed his eyes
from her, and now as she turned to speak to Virdow, he
came and stood by her side, and lifting gently one of her
brown curls gazed wonderingly upon it. She was embarrassed, but her good sense came to the rescue.

"See the light upon it come and go," he said. "We call
it the reflected light; but it is life itself glimmering there.
The eye holds the same ray."

"You have imagination," she said, smiling, "and it is
fortunate. Here you must be lonely." He shook his head.

"Imagination is often a curse. The world generally is
happy, I think, and the happiest are those who touch life
through the senses alone and who do not dream. I am
never alone! Would to God sometimes I were." A look
of anguish convulsed his face. She laid her hand upon
his wrist as he stood silently struggling for self-pos-
session.

"I am so sorry," she said, softly; "I have pained you."
The look, the touch, the tender voice—which was it? He
shuddered and gazed upon the little hand and then into
her eyes. Mary drew back, wondering; she read him
aright. Love in such natures is not a growth. It is born
as a flash of light. Yet she did not realize the full significance of the discovery. Then, oh, wonderful power of
nature, she turned upon him her large, melting eyes and
gave him one swift message of deepest sympathy. Again
he shuddered and the faintest crimson flushed his cheeks.

They went with Virdow to see the wing-room, of which

she had heard so much, to look into the little cabinets, where he made his photographs, to handle his weapons, view his favorite books and all the curious little surroundings of his daily life; she went with an old man and a child. Her girlish interest was infectious; Virdow threw off his speculations and let himself drift with the new day, and Gerald was as a smiling boy.

They even ventured with unconventional daring to peep into the glass-room. Standing on the threshold, the girl gazed in with surprise and delight.

"How novel and how simple!" she exclaimed; "and to think of having the stars for friends all night!" He laughed silently and nodded his head; here was one who understood.

And then her eyes caught a glimpse of the marble bust, which Gerald had polished and cleared of its discolorations. She made them bring it and place it before her. A puzzled look overspread her face as she glanced from Gerald to the marble and back again.

"Strange, strange," she said; "sit here, Mr. Gerald, sit here, with your head by this one, and let me see." White now as the marble itself, but controlled by the new power that had enthralled, he obeyed; the two faces looked forward upon the girl, feature for feature. Even the pose was the same.

"It was well done," she said. "I never saw a more perfect resemblance, and yet"—going to one side—"the profile is that of Mr. Edward!" The young man uttered no sound; he was, in the swift passing of the one bright hour of his life, as the marble itself. But as he remained a moment under the spell of despair that overrun him, Gen. Evan stood in the door. Only Mary caught the words in his sharp, half-smothered exclamation as he started back. They were: "It is true!" He came forward and, taking up the marble, looked long and tenderly into the face, and bowing his head gave way to his tears.

One by one they withdrew—Virdow, Mary, Edward. Only Gerald remained, gazing curiously into the general's face and thinking. Then tenderly the old man replaced the bust upon the table, and, standing above his hearer, said with infinite tenderness:

"Gerald, you do not know me; if God wills it you will know me some day! That marble upon the table is the carved face of my daughter—Marion Evan."

"Then you are Gen. Evan." The young man spoke the words coolly and without emotion.

"Yes. Nearly thirty years ago she left me—without a word—without a farewell until too late, with no human being in all the world to love, none to care for me."

"So Rita told me." The words were little more than a whisper.

"I did not curse her; I disowned her and sought to forget. I could not. Then I began to cry out for her in the night—in my loneliness—do you know what that word means?"

"Do I know?" The pathos in the echo was beyond description.

"And then I began a search that ended only when ten years had buried all hopes. No tidings, no word after her first letter ever reached me. She is dead, I believe; but recently some of the mystery has been untangled. I begin to know, to believe that there has been an awful error somewhere. She did come back. Her child was born and Rita cared for it. As God is my judge, I believe that you are that child! Tell me, do you remember, have you any knowledge that will help me to unravel this tangled——"

"You are simply mistaken, general," said the young man, without moving other than to fold his arms and sink back into his chair. "I am not the son of Marion Evan." Speechless for a moment, the general gazed upon his companion.

"I thought I was," continued Gerald; "I hoped I was. My God! My God! I tried to be! I have exhausted almost life itself to make the truth a lie, and the lie a truth! I have struggled with this secret here for twenty years or more; I have studied every phase of life; I well-nigh broke Rita's heart. Poor, honest Rita!

"She told me what they claimed—she was too honest to conceal that—and what she believed; she was too human to conceal that; and then left me to judge. The woman they would have me own as my mother left me, a lonely babe, to the care of strangers; to grow up ill-taught, unguided, frail and haunted with a sickening fear. She has left me twenty-seven years! Rita stayed. If I were sick, Rita was by me. If I was crazed Rita was there to calm. Sleepless by night, sleepless by day, she loved and comforted and blessed me." He had risen in his growing excitement. "I ask you, general, who have known life better than I, which of the two was my mother? Let me answer; you will not. The woman of thirty years ago is nothing to me; she was once. That has passed. When Rita lay dead in her coffin I kissed her lips at last and called her mother. I would have killed myself afterward —life seemed useless—but not so now. It may be a terrible thing to be Rita's son; I suppose it is, but as before God, I thank Him that I have come to believe that there are no ties of blood between me and the woman who was false to both father and child, and in all probability deserted her husband."

Gen. Evan turned abruptly and rushed from the room. Edward saw his face as he passed out through the hall and did not speak. With courtly dignity he took Mary to the buggy and stood with bowed head until they were gone. He then returned to the glass-room. Gerald stood among the ruins of a drawing and the fragments of the marble bust lay on the floor. One glance at this scene and the blazing eyes of the man was sufficient. Evan had failed.

"Tell them," exclaimed Gerald, "that even the son of a slave is dishonored, when they seek to link him to a woman who abandons her child."

"What is it," asked Virdow, in a whisper, coming to Edward's side. Edward shook his head and drew him from the room.

"He does not know what he is saying."

CHAPTER XXXVIII.

UNDER THE SPELL.

The autumn days ran out and in the depths of the southern woods, here and there, the black gums and sweet gums began to flame. And with them came the day when the bandages were to be removed from the eyes of the gentle woman at the hall. The family gathered about the little figure in the sitting-room. Edward Morgan with them, and Col. Montjoy lowered the bandage. The room had been darkened and all light except what came through one open shutter had been excluded. There was a moment of painful silence; Mary was tightly clasping her mother's hands. The invalid turned her face to the right and left, and then to the window.

"Light," she said, gently. "I see!"

"Thank God!" The words burst from the old man's lips and his arms went around mother and daughter at once. For quicker than he the girl had glided in between them and was clasping the beloved form. Edward said a few words of congratulation and passed outside. The scene was sacred.

Then came days of practice. The eyes so long darkened must be accustomed to the light and not strained. Upon that weak vision, little by little, came back the world, the trees and flowers, the faces of husband and daughter and friends. It was a joyful season at the hall.

A little sadder, a little sterner than usual, but with his fine face flushed in sympathetic feeling, the old general came to add his congratulations. Now nothing remained but to prepare for Paris, and all was bustle.

A few more nights and then—departure!

Mary was at the piano, playing the simple music of the south and singing the songs which were a part of the air she had breathed all her life—the folk songs of the blacks.

Col. Montjoy had the Duchess on his lap to hear "the little boy in his watch crack hickory nuts" and the monotonous cracking of the nuts mingling with the melody of the musician had put both asleep.

Mary and Edward went to the veranda, and to them across the field came the measured tread of feet, the call of the fiddler, and now and then strains of music, such as the negro prefers.

Edward proposed an excursion to witness the dance, and the girl assented gladly. She was herself a born dancer; one whose feet were set to rhythm in infancy.

They reached the long house, a spacious one-room edifice, with low rafters but a broad expanse of floor, and stood at the door. Couple after couple passed by in the grand promenade, the variety and incongruities of colors amusing Edward greatly. Every girl in passing called repeatedly to "missy," the name by which Mary was known on the plantation, and their dusky escorts bowed awkwardly and smiled.

Suddenly the lines separated and a couple began to dance. Edward, who had seen the dancers of most nations, was delighted with the abandon of these. The man pursued the girl through the ranks, she eluding him with ease, as he was purposely obstructed by every one. His object was to keep as near her as possible for the final scene. At last she reappeared in the open space and hesitating a moment, her dusky face wreathed in smiles, darted through the doorway. There was a shout as her escort followed. If he could catch her before she reentered at the opposite door she paid the penalty. Before Edward realized the situation the girl was behind him. He stepped the wrong way, there was a collision, and ere she could recover, her pursuer had her in his arms. There was a moment's struggle; his distinct smack proved his success, and if it had not, the resounding slap from the broad hand of his captive would have betrayed matters.

On went the dance. Mary stood patting time to the music of the violin in the hands of old Morris, the presiding genius of the festival, who bent and genuflected to suit the requirements of his task. As the revel grew wilder, as it always does under the stimulus of a spectator's presence, she motioned to Edward, and entering, stood by the player.

"In all your skill," she said, "you cannot equal this." For reply the young man, taking advantage of a pause in the rout, reached over and took the well-worn instrument from the hands of the old man. There was a buzz of interest. Catching the spirit of the scene he drew the bow and gave them the wild dance music of the Hungarians. They responded enthusiastically and the player did not fail.

Then, when the tumult had reached its climax, there was a crash, and with bow in air Edward, flushed and excited, stood gazing upon the crowd. Then forty voices shouted:

"Missy! Missy!" On the impulse of the moment they cheered and clapped their hands.

All eyes were turned to Mary. She looked into the face of the player; his eyes challenged hers and she responded, instinctively the dusky figures shrunk to the wall and alone, undaunted, the slender girl stood in the middle of the deserted floor. Edward played the gypsy dance, increasing the time until it was a passionate melody, and Mary began. Her lithe form swayed and bent and glided in perfect response to his power, the little feet twinkling almost unseen upon the sandy boards. Such grace, such allurements, he had never before dreamed of. And finally, breathless, she stood one moment, her hand uplifted, the triumphant interpreter of his melody. With a mischievous smile, she sprung from the open door, her face turned backward for one instant.

Releasing the instrument Edward followed in perfect forgetfulness of self and situation. But when, puzzled, he appeared alone at the opposite door, he heard her laugh in the distance—and memory overwhelmed him with her tide.

He was pale and startled and the company was laughing. He cast a handful of money among them and in the confusion that followed made his escape. Mary was waiting demurely in the path.

"It was perfect," he said, breaking the awkward silence.

"Any one could dance to that music," was her reply.

Silently they began their return. An old woman sat in her cabin door, a fire of chunks making a red spot in the gloom behind.

"We go to-morrow, Aunt Sylla. Is it for good or ill?" The woman was old and wrinkled. She was the focus of all local superstition; one of the ante-bellum voodoos. If her pewter spoons had been gold, her few beads diamonds, she might have left the doors unbarred without danger.

Mary had paused and asked the question to draw out the odd character for her friend.

"In the woods the clocks of heaven strike 11! Jeffers, who was never born, speaks out," was the strange reply.

"In the woods," said Mary, thoughtfully, "the dew drips tinkling from the leaves; Jeffers, the redbird, was never born, but hatched. What does he say, Aunt Sylla?" The woman was trying to light her pipe. Absence of tobacco was the main cause of her failure. Edward crushed a cigar and handed it to her. When she had lighted it she lifted the blazing chunk and her faded eyes looked steadily upon the young man.

"He says the gentleman will come some day and bring much tobacco." The girl laughed, but the darkness hid her blushes.

"In the meantime," said Edward, cheerfully, placing a silver coin in her hand, "you can tell your friend Jeffers that you are supplied."

The negro's prophecy is usually based on shrewd guesses. Sylla grasped the coin with the eagerness of a child receiving a new doll. She pointed her finger at him and looked to the girl. Mary laughed.

"Keep still a moment, Mr. Morgan," she said, "I must rob you." She took a strand or two of his hair between her little fingers and plucked them out. Edward would not have flinched had there been fifty. "Now something you have worn—what can it be? Oh, a button." She took his penknife and cut from his coat sleeve one of its buttons. "There, Aunt Sylla, if you are not successful with them I shall never forgive you." The old woman took the hair and the button and relapsed into silent smoking.

"I am a little curious to know what she is going to do with those things," said Edward. Mary looked at him shyly.

"She is going to protect you," she said. "She will mix a little ground glass and a drop of chicken blood with them, and sew all in a tiny bag. No negro alive or dead would touch you then for the universe, and should you touch one of them with that charm it would give them catalepsy. You will get it to-morrow."

"She is arming me with a terrible power at small cost," he replied, dryly.

"Old Sylla is a prophetess," said the girl, "as well as a voodoo, and there is with us a tradition that death in the family will follow her every visit to the house. It is strange, but within our memory it has proved true. My infant brother, my only sister, mamma's brother, papa's sister, an invalid northern cousin spending the winter here—all their deaths were preceded by the appearance of old Sylla."

"And is her success in prophecy as marked?"

"Yes, so far as I know." She hesitated a moment. "Her prediction as to myself has not had time to mature."

"And what was the prediction?"

"That some day a stranger would carry me into a strange land," she said, smiling; "and—break my heart."

They had reached the gate; except where the one light burned in the sitting-room all was darkness and silence. Edward said gently, as he stood holding open the gate:

"I am a stranger and shortly I will take you into a strange land, but may God forget me if I break your heart." She did not reply, but with face averted passed in. The household was asleep. She carried the lamp to his door and opened it. He took it and then her hand. For a moment they looked into each other's eyes; then, gravely lifting the little hand, he kissed it.

"May God forget me," he said again, "if I break your heart." He held the door open until she had passed down the stairs, her flushed face never lifted again to his.

CHAPTER XXXIX.

THE HIDDEN HAND.

It matters little what kind of seed is planted, it finds its proper elements in the soil. So with rumors. There is never a rumor so wild, but that it finds a place for its roots.

It soon reached the coroner, that zealous officer whose compensation is based upon fees, that his exchequer had been defrauded by the improper burial of a woman out at Ilexhurst. She had dropped dead, and there had not been a witness. An inquest was proper; was necessary. He began an investigation. And then appeared in the brevity columns of one of the papers the incipient scandal:

"It is whispered that suspicions of foul play are entertained in connection with Rita, the housekeeper of the late John Morgan at Ilexhurst. The coroner will investigate."

And the next day the following:

"Our vigilant coroner has made inquiry into the death and burial of Rita Morgan, and feels that the circumstances demand a disinterment and examination of the body. So far the rumors of foul play come from negroes only. It seems that Mr. Edward Morgan found the woman lying in his yard, and that she died almost immediately after the discovery. It was upon the night but one preceding his meeting with Mr. Royson on the field of honor, and during his absence next day the body was hurriedly interred. There is little doubt that the woman came to her death from natural causes, but it is known that she had few if any friends among her race, and other circumstances attending her demise are such that the body will be disinterred and examined for evidence."

Even this did not especially interest the public. But when next day the morning papers came out with triple

headlines the first of which was "Murdered," followed by
a succinct account of the disinterment of Rita Morgan,
as she was called, with the discovery of a cut on the left
temple and a wound in the back of the head that had
crushed in the skull, the public was startled. No charge
was made against Edward Morgan, no connection hinted
at, but it was stated in the history of the woman that
she was the individual referred to in Royson's famous
letter on which the duel had been fought, and that she
died suddenly upon the day it was published. The
paper said that it was unfortunate that Mr. Morgan had
left several days before for Paris, and had sailed that
morning from New York.

Then the public tongue began to wag and the public
mind to wait impatiently for the inquest.

The inquest was held in due form. The surgeons designated to examine the supposed wounds reported them
genuine, the cut in the temple trifling, the blow in the
back of the head sufficient to have caused death.

A violent discussion ensued when the jury came to
make up its verdict, but the conservative members carried the day. A verdict of "death by a blow upon the
head by a weapon in the hands of a person or persons
unknown to the jury" was rendered; the body reinterred
and the crowds of curiosity seekers withdrew from Ilexhurst.

Unfortunately during the era of excitement Gerald
was locked in his room, lost in the contemplation of
some question of memory that had come upon him, and
he was not summoned as a witness, from the fact that
in no way had he been mentioned in the case, except
by Gen. Evan, who testified that he was asleep when the
death occurred. The German professor and Gen. Evan
were witnesses and gave their testimony readily.

Evan explained that, although present at the finding
of the body, he left immediately to meet a gentleman
who had called, and did not return. When asked as to
Edward's actions he admitted that they were excited,
but stated that other matters, naming them briefly, were
engaging them at the same time and that they were of a
disturbing nature. The woman, he said, had first at-

tracted Edward's attention by falling against the glass, which she was evidently looking through, and which she broke in her fall. If she was struck, it was probably at that moment.

He was positive in his belief that at the time the sound of falling glass was heard Edward was in the room, but he would not state it under oath as a fact. It was this evidence that carried the day.

When asked where was Edward Morgan and the reason for his absence, he said that he had gone as the escort of Mrs. Montjoy to Paris, where her eyes were to be examined, and that the trip had been contemplated for several weeks. Also that he would return in less than a month. •

Nevertheless, the gravest of comments began to be heard upon the streets, and prophecies were plenty that Edward would never return.

And into these began to creep a word now and then for Royson. "He knew more than he could prove," "was the victim of circumstances," "a bold fellow," etc., were fragments of conversations connected with his name.

"We fought out that issue once," he said, briefly, when asked directly about the character of the woman Rita, "and it is settled so far as I am concerned." And the public liked the answer.

No charge, however, had been brought against Edward Morgan; the matter was simply one that disturbed the public; it wanted his explanation and his presence. But behind it all, behind the hesitancy which the stern, open championship of Evan and Montjoy commanded, lay the proposition that of all people in the world only Edward Morgan could have been benefited by the death of the woman; that he was the only person present and that she died a violent death. And people would talk.

Then came a greater shock. A little paper, the Tell-Tale, published in an adjoining city and deriving its support from the publication of scandals in which the victim was described without naming, was cried upon the street. Copies were sold by the hundreds, then thousands. It practically charged that Edward Morgan was the son of Rita Morgan; that upon finding Royson possessed of his secret he first killed the woman and then tried to kill that gentleman in a duel into which Morgan went with everything to gain and nothing to lose; that upon seeing the storm gathering he had fled the country, under the pretense of escorting a very estimable young lady and her mother abroad, the latter going to have her eyes examined by a Parisian expert, the celebrated Moreau.

It proceeded further; the young man had completely hoodwinked and deceived the family to which these ladies belonged, and, it was generally understood, would some day become the husband and son-in-law. Every sensational feature that could be imagined was brought out —even Gerald did not escape. He was put in as the legitimate heir of John Morgan; the child of a secret marriage, a non compos mentis whose property was being enjoyed by the other.

The excitement in the city reached white heat. Col. Montjoy and Gen. Evan came out in cards and denounced the author of the letter as an infamous liar, and made efforts to bring the editor of the sheet into court. He could not be found.

Days slipped by, and then came the climax! One of the sensational papers of New York published a four-column illustrated article headed "A Southern Tragedy," which pretended to give the history of all the Morgans for fifty years or more. In this story the writer displayed considerable literary ability, and the situations were dramatically set forth. Pictures of Ilexhurst were given; the murder of a negro woman in the night and a fancy sketch of Edward. The crowning shame was a picture of Mary. While this latter did not bear much resemblance to Mary, it bore her name in bold type. No such sensation had been known since the race riots of 1874.

In reply to this Montjoy and Evan also telegraphed fiery denunciations and demanded the author's name. Their telegrams were published, and demands treated with contempt. Norton Montjoy, in New York, had himself interviewed by rival papers, gave the true history of Morgan and denounced the story in strong terms.

He consulted lawyers and was informed that the Mont-joys had no right of action.

Court met and the grand jury conferred. Here was evidence of murder, and here was a direct published charge. In vain Evan and Virdow testified before it. The strong influence of the former could not carry the day. The jury itself was political. It was part of the Swearingen ring. When it had completed its labors and returned its batch of true bills, it was known in a few hours that Edward Morgan had been indicted for the murder of Rita Morgan.

Grief and distress unspeakable reigned in the houses of Gen. Evan and Col. Montjoy, and in his bachelor quarters that night one man sat with his face upon his hands and thought out all of the details of the sad catastrophe. An unspeakable sorrow shone in his big eyes. Barksdale had been touched in the tenderest part of his life. Morgan he admired and respected, but the name of the woman he loved had been bespattered with mud. With him there rested no duty. Had the circumstances been different, there would have been a tragedy at the expense of his last dollar—and he was rich.

At the expense even of his enterprise and his business reputation, he would have found the author of those letters and have shot him to death at the door of a church, if necessary. There is one point on which the south has suffered no change.

Morgan, he felt, would do the same, but now, alas, Morgan was indicted for another murder, and afterward it would be too late. Too late! He sprang to his feet and gave vent to a frightful malediction; then he grew calm through sheer astonishment. Without knock or inquiry his door was thrown open and Gerald Morgan rushed into the room.

When Barksdale had last seen this man he doubted his ability to stand the nervous strain put upon him, but here was evidence of an excitement tenfold greater. Gerald quivered like an overtaxed engine, and deep in the pale face the blazing eyes shone with a horrible fierceness. The cry he uttered as he paused before Barksdale was so unearthly that he unconsciously drew back. The young man was unrolling some papers. Upon them were the scenes at the grave as he drew them—the open coffin, the shrunken face of the woman—and then, in all its repulsive exactness, the face of the man who had turned upon the artist under the electric light!

"What does it mean, my friend?" said Barksdale, seeking by a forced calmness to reduce the almost irrational visitor to reason again.

"What?" exclaimed Gerald; "don't you understand? The man uncovered that coffin; he struck that blow upon poor dead Rita's head! I saw him face to face and drew those pictures that night. There is the date."

"You saw him?" Barksdale could not grasp the truth for an instant.

"I saw him!"

"Where is he now?"

"I do not know; I do not know!" A thrill ran through the now eager man, and he felt that instead of calming the excitement of his visitor he was getting infected by it. He sat down deliberately.

"Take a seat, Mr. Morgan, and tell me about it." But Gerald dropped the pictures and stood over them.

"There was the grave," he said, "and the man was down in it; I stood up here and lifted a spade, but then he had struck and was arranging her hair. If he had struck her again I would have killed him. I wanted to see what it was about. I wanted to see the man. He fled, and then I followed. Downtown I saw him under an electric light and got his face. He was the man, the infamous, cowardly scoundrel who struck poor Rita in her coffin; but why—why should any one want to strike Rita? I can't see. I can't see. And then to charge Edward with it!"

Barksdale's blood ran cold during the recital, the scene so vividly pictured, the uncanny face before him. It was horrible. But over all came the realization that some hidden hand was deliberately striking at the life of Edward Morgan through the grave of the woman. The cowardliness, the infamy, the cruelty was overpowering. He turned away his face.

But the next instant he was cool. It was a frail and

doubtful barrier between Edward and ruin, this mind unfolding its secret. If it failed there was no other witness.

"What became of the man, did you say?"

"I do not know. I wanted his face; I got it."

"Where did you last see him?"

"On the street." Barksdale arose deliberately.

"Mr. Morgan, how did you come here?"

"I suppose I walked. I want you to help me find the man who struck the blow."

"You are right, we must find the man. Now, I have a request to make. Edward trusted to my judgment in the other affair, and it came out right, did it not?"

"Yes. That is why I have come to you."

"Trust me again. Go home now and take that picture. Preserve it as you would your life, for on it may hang the life of Edward Morgan. You understand? And do not open your lips on this subject to any one until I see you again."

Gerald rolled up the paper and turned away abruptly. Barksdale followed him down the steps and called a hack.

"Your health," he said to Gerald, as he gently forced him into the carriage, "must not be risked. And to the driver, slipping a fee in his hand: "Take Mr. Morgan to Ilexhurst. Remember, Mr. Morgan," he called out.

"I remember," was the reply. "I never forget. Would to God I could."

Barksdale walked rapidly to the livery stable.

CHAPTER XL.

WITH THE WOMAN THAT LOVED HIM.

Edward Morgan gave himself up to the dream. The flying train sped onward, out of the pine forests, into the hills and the shadow of mountains, into the broad world of life and great cities.

16

They had the car almost to themselves, for the north-ward travel is small at that season.

Before him was the little woman of the motherly face and smooth, soft hand, and behind her, lost in the contemplation of the light literature with which he had surrounded her, was the girl about whom all the tendrils of hungry life were twining. He could see her half-profile, the contour of the smooth cheek, the droop of eyelid, the fluff of curly hair over her brow, and the shapely little head. He was content.

It was a novel and suggestive situation. And yet—only a dream. No matter how far he wandered, how real seemed the vision, it always ended there—it was but a dream, a waking dream. He had at last no part in her life; he would never have.

And yet again, why not? The world was large; he felt its largeness as they rushed from center to center, saw the teeming crowds here, the far-stretching farms and dwellings there. The world was large, and they were at best but a man and a woman. If she loved him what did it matter? It meant only a prolonged and indefinite stay abroad in the land he best knew; all its pleasures, its comforts, his—and hers.

If only she loved him! He lived over every minute detail of their short companionship, from the hour he saw her, the little madonna, until he kissed her hand and promised unnecessarily that he would never break her heart. A strange comfort followed this realization. Come what might, humiliation, disgrace, separation, she loved him!

His fixed gaze as he dreamed had its effect; she looked up from her pictures and back to him.

A rush of emotions swept away his mood; he rose almost angrily; it was a question between him and his Savior only. God had made the world and named its holiest passion love, and if they loved blindly, foolishly, fatally, God, not he, was to blame. He went and sat by her.

"You puzzle me sometimes," she said. "You are animated and bright and—well, charming often—and then you seem to go back into your shell and hide. I am afraid you are not happy, Mr. Morgan."

"Not happy? Hardly. But then no bachelor can be quite happy," he added, returning her smile.

"I should think otherwise," she answered. "When I look about among my married friends I sometimes wonder why men ever marry. They seem to surrender so much for so little. I am afraid if I were a bachelor there isn't a woman living whom I would marry—not if she had the wealth of a Vanderbilt."

Edward laughed outright.

"If you were a bachelor," he answered, "you would not have such thoughts."

"I don't see why," she said, trying to frown.

"Because you are not a bachelor."

"Then," she said, mockingly, "I suppose I never will —since I can't be a bachelor."

"The mystery to me," said Edward, "is why women ever marry."

"Because they love," answered the girl. "There is no mystery about that."

"But they take on themselves so much of care, anxiety, suffering."

"Love can endure that."

"And how often it means—death!"

"And that, too, love does not consider. It would not hesitate if it knew in advance."

"You speak for yourself?"

"Yes, indeed. If I loved, I am afraid I would love blindly, recklessly. It is the way of Montjoy women— and they say I am all Montjoy."

"Would you follow barefooted and in rags from city to city behind a man, drunken and besotted, to sing upon the streets for a crust and sleep under a hedge, his chances your chances, and you with no claim upon him save that you loved him once? I have seen it." She shook her head.

"The man I loved could never sink so low. He would be a gentleman, proud of his name, of his talents, of his honor. If misfortune came he would starve under the first hedge before he would lead me out to face a scorn-

ful world. And if it were misfortune only I would sing
for him—yes, if necessary, beg, unknown to him for
money to help him in misfortune. Only let him keep
the manliness within him undimmed by act of his." He
gazed into her glowing face.

"I thank you," he said. "I never understood a true
woman's heart before."

The express rushed into new and strange scenes. There
were battlefields pointed out by the conductor—mere
landscapes, the names of which only were thrilling.
Manassas glided by, the birthplace of a great hope that
perished. How often she had heard her father and the
general tell of that battle!

And then the white shaft of the Washington monu-
ment, and the capitol dome rose in the distance.

As they glided over the long bridge across the Potomac
and touched the soil of the capital city and the street
lights went past, the young woman viewed the scenes
with intense interest. Washington! But for that infamous assault upon her father, through the man who
had been by her side, he would have walked the streets
again, a Southern congressman!

They took rooms to give the little mamma a good
night's rest, and then, with the same unconventional freedom of the hall, Mary wandered out with Edward to
view the avenue. They went and stood at the foot of
that great white pile which closes one end of the avenue,
and were awed into silence by its grandeur.

She would see grander sights, but never one that would
impress her more. She thought of her father alone,
away back in Georgia, at the old home, sitting just then
upon the porch smoking his pipe. Perhaps the Duchess
was asleep in his lap, perhaps the general had come over
to keep him company, and if so they were talking of
the absent ones. Edward saw her little hand lightly
laid upon her eyes for a moment, and comprehended.

Morning! And now the crowded train sweeps north-
ward through the great cities and opens up bits of marine
views. For the first time the girl sees a stately ship,
with wings unfurled, "go down into the seas," vanishing
upon the hazy horizon, "like some strain of sweet melody

silenced and made visible," as Edward quoted from a far-away poet friend.

"And if you will watch it intently," he added, "and forget yourself you will lose sight of the ship and hear again the melody." And then came almost endless streets of villages and towns, the smoke of factories, the clamor and clangor of life massed in a small compass, a lull of the motion, hurrying crowds and the cheery, flushed face of Norton pressed to his mother's and to hers.

The first stage of the journey was over. Across the river rose, in dizzy disorder and vastness, New York.

The men clasped hands and looked each other in the eyes, Montjoy smiling, Morgan grave. It seemed to the latter that the smile of his friend meant nothing; that behind it lay anxiety, questioning. He did not waver under the look, and in a moment the hand that held his tightened again. Morgan had answered. Half the conversation of life is carried on without words. Morgan had answered, but he could not forget his friend's questioning gaze. Nor could he forget that his friend had a wife.

CHAPTER XLI.

THE SONG THE OCEAN SUNG.

The stay of the party in New York was short. Norton was busy with trade that could not wait. He stole a part of a day, stuffed the pocketbooks of the ladies with gold, showed them around and then at last they looked from the deck of a "greyhound" and saw the slopes of Staten island and the highlands sink low upon the horizon.

The first night at sea! The traveler never forgets it. Scenes of the past may shine through it like ink renewed in the dimmed lines of a palimpsest through later records, but this night stands supreme as if it were the sum of all. For in this night the fatherland behind and the heart grown tender in the realization of its isolation,

come back again the olden experiences. Dreams that
have passed into the seas of eternity meet it and shine
again.   Old loves return and fold their wings, and hopes
grown wrinkled with disappointment throw off dull
Time's imprints and are young once more.

To the impressionable heart of the girl, the vastness
and the solemnity brought strange thoughts.   She stood
by the rail, silenced, sad, but not with the sadness that
oppresses.   By her was the man who through life's hidden current had brought her all unknowing into harmony
with the eternal echoes rising into her consciousness.

At last she came back to life's facts.   She found her
hand in his again, and gently, without protest, disen-
gaged it.   Her face was white and fixed upon nothing-
ness.

"Of what are your thinking?" she asked, gently.   He
started and drew his breath inward with a gasp.

"I do not know—of you, I suppose."   And then, as
she was silent and embarrassed: "There is a tone in the
ocean, a note I have never heard before, and I have listened on all seas.   But here is the new song different
from all.   I could listen forever."

"I have read somewhere," she said, "that all the sound
waves escape to the ocean.   They jostle and push against
each other where men abound, the new crowding out the
old; but out at sea there is room for all.   It may be
that you hear only as your heart is attuned."

He nodded his head, pleased greatly.

"Then I have heard to-night," he said, earnestly, "a
song of a woman to the man she loves."

"But you could not have heard it unless your heart
was attuned to love's melodies.   Have you ever loved a
woman, Mr. Morgan?"

He started and his hand tightened upon the guard.

"I was a boy in heart when I went abroad," he said.
"I had never known a woman's love and sympathy.   In
Switzerland a little girl gave me a glass of goat's milk
at a cottage door in the mountains.   She could not have
been more than 12 years old.   I had heard her singing
as I approached, her voice marvelous in its power and
pathos.   Her simple dress was artistic, her face frank

and eyes confiding. I loved her. I painted her picture and carried her both in my heart and my satchel for three years. I did not love her and yet I believed I did. But I think that I must have loved at some time. As you say, I could not have heard if it were not so." He drew her away and sought the cabin. But when he said good-night he came and walked the deck for an hour, and once he tossed his arms above him and cried out in agony: "I cannot! I cannot! The heart was not made for such a strain!"

*   *   *

Six times they saw the sun rise over the path ahead, ascend to the zenith and sink away, and six times the endless procession of stars glinted on the myriad facets of the sea. The hundreds of strange faces about them grew familiar, almost homelike. The ladies made acquaintances; but Edward none. When they were accessible he never left their presence, devoting himself with tender solicitude to their service, reading to them, reciting bits of adventure, explaining the phenomena of the elements, exhibiting the ship and writing in their journals the record for the father at home. When they were gone he walked the deck, silent, moody, sad; alone in the multitude.

People had ceased to interest him. Once only did he break the silence; from the ship's orchestra he borrowed a violin, and standing upon the deck, as at first, he found the love-song again and linked it forever with his life. It was the ocean's gift and he kept it.

He thought a great deal, but from the facts at home he turned resolutely. They should not mar the only summer of his heart. "Not now," he would say to these trooping memories. "After a while you may come and be heard."

But of the future he thought and dreamed. He pictured a life with the woman he loved, in every detail; discounting its pleasures, denying the possibility of sorrow. There were times when with her he found himself wishing to be alone that he might review the dream and enlarge it. It ceased to be a dream, it became a fact, he lived with it and he lived by it. It was possible no longer; it was certain. Some day he would begin it; he would tell it to her and make it so beautiful she would consent.

All this time the elder lady thought, listened and knitted. She was one of those gentle natures not made for contentions, but for soothing. She was never idle. Edward found himself watching the busy needles as they fought for the endless thread, and marveled. What patience! What continuity! What endurance!

The needles of good women preach as they labor. He knew the history of these. For forty years they had labored, those bits of steel in the velvet fingers. Husband, children, slaves, all had felt upon their feet the soft summings of their calculations. One whole company of soldiers, the gallant company her husband had led into confederate service, had threaded the Wilderness in her socks, and died nearly all at Malvern Hill. Down deep under the soil of the old mother state they planted her work from sight, and the storms of winter removed its imprints where, through worn and wasted leather, it had touched virgin soil as the bleeding survivors came limping home. Forty years had not stilled the thought on which it was based. It was strong and resolute still. Some day the needles would rust out of sight, the hands be folded in rest and the thought would be gone. Edward glanced from the woman to the girl.

"Not so," he said, softly; "the thought will live. Other hands trained under its sweet ministry will take up the broken threads; the needles will flash again. Woman's work is never done, and never will be while love and faith and courage have lodgment upon earth.

"Did you speak, Mr. Morgan?"

"Possibly. I have fallen into the habit of thinking aloud. And I was thinking of you; it must have been a great privilege to call you mother, Mrs. Montjoy." She smiled a little.

"I am glad you think so."

"I have never called any one by that name," he said, slowly, looking away. "I never knew a mother."

"That will excuse a great many things in a man's life," she said, in sympathy. "You have no remembrance, then?"

"None. She died when I was an infant, I suppose, and I grew up, principally, in schools."

"And your father?"

"He also—died." He was reckless for the moment. "Sometimes I think I will ask you to let me call you— mother. It is late to begin, but think of a man's living and dying without once speaking the name to a woman."

"Call me that if you will. You are certainly all that a son could be to me."

"Mother," he said, reflectively, "mother," and then looking toward Mary he saw that, though reading, her face was crimson; "that gives me a sister, does it not?" he added, to relieve the situation. She glanced toward him, smiling.

"As you will, brother Edward—how natural."

"I like the mother better," he said, after a pause. "I have observed that brothers do not wear well. I should hate to see the day when it would not be a pleasure to be with you, Miss Montjoy." He could not control nor define his mood.

"Then," she said, with her eyes upon the book, "let it not be brother. I would be sorry to see you drift away —we are all your friends."

"Friends!" He repeated the word contemplatively. "That is another word I am not fond of. I have seen so many friends—not my own, but friends of others! Friends steal your good name, your opportunities, your happiness, your time and your salvation. Oh, friendship!"

"What is the matter with you to-day, Mr. Morgan?" said Mary. "I don't think I ever saw you in just such a frame of mind. What has made you cynical?"

"Am I cynical? I did not know it. Possibly I am undergoing a metamorphosis. Such things occur about us every day. Have you ever seen the locust, as he is called, come up out of the earth and attach himself to a tree and hang there brooding, living an absolutely worthless life? Some day a rent occurs down his own back and out comes the green cicada, with iridescent wings; no longer a dull plodder, but now a swift wanderer, merry and musical. So with the people about you. Useless and unpicturesque for years, they some day suffer a change; a piece of good luck, success in business; any of these can furnish sunlight, and the change is born. Behold your clodhopper is a gay fellow."

"But," said the girl, laughing, "the simile is poor; you do not see the cicada go back from the happy traveler stage and become a cynic."

"True. What does become of him? Oh, yes; along comes the ichneumon fly and by a skillful blow on the spine paralyzes him and then thrusts under his skin an egg to be warmed into life by its departing heat. That is the conclusion; your gay fellow and careless traveler gets an overwhelming blow; an idea or a fact, or a bit of information to brood upon; and some day it kills him."

She was silent, trying to read the meaning in his words. What idea, what fact, what overwhelming blow were killing him? Something, she was sure, had disturbed him. She had felt it for weeks.

Mrs. Montjoy expressed a desire to go to her state-room, and Edward accompanied her. The girl had ceased reading and sat with her chin in hand, revolving the matter. After he had resumed his position she turned to find his gaze upon her. They walked to the deck; the air was cold and bracing.

"I am sorry you are so opposed to sisters," she said, smiling. "If I were a sister I would ask you to share your trouble with me."

"What trouble?"

"The trouble that is changing the careless traveler to a cynic—is killing his better self."

He ceased to speak in metaphor. "There is a trouble," he said, after reflection; "but one beyond your power to remedy or lighten. Some day I will tell it to you—but not now."

"You do not trust me."

"I do not trust myself." She was silent, looking away. She said no more. Pale and trembling with suppressed emotion, he stood up. A look of determination came into his eyes, and he faced her. At that moment a faint, far cry was heard and every one in sight looked forward.

"What is it?" asked a passenger, as the captain passed.

"The cliffs of England," he said. Edward turned and

walked away, leaving her leaning upon the rail. He
came back smoking. His mood had passed.

The excitement had begun at once. On glided the
good ship. Taller grew the hills, shipping began to appear, and land objects to take shape. And then at last
the deep heart throbbing ceased and the glad voyagers
poured forth upon the shore.

CHAPTER XLII.

THE DEATH OF GASPARD LEVIGNE.

Paris!

With emotions difficult to appreciate Edward found
himself at home, for of all places Paris meant that to
him. He went at once to his old quarters; a suite of
rooms in a quiet but accessible street, where was combined something of both city and suburban life. The
concierge almost overwhelmed him with his welcome.

In obedience to his letters, everything had been
placed in order, books and furniture dusted, the linen
renewed, the curtains laundered and stiffened anew, and
on the little center table was a vase of crimson roses—
a contribution for madame and mademoiselle.

His own, the larger room, was surrendered to the
ladies; the smaller he retained. There was the little
parlor between, for common use. Outside was the
shady vista of the street and in the distance the murmur
of the city.

Mrs. Montjoy was delighted with the arrangement
and the scene. Mary absorbed all the surroundings of
the owner's past life; every picture, every book and bit
of bric-a-brac, all were parts of him and full of interest.
The very room seemed imbued with his presence. Here
was his shaded student's lamp, there the small upright
piano, with its stack of music and, in place ready for the
player, an open sheet. It might have been yesterday
that he arose from its stool, walked out and closed the
door.

It was a little home, and when coming into the parlor
from his toilet, Edward saw her slender figure, he
paused, unwilling to disturb the scene. His heart beat
faster, and then the old depression returned.

She found him watching her, and noted the troubled
look upon his face.

"It is all so cozy and beautiful," she said. "I am so
glad that you brought us here rather than to a hotel."

"And I, too, if you are pleased."

"Pleased! It is simply perfect!"

A note lay upon the center table. He noticed that it
was addressed to him, and, excusing himself, opened it
and read:

"M. Morgan. Benoni, the maestro, is ill and desires
monsieur. It will be well if monsieur comes quickly.
                                            "Annette."

He rang the bell hurriedly and the concierge appeared.

"This note," said Edward, speaking rapidly in French;
"has it been long here?"

"Since yesterday. I sent it back, and they returned it.
Monsieur is not disappointed, I trust." Edward shook
his head and was seeking his hat and gloves.

"You recall my old friend, the maestro, who gave me
the violin," he said, remembering Mary. "The note says
he is very ill. It was sent yesterday. Make my excuses
to your mother; I will not stay long. If I do not see
you here, I will seek you over yonder in the park, where
the band may be playing shortly; and then we will find
a supper."

Walking rapidly to a cab stand he selected one with a
promising horse, and gave directions. He was carried
at a rapid rate into the region of the Quartier Latin and
in a few moments found the maestro's home.

One or two persons were by him when he entered the
room, and they turned and looked curiously. "Edward!"
exclaimed the old man, lifting his sightless eyes toward
the door; "there is but one who steps like that!"

Edward approached and took his hand. The sick man
was sitting in his arm-chair, wrapped in his faded dress-

ing-gown. "My friends," he continued, lifting his hand with a slight gesture of dismissal, "you have been kind to Benoni; God will reward you; farewell!"

The friends, one a woman of the neighborhood, the other the wife of the concierge, came and touched his hand, and, bowing to Edward, withdrew, lifting their white aprons to their faces as they passed from the room.

"You are very ill," said Edward, placing his hand upon the old man's arm; "I have just returned to Paris and came at once."

"Very ill, indeed." He leaned back his head wearily. "It will soon be over."

"Have you no friends who should know of this, good Benoni; no relatives? You have been silent upon this subject, and I have never questioned you. I will bring them if you will let me." Benoni shook his head.

"Never. I am to them already dead." A fit of coughing seized him, and he became greatly exhausted. Upon the table was a small bottle containing wine, left by one of the women. Edward poured out a draught and placed it to the bloodless lips.

"One is my wife," said the dying man, with sudden energy; "my own wife."

"I will answer that she comes; she cannot refuse."

"Refuse? No, indeed! She has been searching for me for a lifetime. Many times she has looked upon me without recognition. She would come; she has been here—she has been here!"

"And did not know you? Is it possible?"

"She did not know."

"You told her, though?"

"No."

"You never told her—" There was a pause. The sick man said, gasping:

"I am a convict!" A cry of horror broke from the lips of the young man. The old violinist resented his sudden start and exclamation. "But a convict innocent. I swear it before my Maker!" Edward was deeply touched.

"None can doubt that who knows you, Benoni."

"He threatened my life; he struck at me with his knife;

I turned it on him, and he fell dead. I did what I could;
I was stanching the wound when they seized me. His
ring jewel had cut my face; but for that I would have
been executed. I had no friends, even my name was not
my own. I went to prison and labor for twenty years."

He named the length of his sentence in a whisper. It
was a horror he could never understand. He stretched
out his hand. "Wine." Again Edward restored something of the fleeting strength.

"She came," he said, "searching for me. I was blind
then; they had been careless with their blasting—my
eyes were gone, my hair white, my face scarred. She
did not know me. Her voice was divine! Her name has
been in the mouths of all men. She came and sang at
Christmas, to the prisoners, the glorious hymns of her
church, and she sang to me. It was a song that none,
there knew but me—my song! Had she watched my
face, then, she would have known; but how could she
suspect me, the blind, the scarred, the gray? She passed
out forever. And I, harmless, helpless, soon followed—
pardoned. I knew her name; I made my way to Paris
to be near that voice; and the years passed; I was poor
and blind. It cost money to hear her."

Trembling with emotion, Edward whispered: "Her
name?" Benoni shook his head and slowly extended his
withered arms. The woolen wristlets had been removed,
there were the white scars, the marks of the convict's
long-worn irons.

"I have forgiven her; I will not bring her disgrace."

"Cambia?" said Edward, unconsciously. There was a
loud cry; the old man half-rose and sunk back, baffled
by his weakness.

"Hush! Hush!" he gasped; "it is my secret; swear to
me you will keep it; swear to me, swear!"

"I swear it, Benoni, I swear it." The old man seemed
to have fallen asleep; it was a stupor.

"She came," he said, "years ago and offered me gold.
It was to be the last effort of her life. She could not believe but that her husband was in Paris and might be
found. She believed the song would find him. I had
been suggested to her because my music and figure were

known to all the boulevards. I was blind and could never
know her. But I knew her voice.

"We went, veiled to avoid recognition; she stood by
me at a certain place on the boulevard where people
gather in the evening and sung. What a song! The
streets were blocked, and men, I am told, uncovered before the sacred purity of that voice, and when all were
there who could hear she sung our song; while I, weeping, played the accompaniment, ay, as no man living or
dead could have played it. Always in the lines—

> "Cceans may roll between
> Thy home and thee."

—her voice gave way. They called it art.

"Well, I thought, one day I will tell; it was always the
next day, but I knew, as she sung, in her mind must have
arisen the picture of that husband standing by her side—
ah, my God, I could not, I could not; blind, scarred, a
felon, I could not; I was dead! It was bitter!

"And then she came to me and said: 'Good Benoni,
your heart is true and tender; I thank you; I have wealth
and plenty; here is gold, take it in memory of a broken
heart you have soothed.' I said:

"'The voice of that woman, her song, are better than
gold. I have them.' I went and stood in the door as she,
weeping, passed out. She lifted her veil and touched the
forehead of the old musician with her lips, and then—I
hardly knew! I was lying on the floor when Annette came
to bring my tea."

For a long time he sat without motion after this recital.
Edward loosened the faded cords of his gown. The old
man spoke again in a whisper:

"Come closer; there is another secret. I knew then that
I had never before loved her.   My marriage had been
an outrage of heart-faith.   I mistook admiration, sympathy, memory, for love. I was swept from my feet by her
devotion, but it is true—as God is my judge, I never loved
her until then—until her sad, ruined life spoke to me in
that song on the streets of Paris." Edward still held his
hand.

"Benoni," he said, simply, "there is no guilt upon your

soul to have deserved the convict's irons. Believe me, it is better to send for her and let her come to you. Think of the long years she has searched; of the long years of uncertainty that must follow. You cannot, you cannot pass away without paying the debt; it was your fault in the beginning——"

The old man had gradually lifted his head; now he bowed it. "Then you owe her the admission. Oh, believe me, you are wrong if you think the scars of misfortune can shame away love. You do not know a true woman's heart. You have not much time, I fear; let me send for her." There was no reply. He knelt and took one withered hand in his. "Benoni, I plead for you as for her. There will come a last moment—you will relent; and then it will be too late."

"Send!" It was a whisper. The lips moved again; it was an address. Upon a card Edward wrote hurriedly:

"The blind musician who once played for you is dying. He has the secret of your life. If you would see your husband alive lose no minute.   A Friend."

He dashed from the room and ran rapidly to a cab stand.

"Take this," he said, "bring an answer in thirty minutes, and get 100 francs. If the police interfere, say a dying man waits for his friend."

The driver lashed his horses, and was lashing them as he faded into the distance.

Edward returned; he called for hot water and bathed the dying man's feet; he rubbed his limbs and poured brandy down his throat. He laid his watch upon the little table; five, ten, fifteen, twenty, twenty-five—would she never come?"

Death had already entered; he was hovering over the doomed man.

The door opened; a tall woman of sad but noble countenance stepped in, thrusting back her veil. Edward was kneeling by Benoni's side. Cambia's eyes were fastened upon the face of the dying man.

Edward passed out, leaving them alone. A name escaped her.

"Gaspard."

Slowly, leaning upon the arm of his chair, the old man arose and listened.

"It was a voice from the past," he said, clearly. "Who calls Gaspard Levigne?"

"Oh, God in heaven!" she moaned, dropping to her knees. "Is it true? What do you know of Gaspard Levigne?"

"Nothing that is good; but I am he, Marie!" The woman rushed to his side; she touched his face and smoothed the disordered hair. She held his hand after he had sunk into his chair.

"Tell me, in God's name," she said. "Tell me where are the proofs of our marriage? Oh, Gaspard, for my sake, for the sake of your posterity! You are dying; do not deny me!"

"Ah," he said, in a whisper. "I did not know—there—was—another—I did not know. The woman—she wrote that it died!" He rose again to his feet, animated by a thought that gave him new strength. Turning his face toward her in horror, he said:

"It is for you that you search, then—not for me!"

He tore wildly at his throat and dropped to the floor. She caught his hand.

"Speak, Gaspard, my husband, for my sake, for the sake of your Marie, who loved and loves you, speak!" His lips moved. She placed her ear to them:

"Dear heaven," she cried in despair. "I cannot hear him! I cannot hear him! Gaspard! Gaspard! Gaspard! Ah——" The appeal ended in a shriek. She was staring into his glazing eyes. Then over the man's face came a change. Peace settled there. The eyes closed and he whispered: "Freda!"

Hearing her frantic grief, Edward rushed in and now stood looking down in deep distress upon the scene.

"He is dead, madame," he said, simply. "Let me see you to your home." She arose, white and calm, by a mighty effort.

"What was he to you? Who are you?" she asked.

"He was my friend and master." He laid his hands lovingly on the eyes, closing them. "I am Edward Morgan!" Her eyes never left him. There was no motion

17

of her tall figure; only her hand upon the veil closed tightly and her features twitched. They stood in silence but a moment; it was broken by Cambia. She had regained something of the bearing of the dramatic soprano. With a simple dignity she said:

"Sir, you have witnessed a painful scene. On the honor of a gentleman give me your pledge to secrecy. There are tragedies in all lives; chance has laid bare to you the youth of Cambia." He pointed downward to where the still form lay between them.

"Above the body of your husband—my friend—I swear to you that your secret is safe."

"I thank you."

She looked a moment upon the form of the sleeper, and then her eyes searched the face of the young man. "Will you leave me alone with him a few moments?" He bowed and again withdrew into the little hall.

When he was gone she knelt above the figure a long time in prayer, and then, looking for the last time upon the dead face, sadly withdrew. The young man took her to the carriage. A policeman was guarding it.

"The driver broke the regulation by my orders," Edward said; "he was bringing this lady to the bedside of a dying friend. Here is enough to pay his fine." He gave a few napoleons to the cabman and his card, on which he placed his address.

"Adieu, madame. I will arrange everything, and if you will attend the funeral I will notify you."

"I will attend," said Cambia; "I thank you. Adieu."

CHAPTER XLIII.

THE HEART OF CAMBIA.

It was a simple burial. Edward sent a carriage for Cambia, one for the concierge and his wife, and in the other he brought Mrs. Montjoy and Mary, to whom he had related a part of the history of Benoni, as he still called him. Out in Pere la Chaise they laid away the body of the old master, placed on it their flowers and the beautiful wreath that Cambia brought, and were ready to return.

As they approached their carriage, Edward introduced the ladies, to whom he had already told of Cambia's career.

They looked with sympathetic pleasure upon the great singer and were touched by her interest in and devotion to the old musician, "whom she had known in happier days."

Cambia studied their faces long and thoughtfully and promised to call upon them. They parted to meet again.

When Edward went to make an engagement for Mrs. Montjoy with Moreau, the great authority on the eye, he was informed that the eminent specialist had been called to Russia for professional services in the family of the czar, and would not return before a date then a week off. The ladies accepted the delay philosophically. It would give them time to see something of Paris.

And see it they did. To Edward it was familiar in every feature. He took them to all the art centers, the historical points, the great cathedral, the environments of Malmaison and Versailles, to the promenades, the palaces and the theater. This last feature was the delight of both. For the dramatic art in all its perfection both betrayed a keen relish, and just then Paris was at its gayest. They were never jostled, harrassed, nor disappointed. They were in the hands of an accomplished cosmopolitan.

To Mary the scenes were full of never-ending delight. The mother had breathed the same atmosphere before, but to Mary all was novel and beautiful.

Throughout all Edward maintained the sad, quiet dignity peculiar to him, illumined at times by flashes of life as he saw and gloried in the happiness of the girl at his side.

Then came Cambia! Mary had gone out with Edward, for a walk, and Mrs. Montjoy was knitting in the parlor in silent reverie when a card was brought in, and almost immediately the sad, beautiful face of the singer appeared in the door.

"Do not arise, madame," she said, quickly, coming

forward upon seeing the elderly lady beginning to put
aside her knitting, "nor cease your work. I ask that you
let me forget we are almost strangers and will sit here by
your side. You have not seen Moreau yet?"

"No," said Mrs. Montjoy, releasing the white hand
that had clasped hers; "he is to return to-day."

"Then he will soon relieve your anxiety. With Moreau
everything is possible."

"I am sure I hope your trust is not misplaced; success
will lift a great weight from my family." Cambia was silent, thinking; then she arose and, sinking upon the little
footstool, laid her arms upon the knees of her hostess,
and with tearful eyes raised to her face she said:

"Mrs. Montjoy, do you not know me? Have I indeed
changed so much?"

The needles ceased to contend and the work slipped
from the smooth little hands. A frightened look overspread the gentle face.

"Who is it speaks? Sometime I must have known
that voice."

"It is Marion Evan." The visitor bent her head upon
her own arms and gave way to her emotion. Mrs. Montjoy had repeated the name unconsciously and was silent.
But presently, feeling the figure bent before her struggling in the grasp of its emotion, she placed both hands
upon the shapely head and gently stroked its beautiful
hair, now lined with silver.

"You have suffered," she said, simply. "Why did you
leave us? Why have you been silent all these years?"

"For my father's sake. They have thought me cold,
heartless, abandoned. I have crucified my heart to save
his." She spoke with vehement passion.

"Hush, my child," said the elder lady; "you must calm
yourself. Tell me all; let me help you. You used to tell
me all your troubles and I used to call you daughter in
the old times. Do you remember?"

"Ah, madame, if I did not I would not be here now.
Indeed you were always kind and good to Marion."

And so, living over the old days, they came to learn
again each other's hearts and find how little time and the
incidents of life had changed them. And sitting there

beneath the sympathetic touch and eyes of her lifetime friend, Cambia told her story.

"I was not quite 17, madame, you remember, when it happened. How, I do not know; but I thought then I must have been born for Gaspard Levigne. From the moment I saw him, the violin instructor in our institution, I loved him. His voice, his music, his presence, without effort of his, deprived me of any resisting power; I did not seek to resist. I advanced in my art until its perfection charmed him. I had often seen him watching me with a sad and pensive air and he once told me that my face recalled a very dear friend, long dead. I sung a solo in a concert; he led the orchestra; I sung to him. The audience thought it was the debutante watching her director, but it was a girl of 17 singing to the only man the world held for her. He heard and knew.

"From that day we loved; before, only I loved. He was more than double my age, a handsome man, with a divine art; and I—well, they called me pretty—made him love me. We met at every opportunity, and when opportunities did not offer we made them, those innocent, happy trysts.

"Love is blind not only to faults but to all the world. We were discovered and he was blamed. The great name of the institution might be compromised—its business suffer. He resigned.

"Then came the terrible misstep; he asked me to go with him and I consented. We should have gone home; he was afraid of the legal effects of marrying a minor, and so we went the other way. Not stopping in New York we turned northward, away from the revengeful south; from police surveillance, and somewhere we were married. I heard them call us man and wife, and then I sank again into my dream.

"It does not seem possible that I could not have known the name of the place, but I was no more than a child looking from a car window and taken out for meals here and there. I had but one thought—my husband.

"We went to Canada, then abroad. Gaspard had saved considerable money; his home was in Silesia and thither we went; and that long journey was the happiest honeymoon a woman could know."

"I spent mine in Europe wandering from point to point. I understand," said Mrs. Montjoy, gently.

"Ah, you do understand. We reached the home and then my troubles began. My husband, the restraints of his professional engagement thrown off, fell a victim to dissipation again. He had left his country to break up old associations and this habit.

"His people were high-class but poor. He was Count Levigne. Their pride was boundless. They disliked me from the beginning. I had frustrated the plans of the family, whose redemption was to come from Gaspard. Innocent though I was, and soon demanding the tenderness, the love, the gentleness which almost every woman receives under like circumstances, I received only coldness and petty persecution.

"Soon came want; not the want of mere food, but of clothing and minor comforts. And Gaspard had changed —he who should have defended me left me to defend myself. One night came the end. He reproached me— he was intoxicated—with having ruined his life and his prospects." The speaker paused. With this scene had come an emotion she could with difficulty control; but, calm at last, she continued with dignity:

"The daughter of Gen. Albert Evan could not stand that. I sold my diamonds, my mother's diamonds, and came away. I had resolved to come back and work for a living in my own land until peace could be made with father. At that time I did not know the trouble. I found out, though.

"Gaspard came to his senses then and followed me. Madame, can you imagine the sorrow of that coming back? But a few months before I had gone over the same route the happiest woman in all the to me beautiful world, and now I was the most miserable; life had lost its beauty!

"We met again—he had taken a shorter way, and, guessing my limited knowledge correctly, by watching the shipping registers found me. But all eloquence could not avail then; there had been a revulsion. I no longer loved him. He would never reform; he would live by fits and starts and he could not support me. At that time he had but one piece of property in the world—a magnificent Stradivarius violin. The sale of that would have brought many thousand francs to spend, but on that one thing he was unchanging. It had come to him by many generations of musicians. They transmitted to him their divine art and the vehicle of its expression. A suggestion of sale threw him into the most violent of passions, so great was the shock to his artistic nature and family pride. If he had starved to death that violin would have been found by his side.

"I believe it was this heroism in his character that touched me at last; I relented. We went to Paris and Gaspard secured employment. But, alas, I had not been mistaken. I was soon penniless and practically abandoned. I had no longer the ability to do what I should have done at first; I could not go home for want of means."

"You should have written to us."

"I would have starved before I would have asked. Had you known, had you offered, I would have received it. And God sent me a friend, one of His noblemen—the last in all the world of whom I could ask anything. When my fortunes were at their lowest ebb John Morgan came back into my life."

"John Morgan!"

"He asked no questions. He simply did all that was necessary. And then he went to see my father. I had written him, but he had never replied; he went, as I learned afterward, simply as a man of business and without sentiment. You can imagine the scene. No other man witnessed it. It was, he told me, long and stormy.

"The result was that I would be received at home when I came with proofs of my marriage.

"I was greatly relieved at first; I had only to find my husband and get them. I found him, but I did not get them. It happened to be a bad time to approach him. Then John Morgan tried, and that was unfortunate. In my despair I had told my husband of that prior engagement. An insane jealousy now seized him. He thought it was a plot to recover my name and marry me to Mr. Morgan. He held the key to the situation and swore that in an action for divorce he would testify there had been no marriage!

"Then we went forward to find the record. We never found it. If years of search and great expense could have accomplished it, we would have succeeded. It was, however, a fact; I remembered standing before the officiating officer and recalled my trembling responses, but that was all. The locality, the section, whether it was the first or second day, I do not recall. But, as God is my judge, I was married."

She became passionate. Her companion soothed her again.

"Go on, my child. I believe you."

"I cannot tell you a part of this sad story; I have not been perfectly open. Some day I will, perhaps, and until that time comes I ask you to keep my secret, because there are good reasons now for silence; you will appre-ciate them when you know. Gaspard was left—our only chance. Mr. Morgan sought him, I sought him; he would have given him any sum for his knowledge. Gaspard would have sold it, we thought; want would have made him sell, but Gaspard had vanished as if death itself had carried him off.

"In this search I had always the assistance of Mr. Morgan, and at first his money defrayed all expense; but shortly afterward he influenced a leading opera master to give me a chance, and I sung in Paris as Cambia, for the first time. From that day I was rich, and Marion Evan disappeared from the world.

"Informed weekly of home affairs and my dear father, my separation was lessened of half its terrors. But year after year that unchanging friend stood by me. The time came when the stern face was the grandest object on which my eyes could rest. There was no compact be-tween us; if I could have dissolved the marriage tie I would have accepted him and have been happy. But Cambia could take no chances with herself nor with Gen. Evan! Divorce could only have been secured by three months' publication of notice in the papers and if that reached Gaspard his terrible answer would have been filed and I would have been disgraced.

"The American war had passed and then came the French war. And still no news from Gaspard. And

one day came John Morgan, with the proposition that
ten years of abandonment gave me liberty, and offered
me his hand—and fortune. But—there were reasons—
there were reasons. I could not. He received my answer and said simply: 'You are right!' After that we
talked no more upon the subject.

"Clew after clew was exhausted; some led us into a
foreign prison. I sung at Christmas to the convicts.
Sometimes a little song that Gaspard had written for me.
All seemed touched; but none were overwhelmed; Gaspard was not among them.

"I sung upon the streets of Paris, disguised; all Paris
came to know and hear 'the veiled singer,' whose voice,
it was said, equaled the famous Cambia's. A blind violinist accompanied me. We managed it skillfully. He
met me at a new place every evening, and we parted at
a new place, I alighting from the cab we always took, at
some unfrequented place, and sending him home. And
now, madame, do you still believe in God?"

"Implicitly."

"Then tell me why, when, a few days since, I was called
by your friend Mr. Morgan to the bedside of Gaspard
Levigne, the old musician, who had accompanied me on
the streets of Paris, why was it that God in His mercy
did not give him breath to enable his lips to answer my
pitiful question; why, if there is a God in heaven, did He
not——"

"Hush, Marion!" The calm, sweet voice of the elder
woman rose above the excitement and anguish of the
singer. "Hush, my child; you have trusted too little in
Him! God is great, and good and merciful. I can say it
now; I will say it when His shadows fall upon my eyes
as they must some day."

Awed and touched, Cambia looked up into the glorified
face and was silent.

Neither broke that stillness, but as they waited a violent
step was heard without, and a voice:

"Infamous! Infamous!" Edward rushed into the room,
pale and horrified, his bursting heart finding relief only in
such words.

"What is it, my son—Edward!" Mrs. Montjoy looked
upon him reproachfully.

"I am accused of the murder of Rita Morgan!" he cried. He did not see Cambia, who had drawn back from between the two, and was looking in horror at him as she slowly moved toward the door.

"You accused, Edward? Impossible! Why, what possible motive——"

"Oh, it is devilish!" he exclaimed, as he tore the American paper into shreds. "Devilish! First I was called her son, and now her murderer! I murdered her to destroy her evidence, is the charge!" The white face of Cambia disappeared through the door.

CHAPTER XLIV.

THE MAN WITH THE TORCH.

The startling news had been discussed in all its phases in the little parlor, Mary taking no part. She sat with averted face listening, but ever and anon when Edward's indignation became unrestrainable she turned and looked at him. She did not know that the paper contained a reference to her.

The astounding revelation, aside from the accusation, was the wound. Strange that he had not discovered it. Who could have murdered poor Rita? Positively the only person on the immediate premises were Virdow, Evan and Gerald. Virdow was of course out of the question, and the others were in the room. It was the blow that had driven her head through the glass. What enemy could the woman have had?

So far as he was concerned, the charge could amount to nothing; Evan was in the room with him; the general would surely remember that.

But the horror, the mortification—he, Edward Morgan, charged with murder, and the center of a scandal in which the name of Mary Montjoy was mentioned.

The passion left him; depressed and sick from reaction he sat alone in the little parlor, long after the ladies had

retired; and then came the climax. A cablegram reached
the house and was handed in to him. It was signed by
Evan and read:

"You have been indicted. Return."

"Indicted," and for murder, of course. It gave him
no uneasiness, but it thrust all light and sweetness from
life. The dream was over. There could now be no search
for Marion Evan. That must pass, and with it hope.

He had builded upon that idea castles whose minarets
wore the colors of sunrise. They had fallen and his life
lay among the ruins.

He threw himself upon the bed to sleep, but the gray
of dawn was already over the city; there came a rumbling
vehicle in the street; he heard the sound of a softly closing
door—and then he arose and went out. The early morning air and exercise brought back his physical equipoise.
He returned for breakfast, with a good appetite, and
though grave, was tranquil again.

Neither of the ladies brought up the painful subject;
they went with him to see the learned oculist and came
back silent and oppressed. There was no hope.

The diagnosis corresponded with Dr. Campbell's; the
blind eye might have been saved years ago, but an operation would not have been judicious under the circumstances. Continued sight must depend upon her general
health.

All their pleasures and hopes buried in one brief day,
they turned their backs on Paris and started homeward.

Edward saw Cambia no more; Mrs. Montjoy called
alone and said farewell. The next day they sailed from
Havre.

In New York Norton met them, grave and embarrassed
for once in his life, and assisted in their hurried departure
for the fair southern home. There was no exchange of
views between the two men. The paper Norton had sent
was acknowledged; that was all. The subject was too
painful for discussion. And so they arrived in Georgia.
They were met by the Montjoy carriage at a little station
near the city. It was the 11:20 p. m. train. Gen. Evan
was waiting for Edward.

The handshaking over, they rapidly left the station.

Evan had secured from the sheriff a temporary exemption from arrest for Edward, but it was understood that he was to remain out of sight.

They had arrived within a couple of miles of the Cedars, having only broached commonplace subjects, traveling incidents and the like, when a negro stopped them. In the distance they heard a hound trailing.

"Boss, kin air one er you gentlemen gi' me a match? I los' my light back yonder, and hit's too putty 'er night ter go back without a possum." Evan drew rein. He was a born sportsman and sympathetic.

"I reckon so," he said; "and—well, I can't," he concluded, having tried all pockets. "Mr. Morgan, have you a match?" Edward had one and one only. He drew all the little articles of his pockets into his hand to find it.

"Now, hold," said the general; "let's light our cigars, if it's to be the last chance." The negro touched the blazing match to splinters of lightwood, as the southern pitch pine is called when dry, and instantly he stood in a circle of light, his features revealed in every detail. Edward gazed into it curiously. Where had he seen that face? It came back like the lines of some unpleasant dream—the thick lips, the flat nose, the retreating forehead, full eyes and heavy eyelids, and over all a look of infinite stupidity. The negro had fixed his eyes a moment upon the articles in Edward's hand and stepped back quickly. But he recovered himself and with clumsy thanks, holding up his flaming torch, went away, leaving only the uncertain shadows dancing across the road.

At home Gen. Evan threw aside all reserve. He drew their chairs up into the sheltered corner of the porch.

"I have some matters to talk over," he said, "and our time is short. Yours is not a bailable case and we must have a speedy trial. The law winks at your freedom tonight; it will not do to compromise our friends in the court house by unnecessary delay. Edward, where was I when you discovered the body of the woman, Rita Morgan?" Edward looked through the darkness at his friend, who was gazing straight ahead.

"You were standing by Gerald's bed, looking upon him."

"How did you discover her? It never occurred to me to ask; were you not in the room also?"

"I certainly was. She broke the glass by pressing against it, as I thought at the time, but now I see she was struck. I rushed out and picked her up, and you came when I called.

"Exactly. And you both talked loudly out there."

"Why do you ask?"

"Because," said Evan, slowly, "therein lies the defect in our defense. I cannot swear you were in the room upon my own knowledge. I had been astounded by the likeness of Gerald to those who had been dear to me—I was absorbed. Then I heard you cry out, and found you in the yard." There was a long pause. Edward's heart began to beat with sledge-hammer violence.

"Then," he said with a strange voice, "as the case would be presented, I was found with the body of the woman; she had been murdered and I was the only one who had a motive. Is that it?"

"That is it." The young man arose and walked the porch in silence.

"But that is not all," said Gen. Evan. "If it were, I would have cabled you to go east from Paris. There is more. Is there any one on earth who could be interested in your disgrace or death?"

"None that I know of—that is, well, no; none that I know of. You remember Royson; we fought that out. He cannot cherish enmity against a man who fought him in an open field."

"Perhaps you are mistaken."

"From what do you speak?"

"You had been in Paris but a few days when one night as I sat here your friend Barksdale—great man that Barksdale; a trifle heady and confident, but true as steel— Barksdale came flying on his sorrel up the avenue and landed here.

" 'General,' said he, 'I have discovered the most damnable plot that a man ever faced. All this scandal about Morgan is not newspaper sensation as you suppose, it is the first step in a great tragedy.' And then he went on to tell me that Gerald had invaded his room and showed him pictures of an open grave, the face of a dead woman and also the face of the man who opened that grave, drawn with every detail perfect. Gerald declared that he witnessed the disinterment and drew the scene from memory——"

"Hold a minute," said Edward; he was now on his feet, his hand uplifted to begin a statement; "and then—and then——"

"The object of that disinterment was to inflict the false wound and charge you with murder."

"And the man who did it—who made that wound—was the man who begged a match from us on the road. I will swear it, if art is true. I have seen the picture." Evan paused a moment to take in the vital fact. Then there rung out from him a half-shout:

"Thank God! Thank God!" The chairs that stood between him and the door were simply hurled out of the way. His stentorian voice called for his factotum. "John!" and John did not wait to dress, but came.

"Get my horse and a mule saddled and bring that puppy Carlo. Quick, John, quick!" John fled toward the stable. "Edward, we win if we get that negro—we win!" he exclaimed, coming back through the wreck of his furniture.

"But why should the negro have disinterred the body and have made a wound upon her head? There can be no motive."

"Heavens, man, no motive! Do you know that you have come between two men and Mary Montjoy?"

"I, no, indeed! I have never suspected it, even."

"Two have sought her with all the energy of manhood," said Evan. "Two men as different as the east from the west. Royson hates you and will leave no stone unturned to effect your ruin; Barksdale loves her and will leave no stone unturned to protect her happiness! There you have it all. Only one man in the world could have put that black devil up to his infamous deed—and that man is Royson. Only one man in the world could have grasped the situation and have read the riddle correctly—and that man is Barksdale." Edward was dazed. Gradually the depth and villainy of the conspiracy grew clear.

"But to prove it——"

"The negro."

"Will he testify?"

"Will he? If I get my hands on him, young man, he will testify! Or he will hang by the neck from a limb as his possum hangs by the tail."

"You propose to capture him?"

"I am going to capture him." He disappeared in the house and when he came out he had on his army belt, with sword and pistol. The mounts were at the door and for the first time in his life Edward was astride a mule. To his surprise the animal bounded along after the gray horse, with a smooth and even gait, and kept up without difficulty.

Evan rode as a cavalryman and carried across his saddle the puppy. With unerring skill he halted at the exact spot where the match had been struck, and lowered the dog gently to the ground. The intelligent, excited animal at once took up the trail of man or dogs, and opening loudly glided into the darkness. They followed.

Several miles had been covered, when they saw in the distance a glimmer of light among the trees and Evan drew rein.

"It will not do," he said, "to ride upon him. At the sound of horses' feet he will extinguish his light and escape. The dog, he will suppose, is a stray one led off by his own and will not alarm him." They tied their animals and pressed on.

The dog ahead had opened and Carlo's voice could be heard with the rest, as they trailed the fleeing possum. The general was exhausted. "I can't do it, Edward, my boy—go on. I will follow as fast as possible." Without a word Edward obeyed. The dogs were now furious, the man himself running. In the din and clamor he could hear nothing of pursuit. The first intimation he had of danger was a grip on his collar and a man's voice exclaiming excitedly:

"Halt! You are my prisoner!"

The torch fell to the ground and lay sputtering. The negro was terrified for the moment, but his quick eye pierced the gloom and measured his antagonist. He made a fierce effort to break away, and failing, threw himself with immense force upon Edward. Then began a frightful struggle. No word was spoken. The negro was powerful, but the white man was inspired by a memory and a consciousness of his wrongs. They fell and writhed, and rose and fell again. Slippery Dick had got his hand upon Edward's throat. Suddenly his grasp relaxed and he lay with the white of his eyes rolled upward. The muzzle of a cavalry pistol was against his head and the stern face of the veteran was above him.

"Get up!" said the general, briefly.

"Certainly, boss," was the reply, and breathless the two men arose.

The defense had its witness!

"Ef he had'n conjured me," said the negro doggedly, "he couldn't 'er done it." He had recognized among the little things that Edward drew from his pocket on the road the voodoo's charm.

Edward, breathless, took up the torch and looked into Dick's countenance. "I am not mistaken, general, this is the man."

CHAPTER XLV.

WHAT THE SHEET HID.

Slippery Dick was puzzled as well as frightened. He knew Gen. Evan by sight, and his terror lost some of its wildness; the general was not likely to be out upon a lynching expedition. But for what was he wanted? He could not protest until he knew that, and in his past were many dark deeds, for which somebody was wanted. So he was silent.

His attention was chiefly directed to Edward; he could not account for him, nor could he remember to have seen him. Royson had long since trained him to silence; most men convict themselves while under arrest.

Evan stood in deep thought, but presently he prepared for action.

"What is your name, boy?" The negro answered promptly:

"Dick, sah."

"Dick who?"

"Just Dick, sah."

"Your other name?"

"Slippery Dick." The general was interested instantly.

"Oh, Slippery Dick." The career of the notorious negro was partially known to him. Dick had been the reporter's friend for many years and in dull times more than the truth had been told of Slippery Dick. "Well, this begins to look probable, Edward; I begin to think you may be right."

"I am not mistaken, general. If there is a mistake, it is not mine."

"What dey want me for, Marse Evan? I ain't done nothin'."

"A house has been broken into, Dick, and you are the man who did it."

"Who, me? Fo' Gawd, Marse Evan, I ain't broke inter no man's house. It warn't me—no sah, no sah."

"We will see about that. Now I will give you your choice, Dick; you can go with me, Gen. Evan, and I will protect you. If the person who accuses you says you are innocent I will turn you loose; if you are not willing to go there I will take you to jail; but, willing or unwilling, if you make a motion to escape, I will put a bullet through you before you can take three steps."

"I'll go with you, Marse Evan; I ain't de man. I'll go whar you want me to go."

"Get your dogs together and take the road to town. I will show you when we get there." They went with him to where his dogs, great and small, were loudly baying at the root of a small persimmon tree. Dick looked up wistfully.

"Marse Evan, deir he sots; you don't spec me ter leave dat possum up dere?" The old man laughed silently.

"The ruling passion strong in death," he quoted to Edward, and then sternly to Dick: "Get him and be quick about it." A moment more and they were on the way to the horses.

"I had an object," said Evan, "in permitting this. As we pass through the city we present the appearance of a

18

hunting party. Turn up your coat collar and turn down your hat to avoid the possibility of recognition."

They reached the city, passed through the deserted streets, the negro carrying his possum and surrounded by the dogs preceding the riders, and, without attracting more than the careless notice of a policeman or two, they reached the limits beyond.

Still Dick was not suspicious; the road was his own way home; but when finally he was ordered to turn up the long route to Ilexhurst, he stopped. This was anticipated; the general spurted his horse almost against him.

"Go on!" he said, sternly, "or by the Eternal you are a dead man! Edward, if he makes a break, you have the ax——"

"Marse Evan, you said breakin' in 'er house." Dick still hesitated.

"I did; but it was the house of the dead."

The possum came suddenly to the ground, and away went Dick into an open field, the expectation of a bullet lending speed to his legs. But he was not in the slightest danger from bullets; he was the last man, almost, that either of his captors would have slain, nor was it necessary. The great roan came thundering upon him; he lifted his arm to ward off the expected blow and looked up terrified. The next instant a hand was on his coat collar, and he was lifted off his feet. Dragging his prisoner into the road, Evan held his pistol over his wet forehead, while, with the rein, Edward lashed his elbows behind his back. The dogs were fighting over the remains of the unfortunate possum. They left them there.

The three men arrived at Ilexhurst thoroughly tired; the white men more so than the negro. Tying their animals, Edward led the way around to the glass-room, where a light was burning, but to his disappointment on entering he found no occupant. Slippery Dick was placed in a chair and the door locked. Evan stood guard over him, while Edward searched the house. The wing-room was dark and Gerald was not to be found. From the door of the professor's room came the cadenced breathing of a profound sleeper. Returning, Edward communicated these facts to his companion. They discussed the situation.

Evan, oppressed by the memory of his last two visits to these scenes, was silent and distrait. The eyes of the negro were moving restlessly from point to point, taking in every detail of his surroundings. The scene, the hour, the situation and the memory of that shriveled face in its coffin all combined to reduce Dick to a state of abject terror. Had he not been tied he would have plunged through the glass into the night; the pistol in the hands of the old man standing over him would have been forgotten.

What was to be done? Edward went into the wing-room and lighted the lamps preparatory to making better arrangements for all parties. Suddenly his eyes fell upon the lounge. Extended upon it was a form outlined through a sheet that covered it from head to foot. So still, so immovable and breathless it seemed, he drew back in horror. An indefinable fear seized him. White, with unexpressed horror, he stood in the door of the glass-room and beckoned to the general. The silence of his appearance, the inexpressible terror that shone in his face and manner, sent a thrill to the old man's heart and set the negro trembling.

Driving the negro before him, Evan entered. At sight of the covered form Dick made a violent effort to break away, but, with nerves now at their highest tension and muscles drawn responsive, the general successfully resisted. Enraged at last he stilled his captive by a savage blow with his weapon.

Edward now approached the apparition and lifted the cloth. Prepared as he was for the worst, he could not restrain the cry of horror that rose to his lips. Before him was the face of Gerald, white with the hue of death, the long lashes drooped over half-closed eyes, the black hair drawn back from the white forehead and clustering about his neck and shoulders. He fell almost fainting against the outstretched arm of his friend, who, pale and shocked, stood with eyes riveted upon the fatal beauty of the dead face.

It was but an instant; then the general was jerked with irresistible force and fell backward into the room, Edward going nearly prostrate over him. There was the sound of shattered glass and the negro was gone.

Stunned and hurt, the old man rose to his feet and rushed to the door of the glass-room. Then a pain seized him; he drew his bruised limb from the floor and caught the lintel.

"Stop that man! Stop that man!" he said in a stentorian voice; "he is your only witness now!" Edward looked into his face a moment and comprehended. For the third time that night he plunged into the darkness after Slippery Dick. But where? Carlo was telling! Down the hill his shrill voice was breaking the night. Abandoned by the negro's dogs, accustomed to seek their home and that not far away, he had followed the master's footsteps with unerring instinct and whined about the glass door. The bursting glass, the fleeing form of a strange negro, were enough for his excitable nature; he gave voice and took the trail.

The desperate effort of the negro might have succeeded, but the human arms were made for many things; when a man stumbles he needs them in the air and overhead or extended. Slippery Dick went down with a crash in a mass of blackberry bushes, and when Edward reached him he was kicking wildly at the excited puppy, prevented from rising by his efforts and his bonds. The excited and enraged white man dragged him out of the bushes by his collar and brought reason to her throne by savage kicks. The prisoner gave up and begged for mercy.

He was marched back, all breathless, to the general, who had limped to the gate to meet him.

Edward was now excited beyond control; he forced the prisoner, shivering with horror, into the presence of the corpse, and with the ax in hand confronted him.

"You infamous villain!" he cried; "tell me here, in the presence of my dead friend, who it was that put you up to opening the grave of Rita Morgan and breaking her skull, or I will brain you! You have ten seconds to speak!" He meant it, and the ax flashed in the air. Gen. Evan caught the upraised arm.

"Softly, softly, Edward; this won't do; this won't do! You defeat your own purpose!" It was timely; the blow might have descended, for the reckless man was in earnest, and the negro was by this time dumb.

"Dick," said the general, "I promised to protect you on conditions, and I will. But you have done this gentleman an injury and endangered his life. You opened Rita Morgan's grave and broke her skull—an act for which the law has no adequate punishment; but my young friend here is desperate. You can save yourself, but I cannot save you except in one way. If you value your life tell him and tell me who put you up to that job. If you tell I give you my word of honor as a gentleman that no man shall harm you except over my dead body. If you refuse I will stand aside, and when I do you are a dead man." He was during this hurried speech still struggling with the young man.

"I'll tell, Marse Evan! Hold 'im. I'll tell!"

"Who, then?" said Edward, white with his passion; "who was the infamous villain that paid you for the deed?"

"Mr. Royson, Mr. Royson, he hired me." The men looked at each other. A revulsion came over Edward; a horror, a hatred of the human race, of anything that bore the shape of man—but no; the kind, sad face of the old gentleman was beaming in triumph upon him.

And then from somewhere into the scene came the half-dressed form of Virdow, his face careworn and weary, amazed and alarmed.

*   *   *

Virdow wrote the confession in all its details, and the general witnessed the rude cross made by the trembling hand of the negro. And then they stood sorrowful and silent before the still, dead face of Gerald Morgan!

CHAPTER XLVI.

ON THE MARGINS OF TWO WORLDS.

The discovery of Gerald's death necessitated a change of plans. The concealment of Slippery Dick and Edward must necessarily be accomplished at Ilexhurst. There

were funeral arrangements to be made, the property
cared for and Virdow to be rescued from his solitary and
embarrassing position.   Moreover, the gray dawn was
on ere the confession was written, and Virdow had briefly
explained the circumstances of Gerald's death. Exhausted
by excitement and anxiety and the depression of grief, he
went to his room and brought Edward a sealed packet
which had been written and addressed to him during the
early hours of the night.

"You will find it all there," he said; "I cannot talk
upon it." He went a moment to look upon the face of
his young friend and then, with a single pathetic gesture,
turned and left them.

One of the eccentricities of the former owner of Ilexhurst had been a granite smoke-house, not only burglar
and fireproof but cyclone proof, and with its oaken door
it constituted a formidable jail.

With food and water, Dick, freed of his bonds, was
ushered into this building, the small vents in the high roof
affording enough light for most purposes. A messenger
was then dispatched for Barksdale and Edward locked
himself away from sight of chance callers in his upper
room.   The general, thoughtful and weary, sat by the
dead man.

The document that Virdow had prepared was written
in German. "When your eye reads these lines, you will
be grieved beyond endurance; Gerald is no more! He was
killed to-night by a flash of lightning and his death was
instantaneous.   I am alone, heartbroken and utterly
wretched. Innocent of any responsibility in this horrible
tragedy I was yet the cause, since it was while submitting
to some experiments of mine that he received his death
stroke.   I myself received a frightful electric shock, but
it now amounts to nothing.   I would to God that
I and not he had received the full force of the discharge.
He might have been of vast service to science, but my
work is little and now well-nigh finished.

"Gerald was kneeling under a steel disk, in the glass-
room, you will remember where we began our sound experiments, and I did not know that the steel wire which
suspended it ran up and ended near a metal strip, along

the ridge beam of the room. We had just begun our investigation, when the flash descended and he fell dead.

"At this writing I am here under peculiar circumstances; the butler who came to my call when I recovered consciousness assisted me in the attempt at resuscitation of Gerald, but without any measure of success. He then succeeded in getting one or two of the old negroes and a doctor. The latter declared life extinct. There was no disfigurement—only a black spot in the crown of the head and a dark line down the spine, where the electric fluid had passed. That was all."

Edward ceased to read; his chin sunk upon his breast and the lines slipped from his unfocused eyes. The dark line down the spine! His heart leaped fiercely and he lifted his face with a new light in his eyes. For a moment it was radiant; then shame bowed his head again. He laid aside the paper and gave himself up to thought, from time to time pacing the room. In these words lay emancipation. He resumed the reading:

"We arranged the body on the lounge and determined to wait until morning, and sent for the coroner and undertaker, but one by one your negroes disappeared. They could not seem to withstand their superstition, the butler told me, and as there was nothing to be done I did not worry. I came here to the library to write, and when I returned, the butler, too, was gone. They are a strange people. I suppose I will see none of them until morning, but it does not matter; my poor friend is far beyond the reach of attention. His rare mind has become a part of cosmos; its relative situation is our mystery.

"I will, now, before giving you a minute description of our last evening together, commit for your eye my conclusions as to some of the phenomena and facts you have observed. I am satisfied so far as Gerald's origin is concerned, that he is either the son of the woman Rita or that they are in some way connected by ties of blood. In either case the similarity of their profiles would be accounted for. No matter how remote the connection, nothing is so common as this reappearance of tribal features in families. The woman, you told me, claimed him as her child, but silently waived that claim for his sake.

I say to you that a mother's instinct is based upon something deeper than mere fancy, and that intuitions are so nearly correct that I class them as the nearest approach to mind memory to be observed.

"The likeness of his full face to the picture of the girl you call Marion Evan may be the result of influences exerted at birth. Do you remember the fragmentary manuscript? If that is a history, I am of the opinion that it is explanation enough. At any rate, the profile is a stronger evidence the other way.

"The reproduction of the storm scene is one of the most remarkable incidents I have ever known, but it is not proof that he inherited it as a memory. It is a picture forcibly projected upon his imagination by the author of the fragment—and in my opinion he had read that fragment. It came to him as a revelation, completing the gap. I am sure that from the day that he read it he was for long periods convinced that he was the son of Rita Morgan; that she had not lied to him. In this I am confirmed by the fact that as she lay dead he bent above her face and called her 'mother.' I am just as well assured that he had no memory of the origin of that picture; no memory, in fact, of having read the paper. This may seem strange to you, but any one who has had the care of victims of opium will accept the proposition as likely.

"The drawing of the woman's face was simple. His hope had been to find himself the son of Marion Evan; his dreams were full of her. He had seen the little picture; his work was an idealized copy, but it must be admitted a marvelous work. Still the powers of concentration in this man exceeded the powers of any one I have ever met.

"And that brings me to what was the most wonderful demonstration he gave us. Edward, I have divined your secret, although you have never told it. When you went to secure for me the note of the waterfall, the home note, you were accompanied by your friend Mary. I will stake my reputation upon it. It is true because it is obliged to be true. When you played for us you had her in your mind, a vivid picture, and Gerald drew it. It was a case of pure thought transference—a transference of a mental conception, line for line. Gerald received his conception from you upon the vibrating air. To me it was a demonstration worth my whole journey to America.

"And here let me add, as another proof of the sympathetic chord between you, that Gerald himself had learned to love the same woman. You gave him that, my young friend, with the picture.

"You have by this time been made acquainted with the terrible accusation against you—false and infamous. There will be little trouble in clearing yourself, but oh, what agony to your sensitive nature! I tried to keep the matter from Gerald, as I did the inquest, by keeping him busy with investigations; but a paper fell into his hands and his excitement was frightful. Evading me he disappeared from the premises one evening, but while I was searching for him he came to the house in a carriage, bringing the picture of that repulsive negro, which you will remember. Since then he has been more calm. Mr. Barksdale, your friend, I suppose, was with him once or twice.

"And now I come to this, the last night of our association upon earth; the night that has parted us and rolled between us the mystery across which our voices cannot reach nor our ears hear.

"Gerald had long since been satisfied with the ability of living substance to hold a photograph, and convinced that these photographs lie dormant, so to speak, somewhere in our consciousness until awakened again—that is, until made vivid. He was proceeding carefully toward the proposition that a complete memory could be inherited, and in the second generation or even further removed; you know his theory. There were intermediate propositions that needed confirmation. When forms and scenes come to the mind of the author, pure harmonies of color to that of the artist, sweet co-ordinations of harmonies to the musician. Whence do they come? Where is the thread of connection? Most men locate the seat of their consciousness at the top of the head; they seem to think in that spot. And strange, is it not, that when life passes out and all the beautiful structure of the body ˙

claimed by the frost of death, that heat lingers longest at that point! It is material in this letter, because explaining Gerald's idea. He wished me to subject him to the finest vibrations at that point.

"The experiment was made with a new apparatus, which had been hung in place of the first in the glass-room; or, rather, to this we made an addition. A thin steel plate was fixed to the floor, directly under the wire and elevated upon a small steel rod. Gerald insisted that as the drum and membrane I used made the shapes we secured, a new experiment should be tried, with simple vibrations. So we hung in its place a steel disk with a small projection from the center, underneath. Kneeling upon the lower disk Gerald was between two plates subject to the finest vibration, his sensitive body the connection. There was left a gap of one inch between his head and the projection under the upper disk and we were to try first with the gap closed, and then with it opened.

"You know how excitable he was. When he took his position he was white and his large eyes flashed fire. His face settled into that peculiarly harsh, fierce expression, for which I have never accounted except upon the supposition of nervous agony. The handle to his violin had been wrapped with fine steel wire, and this, extending a yard outward, was bent into a tiny hook, intended to be clasped around the suspended wire, that it might convey to it the full vibrations from the sounding board of the instrument. I made this connection, and, with the violin against my ear, prepared to strike the 'A' note in the higher octave, which if the vibrations were fine enough should suggest in his mind the figure of a daisy.

"Gerald, his eyes closed, remained motionless in his kneeling posture. Suddenly a faint flash of light descended into the room and the thunder rolled. And I, standing entranced by the beauty and splendor of that face, lost all thought of the common laws of physics. A look of rapture had suffused it, his eyes now looked out upon some vision, and a tender smile perfected the exquisite curve of his lips. There was no need of violin outside, the world was full of the fine quiverings of electricity, the earth's invisible envelope was full of vibrations!

Nature was speaking a language of its own. What that mind saw between the glories of this and the other life as it trembled on the margins of both, is not given to me to know; but a vision had come to him—of what?

"Ah, Edward, how different the awakening for him and me! I remember that for a moment I seemed to float in a sea of flame; there was a shock like unto nothing I had ever dreamed, and lying near me upon the floor, his mortal face startled out of its beautiful expression, lay Gerald—dead!"

The conclusion of the letter covered the proposed arrangements for interment. Edward had little time to reflect upon the strange document. The voice of Gen. Evan was heard calling at the foot of the stair. Looking down he saw standing by him the straight, manly figure of Barksdale. The hour of dreams had ended; the hour of action had arrived!

CHAPTER XLVII.

WAR TO THE KNIFE.

Barksdale heard the events of the night, as detailed by the general, without apparent emotion. He had gone with them to look upon the remains of Gerald. He brought from the scene only a graver look in his face, a more gentle tone in his voice. These, however, soon passed. He was again the cold, stern, level-headed man of affairs, listening to a strange story. He lost no detail and his quick, trained mind gave each matter its true position.

The death of Gerald was peculiarly unfortunate for Edward. They had now nothing left but the negro, and negro testimony could be bought for little money. He would undertake to buy just such evidence as Dick had given from a dozen men in ten days and the first man he would have sought would be Slippery Dick, and the public would be thrown into doubt as to Royson by the fact of deadly enmity between the men. To introduce Dick upon the stand to testify and not support his testimony would be almost a confession of guilt. The negro was too well known. Gerald's statement would not be admissible, though his picture might. But of what avail would the picture be without the explanation?

Barksdale pointed out this clearly but briefly. Gen. Evan was amazed that such a situation had not already presented itself. The court case would have been Dick's word against Royson's; the result would not have been doubtful. The least that could be hoped for, if the state made out a case against Edward, was imprisonment.

But there was more; a simple escape was not sufficient; Edward must not only escape but also show the conspiracy and put it where it belonged. He, Barksdale, had no doubt upon that point. Royson was the guilty man.

This analysis of the situation, leaving as it did the whole matter open again, and the result doubtful, filled Evan with anxiety and vexation.

"I thought," said he, walking the floor, "that we had everything fixed; that the only thing necessary would be to hold to the negro and bring him in at the right time. If he died or got away we had his confession witnessed." Barksdale smiled and shook his head.

"It is of the utmost importance," he said, "to hold the negro and bring him in at the right time, but in my opinion it is vital to the case that the negro be kept from communicating with Royson, and that the fact of his arrest be concealed. Where have you got him?"

"In the stone smoke-house," said Edward.

"Tied."

"No."

"Then," said Barksdale, arising at once, "if not too late you must tie him. There is no smoke-house in existence and no jail in this section that can hold Slippery Dick if his hands are free." Thoroughly alarmed, Gen. Evan led the way and Edward followed. Barksdale waved the latter back.

"Don't risk being seen; we can attend to this." They opened the door and looked about the dim interior; it was empty. With a cry the general rushed in.

"He is gone!" Barksdale stood at the door; the building was a square one, with racks overhead for hanging meat. There was not the slightest chance of concealment. A mound of earth in one corner aroused his suspicions. He went to it, found a burrow and, running his arm into this, he laid hold of a human leg.

"Just in time, general, he is here!" With a powerful effort he drew the negro into the light. In one hour more he would have been under the foundations and gone. Dick rose and glanced at the open door as he brushed the dirt from his eyes, but there was a grip of steel upon his collar, and a look in the face before him that suggested the uselessness of resistance. The general recovered the strap and bound the elbows as before.

"I will bring up shackles," said Barksdale, briefly. "In the meantime, this will answer. But you know the stake! Discharge the house servant, and I will send a man of my own selection. In the meantime look in here occasionally." They returned to the house and into the library, where they found Edward and informed him of the arrangements.

"Now," said Barksdale, "this is the result of my efforts in another direction. The publication of libelous articles is almost impossible, with absolute secrecy as to the authorship. A good detective, with time and money, can unravel the mystery and fix the responsibility upon the guilty party. I went into this because Mr. Morgan was away, and the circumstances were such that he could not act in the simplest manner if he found the secret. He had drawn from his pocket a number of papers, and to these, as he proceeded, he from time to time referred.

"We got our first clew by purchase. Sometimes in a newspaper office there is a man who is keen enough to preserve a sheet of manuscript that he 'sets up,' when reflection suggests that it may be of future value. Briefly, I found such a man and bought this sheet"—lifting it a moment—"of no value except as to the handwriting.

"The first step toward discovering the name of the Tell-Tale correspondent was a matter of difficulty, from the nature of the paper. There was always in this case the dernier ressort; the editor could be forced at the point of a pistol. But that was hazardous. The correspondent's name was discovered in this way: We offered and paid a person in position to know, for the addresses of all letters from the paper's office to persons in this city. One man's name was frequently repeated. We got a specimen of his handwriting and compared it with the sheet of manuscript; the chirography was identical.

"A brief examination of the new situation convinced me that the writer did not act independently; he was a young man not long in the city and could not have known the facts he wrote of nor have obtained them on his own account without arousing suspicion. He was being used by another party—by some one having confidential relations or connections with certain families, Col. Montjoy's included. I then began to suspect the guilty party.

"The situation was now exceedingly delicate and I called into consultation Mr. Dabney, one of our shrewdest young lawyers, and one, by the way, Mr. Morgan, I will urge upon you to employ in this defense; in fact, you will find no other necessary, but by all means hold to him. The truth is," he added, "I have already retained him for you, but that does not necessarily bind you."

"I thank you," said Edward. "We will retain him."

"Very good. Now we wanted this young man's information and we did not wish the man who used him to know that anything was being done or had been done, and last week, after careful consultation, I acted. I called in this young fellow and appointed him agent at an important place upon our road, but remote, making his salary a good one. He jumped at the chance and I did not give him an hour's time to get ready. He was to go upon trial, and he went. I let him enjoy the sensation of prosperity for a week before exploding my mine. Last night I went down and called on him with our lawyer. We took him to the hotel, locked the door and terrorized him into a confession, first giving him assurance that no harm should come to him and that his position would not be affected. He gave away the whole plot and conspiracy.

"The man we want is Amos Royson!"

The old general was out of his chair and jubilant. He was recalled to the subject by the face of the speaker, now white and cold, fixed upon him.

"I did not have evidence enough to convict him of conspiracy, nor would the evidence help Mr. Morgan's case, standing alone as it did. The single witness, and he in my employ then, could not have convicted, although he might have ruined, Royson. I am now working upon the murder case. I came to the city at daylight and had just arrived home when your note reached me. My intention was to go straight to Royson's office and give him an opportunity of writing out his acknowledgment of his infamy and a retraction. If he had refused I would have killed him as surely as there is a God in heaven."

Edward held out his hand silently and the men understood each other.

"Now," continued Barksdale, "the situation has changed. There is evidence enough to convict Royson of conspiracy, perhaps. We must consult Dabney, but I am inclined to believe that our course will be to go to trial ourselves and spring the mine without having aroused suspicion. When Slippery Dick goes upon the stand he must find Royson confident and in my opinion he will convict himself in open court, if we can get him there. The chances are he will be present. The case will attract a great crowd. He would naturally come. But we will take no chances; he shall come!

"Just one thing more now; you perceive the importance, the vital importance, of secrecy as to your prisoner; under no consideration must his presence here be known outside. To insure this it seems necessary to take one trusty man into our employ. Have you considered how we would be involved if Mr. Morgan should be arrested?"

"But he will not be. Sheriff——"

"You forget Royson. He is merciless and alert. If he discovers Mr. Morgan's presence in this community he will force an arrest. The sheriff will do all in his power for us, but he is an officer under oath, and with an eye, of course, to re-election. I would forestall this; I would let the man who comes to guard Dick guard Mr. Morgan also. In other words, let him go under arrest and accept a guard in his own house. The sheriff can act in this upon his own discretion, but the arrest should be made." Edward and the general were for a moment silent.

"You are right," said the former. "Let the arrest be made." Barksdale took his departure.

The butler appeared and was summarily discharged for having abandoned Virdow during the night.

And then came the deputy, a quiet, confident man of few words, who served the warrant upon Edward, and then, proceeding with his prisoner to the smoke-house, put shackles upon Slippery Dick, and supplemented them with handcuffs.

CHAPTER XLVIII.

PREPARING THE MINE.

This time the coroner was summoned. He came, examined the body of Gerald, heard Virdow's statement and concluded that he could not hold an inquest without subjecting himself to unpleasant criticism and giving candidates for his office something to take hold of.

The funeral was very quiet. Col. Montjoy, Mrs. Montjoy and Mary came in the old family carriage and the general on horseback.

The little group stood around the open coffin and gazed for the last time upon the pale, chaste face. The general could not endure more than the one glance. As it lay exposed to him, it was the perfect image of a face that had never dimmed in his memory. Mary's tears fell silently as she laid her little cross of white autumn rosebuds upon the silent breast and turned away. Edward was waiting for her; she took his arm and went upon the portico.

"It is a sad blow to you, Mr. Morgan," she said.

"It removes the only claim upon me," was his answer. "When all is over and this trial ended, I shall very likely return to Europe for good!" They were silent for a while. "I came here full of hope," he continued; "I have met distrust, accusation, assaults upon my character and life, the loss of friends, disappointments and now am accused of murder and must undergo a public trial. It is enough to satisfy most men with—the south."

"And do you count your real friends as nothing?'

"My real friends are few, but they count for much," he said, earnestly; "it will be hard to part with them— with you. But fate has laid an iron hand upon me. I must go." He found her looking at him with something of wonder upon her face.

"You know best," she said, quietly. There was something in her manner that reminded him of the calm dignity of her father.

"You do not understand me," he said, earnestly, "and I cannot explain, and yet I will go this far. My parents have left me a mystery to unfathom; until I have solved it I will not come back, I cannot come back." He took her hand in both of his. "It is this that restrains me; you have been a true friend; it grieves me that I cannot share my troubles with you and ask your woman's judgment, but I cannot—I cannot! I only ask that you keep me always in your memory, as you will always be the brightest spot in mine." She was now pale and deeply affected by his tone and manner.

"You cannot tell me, Mr. Morgan?"

"Not even you, the woman I love; the only woman I have ever loved. Ah, what have I said?" She had withdrawn her hand and was looking away. "Forgive me; I did not know what I was saying. I, a man under indictment for murder, a possible felon, an unknown!"

The young girl looked at him fearlessly.

"You are right. You can rely upon friendship, but under the circumstances nothing can justify you in speaking of love to a woman—you do not trust."

"Do not trust! You cannot mean that!" She had turned away proudly and would have left him.

"I have seen so little of women," he said. "Let that be my excuse. I would trust you with my life, my honor, my happiness—but I will not burden you with my trouble. I have everything to offer you—but a name. It seems to me that I have been given a clear title to everything that a man needed except a name. I have feared to tell you; I have looked to see you turn away in suspicion and distrust—in horror. I could not. But anything, even that, is better than reproach and wrong judging.

19

"I tell you now that I love you as no woman was ever loved before; that I have loved you since you first came into my life, and that though we be parted by half a world of space, and through all eternity, I still will love you. But I will never, so help me heaven, ask the woman I love to share an unknown's lot! You have my reasons now; it is because I do love you that I go away." He spoke the words passionately. And then he found her standing close to his side.

"And I," she said, looking up into his face through tearful but smiling eyes, "do not care anything for your name or your doubts, and I tell you, Edward Morgan, that you shall not go away; you shall not leave me." He caught his breath and stood looking into her brave face.

"But your family—it is proud——"

"It shall suffer nothing in pride. We will work out this little mystery together." She extended her hand and, taking it, he took her also. She drew back, shaking her head reproachfully.

"I did not mean that."

He was about to reply, but at that moment a scene was presented that filled them both with sudden shame. How true it is that in the midst of life we are in death.

The hearse had paused at the gate. Silently they entered the house.

He led her back to the side of the dead man.

"He loved you," he said slowly. "I will speak the truth for him." Mary bent above the white face and left a kiss upon the cold brow.

"He was your friend," she said, fearing to look into his eye.

He comprehended and was silent.

It was soon over. The ritual for the dead, the slow journey to the city of silence, a few moments about the open grave, the sound of dirt falling upon the coffin, a prayer—and Gerald, living and dead, was no longer a part of their lives.

The Montjoys were to go home from the cemetery. Edward said farewell to them separately and to Mary last. Strange paradox, this human life. He came from that new-made grave almost happy.

The time for action was approaching rapidly. He
went with Dabney and the general to see Slippery Dick
for the last time before the trial. There was now but one
serious doubt that suggested itself. They took the man
at night to the grave of Rita and made him go over every
detail of his experience there. Under the influence of the
scene he began with the incident of the voodoo's "conjure
bag" and in reply to queries showed where it had been
inserted in the cedar. Edward took his knife and began
to work at the plug, but this action plunged Dick into
such terror that Dabney cautioned Edward in a low voice
to desist.

"Dick," said the young man finally, with sudden decision, "if you fail us in this matter not only will I remove
that plug but I will put you in jail and touch you with
the bag." Dick was at once voluble with promises. Edward, his memory stirred by the incident, was searching
his pockets. He had carried the little charm obtained
for him by Mary because of the tender memories of the
night before their journey abroad. He drew it out now
and held it up. Dick had not forgotten it; he drew back,
begging piteously. Dabney was greatly interested.

"That little charm has proved to be your protector, Mr.
Morgan," he said aloud for the negro's benefit. "You
have not been in any danger. Neither Dick nor any one
else could have harmed you. You should have told me
before. See how it has worked. The woman who gave
you the bag came to you in the night out on the ocean
and showed you the face of this man; you knew him even
in the night, although he had never before met you nor
you him."

A sound like the hiss of a snake came from the negro;
he had never been able to guess why this stranger had
known him so quickly. He now gazed upon his captor
with mingled fear and awe.

"Befo' Gawd, boss," he said, "I ain't goin' back on you,
boss!"

"Going back on him!" said Dabney, laughing. "I
should think not. I did not know that Mr. Morgan had
you conjured. Let us return; Dick cannot escape that
woman in this world or the next. Give me the little bag,

Mr. Morgan—no, keep it yourself. As long as you have it you are safe."

Edward was a prisoner, but in name only. Barksdale had not come again, for more reasons than one, the main reason being extra precaution on account of the watchful and suspicious Royson. But he acted quietly upon the public mind. The day following the interview he caused to be inserted in the morning paper an announcement of Edward's return and arrest, and the additional fact that although his business in Paris had not been finished, he had left upon the first steamer sailing from Havre. At the club, he was outspoken in his denunciation of the newspaper attacks and his confidence in the innocence of the man. There was no hint in any quarter that it had been suspected that Rita Morgan was really not murdered. It was generally understood that the defense would rely upon the state's inability to make out a case.

But Edward did not suffer greatly from loneliness. The day after the funeral Mrs. Montjoy and Mary, together with the colonel, paid a formal call and stayed for some hours; and the general came frequently with Dabney and Eldridge, who had also been employed, and consulted over their plans for the defense. Arrangements had been made with the solicitor for a speedy trial and the momentous day dawned.

CHAPTER XLIX.

SLIPPERY DICK RIGHTS A WRONG.

The prominence of the accused and of his friends, added to the sensational publication, made the case one of immense interest. The court house was crowded to its utmost and room had to be made within the bar for prominent citizens. There was a "color-line" feature in the murder, and the gallery was packed with curious black faces. Edward, quiet and self-contained, sat by his lawyers, and near him was the old general and Col. Montjoy. Slightly in the rear was Barksdale, calm and observant. The state had subpoenaed Royson as a witness, and, smilingly indifferent, he occupied a seat as a member of the bar, inside the rail. The case was called at last.

"The state versus Edward Morgan, murder. Mr. Solicitor, what do you say for the state?" asked the court.

"Ready."

"What do you say for the defense, gentlemen?"

"Ready."

"Mr. Clerk, call the jury." The panel was called and sworn. The work of striking the jury then proceeded. Eldridge and Dabney were clever practitioners and did not neglect any precaution. The jury list was scanned and undesirable names eliminated with as much care as if the prisoner had small chance of escape.

This proceeding covered an hour, but at last the panel was complete and sworn. The defendant was so little known that this was a simple matter.

The witnesses for the state were then called and sworn. They consisted of the coroner, the physician who had examined the wound, and others, including Gen. Evan, Virdow and Royson. Gen. Evan and Virdow had also been summoned by the defense.

As Royson took the oath it was observed that he was slightly pale and embarrassed, but this was attributed to the fact of his recent conflict and the eager state of the great crowd. No man in the room kept such watch upon him as Barksdale; never once did he take his eyes from the scarred face. Witnesses for the defense were then called—Gen. Evan and Virdow. They had taken the oath. The defense demanded that witnesses for the state be sent out of the room until called. As Royson was rising to comply with the requirement common in such cases Dabney stood up and said:

"Before Mr. Royson goes out, may it please your honor, I would respectfully ask of the solicitor what it is he expects to prove by him?"

"We expect to prove, your honor, that Mr. Royson wrote a certain letter which charged the prisoner with being a man of mixed blood, and that Rita Morgan, the woman who was killed, was the woman in question, and

the only authority; an important point in the case. Mr.
Royson, I should say, is here by subpoena only and occu-
pying a very delicate situation, since he was afterward,
by public report, engaged in a conflict with the prisoner,
growing out of the publication of that letter."

"The solicitor is unnecessarily prolix, your honor. I
asked the question to withdraw our demand in his case
as a matter of courtesy to a member of the bar." Royson
bowed and resumed his seat.

"I now ask," said Dabney, "a like courtesy in behalf of
Gen. Evan and Prof. Virdow, witnesses for both state and
defense." This was readily granted.

There was no demurrer to the indictment. The solicitor advanced before the jury and read the document,
word for word. "We expect to prove, gentlemen of the
jury, that the dead woman, named in this indictment,
was for many years housekeeper for the late John Morgan, and more recently for the defendant in this case,
Edward Morgan; that she resided upon the premises with
him and his cousin, Gerald Morgan; that on a certain
night, to wit, the date named in the indictment, she was
murdered by being struck in the head with some blunt
implement, and that she was discovered almost immediately thereafter by a witness; that there was no one with
the deceased at the time of her death but the defendant,
Edward Morgan, and that he, only, had a motive for her
death—namely, the suppression of certain facts, or certain publicly alleged facts, which she alone possessed;
that after her death, which was sudden, he failed to notify
the coroner, but permitted the body to be buried without
examination. And upon these facts, we say, the defendant is guilty of murder. The coroner will please take
the stand."

The officer named appeared and gave in his testimony.
He had, some days after the burial of the woman, Rita
Morgan, received a hint from an anonymous letter that
foul play was suspected in the case, and acting under advice, had caused the body to be disinterred and he had
held an inquest upon it, with the result as expressed in
the verdict, which he proceeded to read, and which was
then introduced as evidence. The witness was turned

over to the defense; they consulted and announced "no questions."

The next witness was the physician who examined the wound. He testified to the presence of a wound in the back of the head that crushed the skull and was sufficient to have caused death. Dabney asked of this witness if there was much of a wound in the scalp, and the reply was "No."

"Was there any blood visible?"

"No." The defense had no other questions for this officer, but announced that they reserved the right to recall him if the case required it.

The next witness was Virdow. He had seen the body after death, but had not examined the back of the head; had seen a small cut upon the temple, which the defendant had explained to him was made by her falling against the glass in the conservatory. There was a pane broken at the point indicated.

And then Evan was put up.

"Gen. Evan," asked the solicitor, "where were you upon the night that Rita Morgan died?"

"At the residence of Edward Morgan, sir."

"Where were you when you first discovered the death of Rita Morgan?"

"Gentlemen of the jury, at the time indicated, I was standing in the glass-room occupied by the late Gerald Morgan, in the residence of the defendant in this county ———"

"And state?" interrupted the solicitor.

"And state. I was standing by the bedside of Gerald Morgan, who was ill. I was deeply absorbed in thought and perfectly oblivious to my surroundings, I suppose. I am certain that Edward Morgan was in the room with me. I was aroused by hearing him cry out and then discovered that the door leading into the shrubbery was open. I ran out and found him near the head of the woman."

"Did you notice any cuts or signs of blood?"

"I noticed only a slight cut upon the forehead."

"Did you examine her for other wounds?"

"I did not. I understood then that she had, in a fit of

some kind, fallen against the glass, and that seeing her
from within Mr. Morgan had run out and picked her up."

"Did you hear any sound of breaking glass?"

"I think I did. I cannot swear to it; my mind was
completely absorbed at that time. There was a broken
glass at the place pointed out by him."

"That night—pointed out that night?"

"No. I believe some days later."

"Did you hear voices?"

"I heard some one say 'They lied!' and then I heard
Edward Morgan cry aloud. Going out I found him by
the dead body of the woman."

The defense cross-questioned.

"You do not swear, Gen. Evan, that Mr. Morgan was
not in the room at the time the woman Rita was seized
with sudden illness?"

"I do not. It was my belief then, and is now——"

"Stop," said the solicitor.

"Confine yourself to facts only," said the court.

"You are well acquainted with Mr. Morgan?"

"As well as possible in the short time I have known
him."

"What is his character?"

"He is a gentleman and as brave as any man I ever
saw on the field of battle." There was slight applause as
the general came down, but it was for the general himself.

"Mr. Royson will please take the stand," said the solicitor. "You were the author of the letter concerning the
alleged parentage of Edward Morgan, which was published in an extra in this city a few weeks since?" Royson bowed slightly.

"From whom did you get your information?"

"From Rita Morgan," he said, calmly. There was a
breathless silence for a moment and then an angry murmur in the great audience. All eyes were fixed upon
Edward, who had grown pale, but he maintained his
calmness. The astounding statement had filled him with
a sickening horror. Not until that moment did he fully
comprehend the extent of the enmity cherished against
him by the witness. On the face of Barksdale descended
a look as black as night. He did not, however, move a
muscle,

"You say that Rita Morgan told you—when?"

"About a week previous. She declared that her own son had secured his rights at last. I had been consulted by her soon after John Morgan's death, looking to the protection of those rights, she being of the opinion that Gerald Morgan would inherit. When it was found that this defendant here had inherited she called, paid my fee and made the statement as given."

"Why did you fight a duel with the defendant, then—knowing, or believing you knew, his base parentage?"

"I was forced to do so by the fact that I was challenged direct and no informant demanded; and by the fact that my witness was dead; also by the further fact that while my friends were discussing my situation, Gen. Evan, acting under a mistaken idea, vouched for him."

These ingenuous answers took away the general's breath. He had never anticipated such plausible lies. Even Dabney was for the moment bewildered. Edward could scarcely restrain his emotion and horror. As a matter of fact, Rita was not dead when the challenge was accepted. Royson had lied under oath!

"The witness is with you," said the solicitor, with just a tinge of sarcasm in his tones.

"Were the statements of Rita Morgan in writing?" asked Dabney.

"No."

"Then, may it please your honor, I move to rule them out." A debate followed. The statements were ruled out. Royson was suffered to descend, subject to recall.

"The state closes," said the prosecuting officer.

Then came the sensation of the day.

The crowd and the bar were wondering what the defense would attempt with no witnesses, when Dabney arose.

"May it please your honor, we have now a witness, not here when the case was called, whom we desire to bring in and have sworn. We will decide about introducing him within a few moments and there is one other witness telegraphed for who has just reached the city. We ask leave to introduce him upon his arrival." And then turning to the sheriff, he whispered directions. The sher-

iff went to the hall and returned with a negro. Royson
was engaged in conversation, leaning over the back of
his chair and with his face averted. The witness was
sworn and took the stand facing the crowd. A murmur
of surprise ran about the room, for there, looking out
upon them, was the well-known face of Slippery Dick.
The next proceedings were irregular but dramatic. Little Dabney drew himself up to his full height and shouted
in a shrill voice:

"Look at that man, gentlemen of the jury." At the
same time his finger was pointed at Royson. All eyes
were at once fixed upon that individual. His face was as
chalk and the red scar across the nose flamed as so much
fiery paint. His eyes were fastened on the witness with
such an expression of fear and horror that those near him
shuddered and drew back slightly. And as he gazed his
left hand fingered at his collar and presently, with sudden
haste, tore away the black cravat. Then he made an effort to leave, but Barksdale arose and literally hurled him
back in his chair. The court rapped loudly.

"I fine you $50, Mr. Barksdale. Take your seat!"

Dick, unabashed, met that wild, pleading, threatening,
futile gaze of Royson, who was now but half-conscious
of the proceedings.

"Tell the jury, do you know this man?" shouted the
shrill voice again, the finger still pointing to Royson.

"Yes, sah; dat's Mr. Royson."

"Were you ever hired by him?"

"Yes, sah."

"When—the last time?"

" 'Bout three weeks ago."

"To do what?"

"Open 'er grave."

"Whose grave?"

"Rita Morgan's."

"And what else?"

There was intense silence; Dick twisted uneasily.

"And what else?" repeated Dabney.

"Knock her in de head."

"Did you do it?"

"Yes, sah,"

"Where did you knock her in the head?"

"In de back of de head."

"Hard?"

"Hard enough to break her skull."

"Did you see Mr. Gerald Morgan that night?"

"Yes, sah."

"Where?"

"Downtown, jus' fo' I tole Mr. Royson 'all right.' "

"Where did you next see him?"

"After he was killed by de lightnin'."

"The witness is with you," said Dabney, the words ringing out in triumph. He faced the solicitor defiantly. His questions had followed each other with astounding rapidity and the effect on every hearer was profound. The solicitor was silent; his eyes were upon Royson. Some one had handed the latter a glass of water, which he was trying to drink.

"I have no questions," said the solicitor, slowly and gravely.

"You can come down, Dick." The negro stepped down and started out. He passed close to Royson, who was standing in the edge of the middle aisle. Their eyes met. It may have been pure devilishness or simply nervous facial contortion, but at that moment the negro's face took on a grin. Whatever the cause, the effect was fatal to him. The approach of the negro had acted upon the wretched Royson like a maddening stimulant. At sight of that diabolical countenance, he seized him with his left hand and stabbed him frantically a dozen times before he could be prevented. With a moan of anguish the negro fell dead, bathing the scene in blood.

A great cry went up from the spectators and not until the struggling lawyer and the bloody corpse had been dragged out did the court succeed in enforcing order.

The solicitor went up and whispered to the judge, who nodded immediately, but before he announced that a verdict of acquittal would be allowed, the defendant's attorneys drew him aside, and made an appeal to him to let them proceed, as a mere acquittal was not full justice to the accused.

Then the defense put up the ex-reporter and by him

proved the procurement by Royson of the libels and his authorship and gave his connection with the affair from the beginning, which was the reception of an anonymous card informing him that Royson held such information.

Gen. Evan then testified that Rita died while Royson's second was standing at the front door at Ilexhurst, with Royson's note in his pocket.

The jury was briefly charged by the court and without leaving the box returned a verdict of not guilty. The tragedy and dramatic denouement had wrought the audience to the highest pitch of excitement. The revulsion of feeling was indicated by one immense cheer, and Edward found himself surrounded by more friends than he thought he had acquaintances, who shook his hand and congratulated him. Barksdale stalked through the crowd and laid $50 upon the clerk's desk. Smiling up at the court he said:

"Will your honor not make it a thousand? It is too cheap!"

But that good-natured dignitary replied:

"The fine is remitted. You couldn't help it."

CHAPTER L.

A WOMAN'S WIT CONQUERS.

Cambia was greatly disturbed by the sudden departure of the Montjoys. She shut herself up and refused all visitors. Was the great-hearted yet stern Cambia ill or distressed? The maid did not know.

She had called for the "Figaro," to see the passenger list of the steamer. The names were there; the steamer had sailed. And then as she sat gazing upon the sheet another caught her attention in an adjoining column, "Gaspard Levigne." It was in the body of an advertisement, which read:

"Reward—A liberal reward will be paid for particulars of the death of Gaspard Levigne, which occurred recently in Paris. Additional reward will be paid for the address

of the present owner of the Stradivarius violin lately
owned by the said Gaspard Levigne and the undersigned
will buy said violin at full value, if for sale."

Following this was a long and minute description of
the instrument. The advertisement was signed by Louis
Levigne, Breslau, Silesia.

Cambia read and reread this notice with pale face and
gave herself up to reflection. She threw off the weight of
the old troubles which had swarmed over her again and
prepared for action. Three hours later she was on her
way to Berlin; the next day found her in Breslau. A few
moments later and she was entering the house of the ad-
vertiser.

In a dark, old-fashioned living-room, a slender, gray-
haired man came forward rather suspiciously to meet her.
She knew his face despite the changes of nearly thirty
years; he was the only brother of her husband and one
of her chief persecutors in those unhappy days. It was
not strange that in this tall, queenlike woman, trained to
face great audiences without embarrassment, he should
fail to recognize the shy and lonely little American who
had invaded the family circle. He bowed, unconsciously
feeling the influence of her fine presence and command-
ing eyes.

"You, I suppose, are Louis Levigne, who advertised
recently for information of Gaspard Levigne?" she said.

"Yes, madame; my brother was the unfortunate Gaspard. We think him dead. Know you anything of him?"

"I knew him years ago; I was then a singer and he was
my accompanist. Recently he died." The face of the
man lighted up with a strange gleam. She regarded him
curiously and continued: "Died poor and friendless."

"Ah, indeed! He should have communicated with us;
he was not poor and would not have been friendless."

"What do you mean?"

"You know, madame, the new age is progressive. Some
lands we had in northern Silesia, worthless for 200 years,
have developed iron and a company has purchased." The
woman smiled sadly.

"Too late," she said, "for poor Gaspard. This is why
you have advertised?"

"Yes, madame. There can be no settlement until we have proofs of Gaspard's death."

"You are the only heir aside from Gaspard?"

"Yes, madame." The count grew restless under these questions, but circumstances compelled courtesy to this visitor.

"Excuse my interest, count, but Gaspard was my friend and I knew something of his affairs. Did he not leave heirs?" The man replied with gesture, in which was mingled every shade of careless contempt that could be expressed.

"There was a woman—a plaything of Gaspard's calling herself his wife—but they parted nearly thirty years ago. He humored her and then sent her back where she came from—America, I believe."

"I am more than ever interested, count. Gaspard did not impress me as vicious."

"Oh, well, follies of youth, call them. Gaspard was wild; he first left here because of a mock-marriage escapade; when two years after he came back with this little doll we supposed it was another case; at any rate, Gaspard was once drunk enough to boast that she could never prove the marriage." Cambia could restrain herself only with desperate efforts. These were knife blows.

"Were there no heirs?"

"I have never heard. It matters little here. But, madame, you know of Gaspard's death; can you not give me the facts so that I may obtain proofs?" She looked at him steadily.

"I saw him die."

"Ah, that simplifies it all," said the count, pleasantly. "Will you be kind enough to go before an attesting officer and complete the proofs? You have answered the advertisement—do I insult you by speaking of reward?" He looked critically at her simple but elegant attire and hesitated.

"No. But I do not care for money. I will furnish positive proof of the death of Gaspard Levigne for the violin mentioned in the advertisement." The man was now much astounded.

"But, madame, it is an heirloom; that is why I have advertised for it. I have not got it."

"Then get it! And let me receive it direct from the hands of the present holder or I will not furnish the proofs." Some doubt of the woman's sanity flashed over the count.

"I have already explained, madame, that it was an heirloom—"

"And I have shown you that I do not consider that as important."

"But of what use can it possibly be to you? There are other Cremonas I will buy—"

"I want this one because it is the violin of Gaspard Levigne, and he was my husband."

The count nearly leaped from the floor.

"When did he marry you, madame?"

"That is a long story; but he did; we were bohemians in Paris. I am heir to his interests in these mines, but I care little for that—very little. I am independent. My husband's violin is my one wish now." The realization of how completely he had been trapped did not add additional courtesy to the brusque old man.

"You married him! I presume you ascertained that the American wife was dead?"

"You have informed me that the American was not his wife."

"But she was, and if she is living to-day madame's claims are very slender."

"You speak positively!"

"I do. I saw the proofs. We would not have given the girl any recognition without them, knowing Gaspard's former escapade."

"Then," said the woman, her face lighting up with a sudden joy, and growing stern again instantly, "then you lied just now, you cowardly hound!"

"Madame!" The count had retreated behind a chair and looked anxiously at the bell, but she was in the way.

"You lied, sir, I say. I am the wife, and now the widow, of Gaspard Levigne, but not a second wife. I am that 'plaything,' as you called her, the American, armed now with a knowledge of my rights and your treachery. You may well shiver and grow pale, sir; I am no longer the trembling child you terrified with brutality, but a woman who could buy your family with its mines thrown in, and not suffer because of the bad investment. From this room, upon the information you have given, I go to put my case in the hands of lawyers and establish my claim. It is not share and share in this country; my husband was the first born, and I am his heir!"

"My God!"

"It is too late to call upon God; He is on my side now! I came to you, sir, a woman to be loved, not a pauper. My father was more than a prince in his country. His slaves were numbered by the hundreds, and his lands would have sufficed for a dozen of your counts. I was crushed and my life was ruined, and my husband turned against me. But he repented—he repented. There was no war between Gaspard and I when he died." The man looked on and believed her.

"Madame," he said, humbly, "has been wronged. For myself, it matters little, this new turn of affairs, but I have others." She had been looking beyond him into space.

"And yet," she said, "it is the violin I would have. It was the violin that first spoke our love; it is a part of me; I would give my fortune to possess it again." He was looking anxiously at her, not comprehending this passion, but hoping much from it.

"And how much will you give?"

"I will give the mines and release all claims against you and your father's estate."

"Alas, madame, I can give you the name of the holder of that violin but not the violin itself. You can make terms with him, and I will pay whatever price is demanded."

"How will I know you are not deceiving me?"

"Madame is harsh, but she will be convinced if she knows the handwriting of her—husband."

"It is agreed," she said, struggling to keep down her excitement. Count Levigne reached the coveted bell and in a few minutes secured a notary, who drew up a formal agreement between the two parties. Cambia then

gave an affidavit setting forth the death of Gaspard Lavigne in proper form for use in court.. Count Levigne
took from his desk an envelope.

"You have read my advertisement, madame. It was
based on this:

"Count L. Lavigne, Breslau: When you receive this
I will be dead. Make no effort to trace me; it will be
useless; my present name is an assumed one. We have
been enemies many years, but everything changes in the
presence of death, and I do not begrudge you the pleasure of knowing that your brother is beyond trouble and
want forever and the title yours. The Cremona, to which
I have clung even when honor was gone, I have given to
a young American named Morgan, who has made my
life happier in its winter than it was in its summer.

"Gaspard Levigne."

The count watched the reader curiously as she examined the letter. Her face was white, but her hand did
not tremble as she handed back the letter.

"It is well," she said. "I am satisfied. Good-morning,
gentlemen."

In Paris, Cambia's mind was soon made up. She privately arranged for an indefinite absence, and one day she
disappeared. It was the sensation of the hour; the newspapers got hold of it, and all Paris wondered.

There had always been a mystery in the life of Cambia.
No man had ever invaded it beyond the day when she
put herself in the hands of a manager and laid the foundation for her world-wide success upon the lyric stage.

And then Paris forgot; and only the circle of her
friends watched and waited.

Meanwhile the swift steamer had carried Mrs. Gaspard
Levigne across the Atlantic and she had begun that journey into the southland, once the dream of her youth—
the going back to father and to friends!

The swift train carried her by towns and villages gorgeous with new paint and through cities black with the
smoke of factories. The negroes about the stations were
not of the old life, and the rushing, curt and slangy young

20

men who came and went upon the train belonged to a new age.

The farms, with faded and dingy houses, poor fences, and uncared-for fields and hedges, swept past like some bad dream. All was different; not thirty years but a century had rolled its changes over the land since her girlhood.

And then comes the alighting. Here was the city, different and yet the same. But where were the great family carriage, with folding steps and noble bays, the driver in livery, the footman to hold the door? Where were father and friends? No human being came to greet her.

She went to the hotel, locked herself in her room, and then Cambia gave way for the first time in a generation to tears.

But she was eminently a practical woman. She had not come to America to weep. The emotion soon passed. At her request a file of recent papers was laid before her, and she went through them carefully. She found that which she had not looked for

CHAPTER LI.

DEATH OF COL. MONTJOY.

It was the morning succeeding the trial, one of those southern days that the late fall steals from summer and tempts the birds to sing in the woodlands. Gen. Evan had borne Virdow and Edward in triumph to the Cedars and, after a good night's sleep and a restless hour following breakfast, Edward had ridden over to the hall, leaving the two old men together. Virdow interested his host with accurate descriptions of the great battles between the Germans and the French; and Evan in turn gave him vivid accounts of the mighty Virginia struggles between federals and confederates.

When they finally came to Edward as a topic the

German was eloquent. He placed him beside himself in learning and ahead of all amateurs as artist and musician.

"Mr. Morgan agreed with me in his estimate of Edward," Virdow said. "They were warm friends. Edward reciprocated the affection bestowed upon him; in Europe they traveled much—"

"Of what Mr. Morgan do you speak?" The general was puzzled.

"The elder, Mr. John Morgan, I think. But what am I saying? I mean Abingdon."

"Abingdon? I do not know him." Virdow reflected a moment.

"Abingdon was the name by which Edward knew John Morgan in Europe. They met annually and were inseparable companions."

"John Morgan—our John Morgan?"

"Yes. I am told he was very eccentric, and this was probably a whim. But it enabled him to study the character of his relative. He seems to have been satisfied, and who wouldn't?"

"You astound me. I had never heard that John Morgan went to Europe. I did hear that he went annually to Canada, for the summer months; that is all."

"Edward never knew of the connection until he came here and saw a picture of John Morgan, drawn by Gerald. We both recognized it instantly." Evan was silent, thinking upon this curious information. At last he asked:

"Was Edward Mr. Morgan's only intimate companion?"

"The only one."

"Did you ever hear why Mr. Morgan concealed his identity under an assumed name?"

"No. We did not connect Abingdon with John Morgan until letters were returned with information that Abingdon was dead; and then Gerald drew his picture from memory."

And as these two old gentlemen chattered about him Edward himself was approaching the Montjoys.

He found Mary upon the porch; his horse's feet had announced his coming. Her face was flushed and a glad light shone in her eyes. She gave him her hand without words; she had intended expressing her pleasure and her congratulations, but when the time came the words were impossible.

"You have been anxious," he said, reading her silence.

"Yes," she replied; "I could not doubt you, but there are so many things involved, and I had no one to talk with. It was a long suspense, but women have to learn such lessons," and then she added, seeing that he was silent: "It was the most unhappy day of my life; papa was gone, and poor mamma's eyes have troubled her so much. She has bandaged them again and stays in her room. The day seemed never-ending. When papa came he was pale and haggard, and his face deceived me. I thought that something had gone wrong—some mistake had occurred and you were in trouble, but papa was ill, and the news—" She turned her face away suddenly, feeling the tears starting.

Edward drew her up to a settee under a spreading oak, and seating himself beside her told her much of his life's story—his doubts, his hopes, his fears. She held her breath as he entered upon his experience at Ilexhurst and Gerald's life and identity were dwelt upon.

"This," said he at last, "is your right to know. It is due to me. I cannot let you misjudge the individual. While I am convinced, that does not make a doubt a fact and on it I cannot build a future. You have my history, and you know that in the heart of Edward Morgan you alone have any part. The world holds no other woman for me, nor ever will; but there is the end. If I stayed by you the day would come when this love would sweep away every resolution, every sense of duty, every instinct of my mind, except the instinct to love you, and for this reason I have come to say that until life holds no mystery for Edward Morgan he will be an exile from you."

The girl's head was sunk upon her arms as it rested upon the settee. She did not lift her face. What could she answer to such a revelation, such a declaration? After a while he ceased to walk the gravel floor of their arbor, and stood by her. Unconsciously he let his hand rest upon the brown curls. "This does not mean," he said, very gently, "that I am going away to mope and wear out life in idle regrets. Marion Evan lives; I will find her. And then—and then—if she bids me, I will come back, and with a clean record ask you to be my wife. Answer me, my love; my only love—let me say these words this once—answer me; is this the course that an honorable man should pursue?"

She rose then and faced him proudly. His words had thrilled her soul.

"It is. I could never love you, Edward, if you could offer less. I have no doubt in my mind—none. A woman's heart knows without argument, and I know that you will come to me some day. God be with you till we meet again—and for all time and eternity. This will be my prayer."

Without object, the silent couple, busy with their thoughts, entered the sitting-room. The colonel was sitting in his arm-chair, his paper dropped from his listless hand, his eyes closed. The Duchess in his lap had fallen asleep, holding the old open-faced watch and its mystery of the little boy within who cracked hickory nuts. They made a pretty picture—youth and old age, early spring and late winter. Mary lifted her hand warningly.

"Softly," she said; "they sleep; don't disturb them." Edward looked closely into the face of the old man, and then to the surprise of the girl placed his arm about her waist.

"Do not cry out," he said; "keep calm and remember that the little mamma's health—"

"What do you mean?" she said, looking with wonder into his agitated face as she sought gently to free herself. "Have you forgotten—"

"This is sleep indeed—but the sleep of eternity."

She sprang from him with sudden terror and laid her hand upon the cold forehead of her father. For an instant she stared into his face, with straining eyes, and then with one frightful scream she sank by his side, uttering his name in agonized tones.

Edward strove tearfully to calm her; it was too late. Calling upon husband and daughter frantically, Mrs. Montjoy rushed from her room into the presence of

death. She was blindfolded, but with unerring instinct
she found the stilled form and touched the dead face.
The touch revealed the truth; with one quick motion
she tore away the bandages from her face, and then in
sudden awe the words fell from her:

"I am blind!" Mary had risen to her side and was
clinging to her, and Edward had assisted, fearing she
might fall to the floor. But with the consciousness of
her last misfortune had soon come calmness. She heed-
ed not the cries of the girl appealing to her, but knelt
with her white face lifted and said, simply:

"Dear Father, Thou art merciful; I have not seen him
dead! Blest forever be Thy holy name!" Edward turned
his back and stood with bowed head. The woman knelt,
the silence broken now only by the sobs of the daughter.
Still sleeping in the lap of the dead, her chubby hand
clasping the wonderful toy, was the Duchess, and at her
feet the streaming sunlight in golden splendor. The little
boy came to the door riding the old man's gold-headed
cane for a horse and carrying the cow horn, which he
had pushed from its nail upon the porch.

"Grandpa, ain't it time to blow the horn?" he said.
"Grandma, why don't grandpa wake up?" She drew him
to her breast and silenced his queries.

And still with a half-smile upon his patrician face—the
face that women and children loved and all men honored
—sat the colonel; one more leaf from the old south
blown to earth.

The little girl awoke at last, sat up and caught sight
of the watch.

"Look, gamma. Little boy in deir cackin' hickeynut,"
and she placed the jewel against the ear of the kneeling
woman.

That peculiarly placid expression, driven away in the
moment of dissolution, had returned to the dead man;
he seemed to hear the Duchess prattle and the familiar
demand for music upon the horn.

Isam had responded to the outcry and rushed in.
With a sob he had stood by the body a moment and then
gone out shaking his head and moaning. And then, as
they waited, there rang out upon the clear morning air

the plantation bell—not the merry call to labor and the sweet summons to rest, which every animal on the plantation knew and loved, but a solemn tolling, significant in its measured volume.

And over the distant fields where the hands were finishing their labors, the solemn sounds came floating. Old Peter lifted his head. "Who dat ring dat bell dis time er day?" he said, curiously; and then, under the lessening volume of the breeze, the sound fell to almost silence, to rise again stronger than before and float with sonorous meaning.

At long intervals they had heard it. It always marked a change in their lives.

One or two of the men began to move doubtfully toward the house, and others followed, increasing their pace as the persistent alarm was sounded, until some were running. And thus they came to where old Isam tolled the bell, his eyes brimming over with tears.

"Old marster's gone! Old marster's gone!" he called to the first, and the words went down the line and were carried to the "quarters," which soon gave back the death chant from excited women. The negroes edged into the yard and into the hall, and then some of the oldest into the solemn presence of the dead, gazing in silence upon the sad, white face and closed eyes.

Then there was a tumult in yard and hall; a shuffling of feet announced a newcomer. Mammy Phyllis, walking with the aid of a staff, entered the room and stood by the side of the dead man. Every voice was still; here was the woman who had nursed him and who had raised him; hers was the right to a superior grief. She gazed long and tenderly into the face of her foster-child and master and turned away, but she came again and laid her withered hand upon his forehead. This time she went, to come no more. In the room of the bereaved wife she took her seat, to stay a silent comforter for days. Her own grief found never a voice or a tear.

One by one the negroes followed her example; they passed in front of the sleeper, looked steadily, silently, into his face and went out. Some touched him with the tips of their fingers, doubtfully, pathetically. For them, although not realized fully, it was the passing of the old regime. It was the first step into that life where none but strangers dwelt, where there was no sympathy, no understanding. Some would drift into cities to die of disease, some to distant cabins, to grow old alone! One day the last of the slaves would lie face up and the old south be no more.

None was left but one. Edward came at last and stood before his host. Long and thoughtfully he gazed and then passed out. He had place in neither the old nor the new. But the dead man had been his friend. He would not forget it.

––––––––––

CHAPTER LII.

THE ESCAPE OF AMOS ROYSON.

When Amos Royson's senses returned to him he was standing in the middle of a room in the county jail. The whirl in his head, wherein had mingled the faces of men, trees, buildings and patches of sky illumined with flashes of intensest light and vocal with a multitude of cries—these, the rush of thoughts and the pressure upon his arteries, had ceased. He looked about him in wonder. Was it all a dream? From the rear of the building, where in their cage the negro prisoners were confined, came a mighty chorus, "Swing low, sweet chariot," making more intense the silence of his own room. That was not of a dream, nor the bare prison walls, nor the barred windows. His hands nervously clutching his lapels touched something cold and wet. He lifted them to the light; they were bloody! He made no outcry when he saw this, but stood a long minute gazing upon them, his face wearing in that half-shadow a confession of guilt. And in that minute all the facts of the day stood forth, clear cut and distinct, and his situation unfolded itself. He was a murderer, a perjurer and conspirator. Not a human being in all that city would dare to call him friend.

The life of this man had been secretly bad; he had deluded himself with maxims and rules of gentility. He was, in fact, no worse at that moment in jail than he had been at heart for years. But now he had been suddenly exposed; the causes he had set in motion had produced a natural but unexpected climax, and it is a fact that in all the world there was no man more surprised to find that Amos Royson was a villain than Royson himself. He was stunned at first; then came rage; a blind, increasing rebellion of a spirit unused to defeat. He threw himself against the facts that hemmed him in as a wild animal against its cage, but he could not shake them. They were still facts. He was doomed by them. Then a tide of grief overwhelmed him; his heart opened back into childhood; he plunged face down upon his bed; silent, oblivious to time, and to the jailer's offer of food returning no reply. Despair had received him! A weapon at hand then would have ended the career of Amos Royson.

Time passed. No human being from the outer world called upon him. Counsel came at last, in answer to his request, and a line of defense had been agreed upon. Temporary insanity would be set up in the murder case, but even if this were successful, trials for perjury and conspiracy must follow. The chances were against his acquittal in any, and the most hopeful view he could take was imprisonment for life.

For life! How often, as solicitor, he had heard the sentence descend upon the poor wretches he prosecuted. And not one was as guilty as he. This was the deliberate verdict of the fairest jury known to man—the convicting instincts of the mind that tries its baser self.

At the hands of the jailer Royson received the best possible treatment. He was given the commodious front room and allowed every reasonable freedom. This officer was the sheriff's deputy, and both offices were political plums. The prisoner had largely shaped local politics and had procured for him the sheriff's bondsmen. Office-holders are not ungrateful—when the office is elective.

The front room meant much to a prisoner; it gave him a glimpse into the free, busy world outside, with its

seemingly happy men and women, with its voices of
school children and musical cries of street venders.

This spot, the window of his room, became Royson's
life. He stood there hour after hour, only withdrawing
in shame when he saw a familiar face upon the street.
And standing there one afternoon, just before dark, he
beheld Annie's little vehicle stop in front of the jail.
She descended, and as she came doubtfully forward she
caught sight of his face. She was dressed in deep black
and wore a heavy crepe veil. There was a few minutes'
delay, and then the room door opened and Annie was
coming slowly toward him, her veil thrown back, her
face pale and her hand doubtfully extended. He looked
upon her coldly without changing his position.

"Are you satisfied?" he said, at length, when she stood
silent before him.

Whatever had been the emotion of the woman, it, too,
passed with the sound of his sentence.

"I would not quarrel with you, Amos, and I might do
so if I answered that question as it deserves. I have but
a few minutes to stop here and will not waste them upon
the past. The question is now as to the future. Have
you any plans?"

"None," he replied, with a sneer. "I am beyond plans.
Life is not worth living if I were out, and the game is
now not worth the candle." The woman stood silent.

"What are your chances for acquittal?" she asked, after
a long silence.

"Acquittal! Absolutely none! Life itself may by a
hard struggle be saved. After that, it is the asylum or
the mines."

"And then?"

"And then? Well, then I shall ask my loving cousin
again to bring me a powder. I will remind her once
more that no Royson ever wore chains or a halter, however much they may have deserved them. And for the
sake of her children she will consent." She walked to the
corridor door and listened and then came back to him.
He smiled and stretched out his hand.

"Amos," she whispered, hurriedly; "God forgive me,
but I have brought it. I am going to New York to-

morrow, and the chance may not come again.   Remember, it is at your request."   She was fumbling nervously at the bosom of her dress.   "The morphine I could not get without attracting attention, but the chloroform I had. I give it to you for use only when life—"   He had taken the bottle and was quietly looking upon the white liquid.

"I thank you, cousin," he said, quietly, with a ghastly little laugh.   "I have no doubt but that I can be spared from the family gatherings and that in days to come perhaps some one will occasionally say 'poor Amos,' when my fate is recalled.   Thanks, a thousand thanks!   Strange, but the thought of death actually gives me new life."   He looked upon her critically a moment and then a new smile dawned upon his face.

"Ah," he said, "your note about Morgan; it will be unfortunate if that ever comes to light.   You were not smart, Annie.   You could have bought that with this bottle."   She flushed in turn and bit her lip.   The old Annie was still dominant.

"It would have been better since Mr. Morgan is to be my brother-in-law.   Still if there is no love between us it will not matter greatly.   Mary seems to be willing to furnish all the affection he will need."

"Where is he?" he asked, hoarsely, not attempting to disguise his suffering.   She was now relentless.

"Oh, at Ilexhurst, I suppose.   The general is to care for the old German until the household is arranged again and everything made ready for the bride."

"Is the marriage certain?"

She smiled cheerfully.   "Oh, yes.   It is to take place soon, and then they are going to Europe for a year." And then as, white with rage, he steadied himself against the window, she said: "Mary insisted upon writing a line to you; there it is.   If you can get any comfort from it, you are welcome."

He took the note and thrust it in his pocket, never removing his eyes from her face. · A ray had fallen into the blackness of his despair.   It grew and brightened until it lighted his soul with a splendor that shone from his eyes and trembled upon every lineament of his face. Not a word had indicated its presence.   It was the silent expression of a hope and a desperate resolve. The woman saw it and drew back in alarm. A suspicion that he was suddenly insane came upon her mind, and she was alone, helpless and shut in with a maniac. A wild desire to scream and flee overwhelmed her; she turned toward the door and in a minute would have been gone.

But the man had read her correctly. He seized her, clapped his hand over her mouth, lifted her as he would a child and thrust her backward on the bed. Before she could tear the grip from her mouth, he had drawn the cork with his teeth and drenched the pillow-case with chloroform. There was one faint cry as he moved his hand, but the next instant the drug was in her nostrils and lungs. She struggled frantically, then faintly, and then lay powerless at the mercy of the man bending over her.

Hardly more than two minutes had passed, but in that time Amos Royson was transformed. He had a chance for life and that makes men of cowards. He stripped away the outer garments of the woman and arrayed himself in them, adding the bonnet and heavy veil, and then turned to go. He was cool now and careful. He went to the bed and drew the cover over the prostrate form. He had occupied the same place in the same attitude for hours. The jailer would come, offer supper from the door and go away. He would, if he got out, have the whole night for flight. And he would need it. The morn might bring no waking to the silent form. The thought chilled his blood, but it also added speed to his movements. He drew off the pillow-case, rolled it into a ball and dropped it out of the window. He had seen the woman approach with veil down and handkerchief to her face. It was his cue. He bent his head, pressed his handkerchief to his eyes beneath the veil and went below. The jailer let the bent, sob-shaken figure in and then out of the office. The higher class seldom came there. He stood bareheaded until the visitor climbed into the vehicle and drove away.

It was with the greatest difficulty only that Royson restrained himself and suffered the little mare to keep a moderate pace. Fifteen minutes ago a hopeless prisoner,

and now free! Life is full of surprises. But where?
Positively the situation had shaped itself so rapidly he
had not the slightest plan in mind. He was free and
hurrying into the country without a hat and dressed in a
woman's garb!

The twilight had deepened into gloom. How long
would it be before pursuit began? And should he keep on
the disguise? He slipped out of it to be ready for rapid
flight, and then upon a second thought put it on again.
He might be met and recognized. His whole manner
had undergone a change; he was now nervous and excited, and the horse, unconsciously urged along, was
running at full speed. A half-hour at that rate would
bear him to the hall. Cursing his imprudence, he
checked the animal and drove on more moderately and
finally stopped. He could not think intelligently. Should
he go on to the hall and throw himself upon the mercy
of his connections? They would be bound to save him.
Mary! Ah, Mary! And then the note thrust itself in
mind. With feverish haste he searched for and drew it
out. He tore off the envelope and helped by a flickering
match he read:

"You must have suffered before you could have sinned
so, and I am sorry for you. Believe me, however others
may judge you, there is no resentment but only forgiveness for you in the heart of   Mary."

Then the tumult within him died away. . No man can
say what that little note did for Amos Royson that night.
He would go to her, to this generous girl, and ask her
aid. But Annie! What if that forced sleep should deepen
into death! Who could extricate her? How would
Mary arrange that? She would get Morgan. He could
not refuse her anything. He could not falter when the
family name and family honor were at stake. He could
not let his wife—his wife! A cry burst from the lips
of the desperate man. His wife! Yes, he would go to
him, but not for help. Amos Royson might die or escape
—but the triumph of this man should be shortlived.

The mare began running again; he drew rein with a

violence that brought the animal's front feet high in air
and almost threw her to the ground. A new idea had
been born; he almost shouted over it. He tore off the
woman's garb, dropped it in the buggy, sprang out and
let the animal go. In an instant the vehicle was out of
sight in the dark woods, and Royson was running the
other way. For the idea born in his mind was this:

"Of all the places in the world for me the safest is Ilexhurst—if—" He pressed his hand to his breast. The .
bottle was still safe! And Annie! The horse returning
would lead to her release.

Amos Royson had a general knowledge of the situation at Ilexhurst. At 12 o'clock he entered through the
glass-room and made his way to the body of the house.
He was familiar with the lower floor. The upper he
could guess at. He must first find the occupied room,
and so, taking off his shoes, he noiselessly ascended the
stairway. He passed first into the boy's room and tried
the door to that known as the mother's, but it was
locked. He listened there long and intently, but heard
no sound except the thumping of his own heart. Then
he crossed the hall and there, upon a bed in the front
room, dimly visible in the starlight, was the man he
sought.

The discovery of his victom, helpless and completely
within his power, marked a crisis in the mental progres-
sion of Royson. He broke down and trembled violently,
not from conscience, but from a realization of the fact
that his escape was now an accomplished fact. This
man before him disposed of, Ilexhurst was his for an
indefinite length of time. Here he could rest and prepare for a distant flight. No one would come, and
should any one come, why, the house was unoccupied.
The mood passed; he went back to the hall, drew out
his handkerchief and saturated it with liquid from the
bottle in his pocket. A distant tapping alarmed him,
and he drew deeper into the shadow. Some one seemed
knocking at a rear door. Or was it a rat with a nut in
the wall? All old houses have them. No; it was the
tapping of a friendly tree upon the weather boards, or a
ventilator in the garret. So he reasoned. There came

a strange sensation upon his brain, a sweet, sickening taste in his mouth and dizziness. He cast the cloth far away and rushed to the stairs, his heart beating violently. He had almost chloroformed himself while listening to his coward fears.

The dizziness passed away, but left him unnerved. He dared not walk now. He crawled to the cloth and thence into the room. Near the bed he lifted his head a little and saw the white face of the sleeper turned to him. He raised the cloth and held it ready; there would be a struggle, and it would be desperate. Would he fail? Was he not already weakened? He let it fall gently in front of the sleeper's face, and then inch by inch pushed it nearer. Over his own senses he felt the languor steal-ing; how was it with the other? The long, regular inspi-rations ceased, the man slept profoundly and noiselessly —the first stage of unconsciousness. The man on the floor crawled to the window and laid his pale cheek upon the sill.

How long Royson knelt he never knew. He stood up at last with throbbing temples, but steadier. He went up to the sleeper and shook him—gently at first, then violently. The drug had done its work.

Then came the search for more matches and then light. And there upon the side table, leaning against the wall, was the picture that Gerald had drawn; the face of Mary, severe and noble, the fine eyes gazing straight into his.

He had not thought out his plans. It is true that the house was his for days, if he wished it, but how about the figure upon the bed? Could he occupy that building with such a tenant? It seemed to him the sleeper moved. Quickly wetting the handkerchief again he laid it upon the cold lips, with a towel over it to lessen evaporation. And as he turned, the eyes of the picture followed him. He must have money to assist his escape; the sleeper's clothing was there. He lifted the garments. An irre-sistible power drew his attention to the little table, and there, still fixed upon him, were the calm, proud eyes of the girl. Angrily he cast aside the clothing. The eyes still held him in their power, and now they were scornful.

They seemed to measure and weigh him: Amos Royson, murderer, perjurer, conspirator—thief! The words were spoken somewhere; they became vocal in that still room. Terrified, he looked to the man upon the bed and there he saw the eyes, half-open, fixed upon him and the towel moving above the contemptuous lips. With one bound he passed from the room, down the steps, toward the door. Anywhere to be out of that room, that house!

CHAPTER LIII.

HOW A DEBT WAS PAID.

On went the spirited mare to the hall, skillfully avoiding obstructions, and drew up at last before the big gate. She had not been gentle in her approach, and old Isam was out in the night holding her bit and talking to her before she realized that her coming had not been expected.

"De Lord bless yer, horse, whar you be'n an' what you done wid young missus?" Mary was now out on the porch.

"What is it, Isam?"

"For Gawd sake, come hyar, missy. Dis hyar fool horse done come erlong back 'thout young missus, an' I spec' he done los' her out in de road somewhar—" Mary caught sight of the dress and bonnet and greatly alarmed drew them out. She could not think of a solution of the mystery. What could have happened? Why was Annie's bonnet and clothing in the buggy? For an instant her heart stood still.

Her presence of mind soon returned. Her mother had retired, and so, putting the maid on guard, she came out and with Isam beside her turned the horse's head back toward the city. But as mile after mile passed nothing explained the mystery. There was no dark form by the roadside. At no place did the intelligent animal scent blood and turn aside. It was likely that Annie had gone to spend the night with a friend, as she declared she would if the hour were too late to enter the jail. But the clothing!

The girl drove within sight of the prison, but could not bring herself, at that hour, to stop there. She passed on to Annie's friends. She had not been there. She tried others with no better success. And now, thoroughly convinced that something terrible had occurred, she drove on to Ilexhurst. As the tired mare climbed the hill and Mary saw the light shining from the upper window, she began to realize that the situation was not very much improved. After all, Annie's disappearance might be easily explained and how she would sneer at her readiness to run to Mr. Morgan! It was the thought of a very young girl.

But it was too late to turn back. She drew rein before the iron gate and boldly entered, leaving Isam with the vehicle. She rapidly traversed the walk, ascended the steps and was reaching out for the knocker, when the door was suddenly thrown open and a man ran violently against her. She was almost hurled to the ground, but frightened as she was, it was evident that the accidental meeting had affected the other more. He staggered back into the hall and stood irresolute and white with terror. She came forward amazed and only half-believing the testimony of her senses.

"Mr. Royson!" The man drew a deep breath and put his hand upon a chair, nodding his head. He had for the moment lost the power of speech.

"What does it mean?" she asked. "Why are you—here? Where is Mr. Morgan?" His ghastliness returned. He wavered above the chair and then sank into it. Then he turned his face toward hers in silence. She read something there, as in a book. She did not cry out, but went and caught his arm and hung above him with white face. "You have not—oh, no, you have not—" She could say no more. She caught his hand and looked dumbly upon it. The man drew it away violently as the horror of a memory came upon him.

"Not that way!" he said.

"Ah, not that way! Speak to me, Mr. Royson—tell

21

me you do not mean it—he is not——" The whisper
died out in that dim hall. He turned his face away a moment and then looked back. Lifting his hand he pointed
up the stairway. She left him and staggered up the steps
slowly, painfully, holding by the rail; weighed upon by
the horror above and the horror below. Near the top
she stopped and looked back; the man was watching her
as if fascinated. She went on; he arose and followed her.
He found her leaning against the door afraid to enter;
her eyes riveted upon a form stretched upon the bed, a
cloth over its face; a strange, sweet odor in the air. He
came and paused by her side, probably insane, for he was
smiling now.

"Behold the bridegroom," he said. "Go to him; he is
not dead. He has been waiting for you. Why are you so
late?" She heard only two words clearly. "Not dead!"

"Oh, no," he laughed; "not dead. He only sleeps, with
a cloth and chloroform upon his face. He is not dead!"
With a movement swift as a bounding deer, she sprung
across the room, seized the cloth and hurled it from the
window. Then she caught the sleeper's shoulders and
shook him and wrung his hands and called him by his
name. She added names that her maiden cheeks would
have paled at, and pressed her face to his, kissing the
still and silent lips and moaning piteously.

The man at the door drew away suddenly, went to the
stairway and passed down. No sound was heard now in
the house except the moaning of the girl upstairs. He
put on a hat in the hall below, closed the door cautiously
and prepared to depart as he had come, when again he
paused irresolute. Then he drew from his pocket a
crumpled paper and read it. And there, under that one
jet which fell upon him in the great hall, something was
born that night in the heart of Amos Royson—something
that proved him for the moment akin to the gods. He
lifted his pale face, then almost transformed. The girl
had glided down the steps and was fleeing past him for
succor. He caught her arm.

"Wait," he said, gently. "I will help you!" She
ceased to struggle and looked appealingly into his face.
"I have not much to say, but it is for eternity. The man

upstairs is now in no immediate danger. Mary, I have loved you as I did not believe myself capable of loving any one. It is the glorious spot in the desert of my nature. I have been remorseless with men; it all seemed war to me, a war of Ishmaelites—civilized war is an absurdity. Had you found anything in me to love, I believe it would have made me another man, but you did not. And none can blame you. To-night, for every kind word you have spoken to Amos Royson, for the note you sent him to-day, he will repay you a thousandfold. Come with me." He half-lifted her up the steps and to the room of the sleeper. Then wringing out wet towels he bathed the face and neck of the unconscious man, rubbed the cold wrists and feet and forced cold water into the mouth. It was a doubtful half-hour, but at last the sleeper stirred and moaned. Then Royson paused.

"He will awaken presently. Give me half an hour to get into a bateau on the river and then you may tell him all. That—" he said, after a pause, looking out of the window, through which was coming the distant clamor of bells—"that indicates that Annie has waked and screamed. And now good-by. I could have taken your lover's life." He picked up the picture from the table, kissed it once and passed out.

Mary was alone with her lover. Gradually under her hand consciousness came back and he realized that the face in the light by him was not of dreams but of life itself—that life which, but for her and the gentleness of her woman's heart, would have passed out that night at Ilexhurst.

And as he drifted back again into consciousness under the willows of the creeping river a little boat drifted toward the sea.

Dawn was upon the eastern hills when Mary, with her rescued sister-in-law, crept noiselessly into the hall. It was in New York that the latter read the account of her mortification.

CHAPTER LIV.

THE UNOPENED LETTER.

Soon it became known that Col. Montjoy had gone to his final judgment. Then came the old friends of his young manhood out of their retreats; the country for twenty miles about gave them up to the occasion. They brought with them all that was left of the old times—courtesy, sympathy and dignity.

There were soldiers among them, and here and there an empty sleeve and a scarred face. There was simply one less in their ranks. Another would follow, and another; the morrow held the mystery for the next.

Norton had returned and with him his wife. He was violently affected, after the fashion of mercurial temperaments, but she was cold and silent. The dead man was nothing to her in life, more than a restraint. She could not be expected to weep. On Edward by accident had fallen the arrangements for the funeral, and with the advice of the general he had managed them well. Fate seemed to make him a member of that household in spite of himself.

The general was made an honorary pall-bearer, and when the procession moved at last into the city and to the church, without forethought it fell to Edward—there was no one else—to support and sustain the daughter of the house. It seemed a matter of course that he should do this, and as they followed the coffin up the aisle, between the two ranks of people gathered there, the fact was noted in silence to be discussed later. This then, read the universal verdict, was the sequel of a romance.

But Edward thought of none of these things. The loving heart of the girl was convulsed with grief. Since childhood she had been the idol of her father, and between them had never come a cloud. To her that white-haired father represented the best of manhood. Edward almost lifted her to and from the carriage, and her weight was heavy upon his arm as they followed the coffin.

But the end came; beautiful voices had lifted the

wounded hearts to heaven and the minister had implored its benediction upon them. The soul-harrowing sound of the clay upon the coffin had followed and all was over.

Edward found himself alone in the carriage with Mary, and the ride was long. He did not know how to lead the troubled mind away from its horror and teach it to cling to the unchanging rocks of faith. The girl had sunk down behind her veil in the corner of the coach; her white hands lay upon her lap. He took these in his own firm clasp and held them tightly. It seemed natural that he should; she did not withdraw them; she may not have known it.

And so they came back home to where the brave little wife, who had promised "though He slay me, yet will I praise Him," sat among the shadows keeping her promise. The first shock had passed and after that the faith and serene confidence of the woman were never disturbed. She would have died at the stake the same way.

The days that followed were uneventful, Norton had recovered his composure as suddenly as he had lost it, and discussed the situation freely. There was now no one to manage the place and he could not determine what was to be done. In the meantime he was obliged to return to business and the next day he went to Edward and, thanking him for all the kindness to mother and sister, hurried back to New York, and Annie went with him for a week's change. Edward had spent one more day with the Montjoy's at Norton's request, and now he, too, took his departure.

When Edward parted from Mary and the blind mother he had recourse to his sternest stoicism to restrain himself. He escaped an awkward situation by promising to be gone only two days before coming again. At home he found Virdow philosophically composed and engaged in the library, a new servant having been provided, and everything proceeding smoothly. Edward went to him and said, abruptly:

"When is it your steamer sails, Herr Virdow?"

"One week from to-day," said that individual, not a little surprised at his friend's manner. "Why do you ask?"

"Because I go with you, never again in all likelihood to enter America. From to-day, then, you will excuse my absences. I have many affairs to settle."

Virdow heard him in silence, but presently he asked:

"Are you not satisfied now, Edward?"

"I am satisfied that I am the son of Marion Evan, but I will have undoubted and unmistakable proof before I set foot in this community again! There is little chance to obtain it. Nearly thirty years—it is a long time, and the back trail is covered up."

"What are your plans?"

"To employ the best detectives the world can afford, and give them carte blanche."

"But why this search? Is it not better to rest under your belief and take life quietly? There are many new branches of science and philosophy—you have a quick mind, you are young—why not come with me and put aside the mere details of existence? There are greater truths worth knowing, Edward, than the mere truth of one's ancestry." Edward looked long and sadly into his face and shook his head.

"These mere facts," he said at length, "mean everything with me." He went to his room; there were hours of silence and then Virdow heard in the stillness of the old house the sound of Gerald's violin, for Edward's had been left in Mary's care. His philosophy could not resist the fatherland appeal that floated down the great hall and filled the night with weird and tender melody. For the man who played worshiped as he drew the bow.

But silence came deep over Ilexhurst and Virdow slept. Not so Edward; he was to begin his great search that night. He went to the wing-room and the glass-room and flooded them with light. A thrill struck through him as he surveyed again the scene and seemed to see the wild face of his comrade pale in death upon the divan. There under that rod still pointing significantly down to the steel disk he had died. And outside in the darkness had Rita also died. He alone was left. The drama could not be long now. There was but one actor.

He searched among all the heaps of memoranda and

writings upon the desk. They were memoranda and notes upon experiments and queries. Edward touched them one by one to the gas jet and saw them flame and blacken into ashes, and now nothing was left but the portfolio—and that contained but four pictures—the faces of Slippery Dick, himself and Mary and the strange scene at the church. One only was valuable—the face of the girl which he knew he had given to the artist upon the song he had played. This one he took, and restored the others.

He had turned out the light in the glass-room, and was approaching the jet in the wing-room to extinguish it, when upon the mantel he saw a letter which bore the address "H. Abingdon, care John Morgan," unopened. How long it had been there no one was left to tell. The postman, weary of knocking, had probably brought it around to the glass-room; or the servant had left it with Gerald. It was addressed by a woman's hand and bore the postmark of Paris, with the date illegible. It was a hurried note:

"Dear Friend: What has happened? When you were called home so suddenly, you wrote me that you had important news to communicate if you could overcome certain scruples, and that you would return immediately, or as soon as pressing litigation involving large interests was settled, and in your postscript you added 'keep up your courage.' You may imagine how I have waited and watched, and read and reread the precious note. But months have passed and I have not heard from you. Are you ill? I will come to you. Are you still at work upon my interests? Write to me and relieve the strain and anxiety. I would not hurry you, but remember it is a mother who waits. Yours, Cambia."

"Cambia!" Edward repeated the name aloud. Cambia. A flood of thoughts rushed over him. What was Cambia—John Morgan to him? The veil was lifting. And then came a startling realization. Cambia, the wife of Gaspard Levigne!

"God in heaven," he said, fervently, "help me now!"

Virdow was gone; only the solemn memories of the room kept him company. He sunk upon the divan and buried his face in his hands. If Cambia was the woman, then the man who had died in his arms—the exile, the iron-scarred, but innocent, convict, the hero who passed in silence—was her husband! And he? The great musician had given him not only the violin but genius! Cambia had begged of his dying breath proofs of marriage. The paling lips had moved to reply in vain.

The mystery was laid bare; the father would not claim him, because of his scars, and the mother—she dared not look him in the face with the veil lifted! But he would face her; he would know the worst; nothing could be more terrible than the mystery that was crushing the better side of his life and making hope impossible. He would face her and demand the secret.

CHAPTER LV.

"WOMAN, WHAT WAS HE TO YOU?"

Edward had formed a definite determination and made his arrangements at once. There had been a coolness between him and Eldridge since the publication of the Royson letter, but necessity drove him to that lawyer to conclude his arrangements for departure. It was a different man that entered the lawyer's office this time. He gave directions for the disposition of Ilexhurst and the conversion of other property into cash. He would never live on the place again under any circumstances.

His business was to be managed by the old legal firm in New York.

The memorandum was completed and he took his departure.

He had given orders for flowers and ascertained by telephone that they were ready. At 3 o'clock he met Mary driving in and took his seat beside her in the old family carriage. Her dress of black brought out the pale, sweet face in all its beauty. She flushed slightly as he greeted her. Within the vehicle were only the few late roses she had been able to gather, with cedar and uonimous. But they drove by the greenhouse and he filled the carriage with the choicest productions of the florist, and then gave the order to the driver to proceed at once to the cemetery.

Within the grounds, where many monuments marked the last resting-place of the old family, was the plain newly made mound covering the remains of friend and father. At sight of it Mary's calmness disappeared and her grief overran its restraints. Edward stood silent, his face averted.

Presently he thought of the flowers and brought them to her. In the arrangement of these the bare sod disappeared and the girl's grief was calmed. She lingered long about the spot, and before she left it knelt in silent prayer, Edward lifting his hat and waiting with bowed head.

The sad ceremony ended, she looked to him and he led the way to where old Isam waited with the carriage. He sent him around toward Gerald's grave, under a wide-spreading live oak, while they went afoot by the direct way impassable for vehicles. They reached the parapet and would have crossed it, when they saw kneeling at the head of the grave a woman dressed in black, seemingly engaged in prayer.

Edward had caused to be placed above the remains simple marble slab, which bore the brief inscription:

GERALD MORGAN.

Died 1888.

They watched until the woman arose and laid a wreath upon the slab. When at last she turned her face and surveyed the scene they saw before them, pale and grief-stricken, Cambia. Edward felt the scene whirling about him and his tongue paralyzed. Cambia, at sight of them gave way again to a grief that had left her pale and haggard, and could only extend the free hand, while with the other she sought to conceal her face. Edward came near, his voice scarcely audible.

"Cambia!" he exclaimed in wonder; "Cambia!" she nodded her head.

"Yes, wretched, unhappy Cambia!"

"Then, madame," he said, with deep emotion, pointing to the grave and touching her arm, "what was he to you?" She looked him fairly in the face from streaming eyes.

"He was my son! It cannot harm him now. Alas, poor Cambia!"

"Your son!" The man gazed about him bewildered. "Your son, madame? You are mistaken! It cannot be!"

"Ah!" she exclaimed; "how little you know. It can be—it is true!"

"It cannot be; it cannot be!" the words of the horrified man were now a whisper.

"Do you think a mother does not know her offspring? Your talk is idle; Gerald Morgan was my son. I have known, John Morgan knew—"

"But Rita," he said, piteously.

"Ah, Rita, poor Rita, she could not know!"

The manner, the words, the tone overwhelmed him. He turned to Mary for help in his despair. Almost without sound she had sunk to the grass and now lay extended at full length. With a fierce exclamation Edward rushed to her and lifted the little figure in his arms. Cambia was at his side.

"What is this? What was she to him?" Some explanation was necessary and Edward's presence of mind returned.

"He loved her," he said. The face of Cambia grew soft and tender and she spread her wrap on the rustic bench.

"Place her here and bring water. Daughter," she exclaimed, kneeling by her side, "come, come, this will never do—" The girl's eyes opened and for a moment rested in wonder upon Cambia. Then she remembered. A strange expression settled upon her face as she gazed quickly upon Edward.

"Take me home, madame," she said; "take me home. I am deathly ill."

They carried her to the carriage, and, entering, Cambia took the little head in her lap. Shocked and now greatly alarmed, Edward gave orders to the driver and entered. It was a long and weary ride, and all the time the girl lay silent and speechless in Cambia's lap, now and then turning upon Edward an indescribable look that cut him to the heart.

They would have provided for her in the city, but she would not hear of it. Her agitation became so great that Edward finally directed the driver to return to the hall. All the way back the older woman murmured words of comfort and cheer, but the girl only wept and her slender form shook with sobs. And it was not for herself that she grieved.

And so they came to the house, and here Mary, by a supreme effort, was able to walk with assistance and to enter without disturbing the household. Cambia supported her as they reached the hall and to the room that had been Mary's all her life—the room opposite her mother's. There in silence she assisted the girl to the bed. From somewhere came Molly, the maid, and together using the remedies that women know so well they made her comfortable. No one in the house had been disturbed, and then as Mary slept Cambia went out and found her way to the side of Mrs. Montjoy and felt the bereaved woman's arms about her.

"You have reconsidered, and wisely," said Mrs. Montjoy, when the first burst of emotion was over. "I am glad you have come—where is Mary?"

"She was fatigued from the excitement and long drive and is in her room. I met her in town and came with her. But madame, think not of me; you are now the sufferer; my troubles are old. But you—what can I say to comfort you?"

"I am at peace, my child; God's will be done. When you can say that you will not feel even the weight of your sorrows. Life is not long, at best, and mine must necessarily be short. Some day I will see again." Cambia bowed her head until it rested upon the hand that clasped hers. In the presence of such trust and courage she was a child.

"My daughter," said Mrs. Montjoy, after a silence, her mind reverting to her visitor's remark; "she is not ill?"

"Not seriously, madame, but still she is not well."

"Then I will go to her if you will lend me your aid. I am not yet accustomed to finding my way. I suppose I will have no trouble after awhile." The strong arm of the younger woman clasped and guided her upon the little journey, and the mother took the place of the maid. Tea was brought to them and in the half-lighted room they sat by the now sleeping figure on the bed, and whispered of Cambia's past and future. The hours passed. The house had grown still and Molly had been sent to tell Edward of the situation and give him his lamp.

But Edward was not alone. The general had ridden over to inquire after his neighbors and together they sat upon the veranda and talked. That is, the general talked, and Edward listened or seemed to listen. The rush of thoughts, the realization that had come over him at the cemetery, now that necessity for immediate action had passed with his charge, returned. Cambia had been found weeping over her son, and that son was Gerald. True or untrue, it was fatal to him if Cambia was convinced.

But it could not be less than true; he, Edward, was an outcast upon the face of the earth; his dream was over; through these bitter reflections the voice of the general rose and fell monotonously, as he spoke feelingly of the dead friend whom he had known since childhood and told of their long associations and adventures in the war. And then, as Edward sought to bring himself back to the present, he found himself growing hot and cold and his heart beating violently; the consequences of the revelation made in the cemetery had extended no further than himself and his own people, but Cambia was Marion Evan! And her father was there, by him, ignorant that in the house was the daughter dead to him for more than a quarter of a century. He could not control an exclamation. The speaker paused and looked at him.

"Did you speak?" The general waited courteously.

"Did I? It must have been involuntarily—a habit!

You were saying that the colonel led his regiment at Malvern Hill." Evan regarded him curiously.

"Yes, I mentioned that some time ago. He was wounded and received the praise of Jackson as he was borne past him. I think Montjoy considered that the proudest moment of his life. When Jackson praised a man he was apt to be worthy of it. He praised me once," he said, half-smiling over the scene in mind.

But Edward had again lost the thread of the narrative. Cambia had returned; a revelation would follow; the general would meet his daughter, and over the grave of Gerald the past would disappear from their lives. What was to become of him? He remembered that John Morgan had corresponded with her, and communicated personally. She must know his history. In the coming denouement there would be a shock for him. He would see these friends torn from him, not harshly nor unkindly, but between them and him would fall the iron rule of caste, which has never been broken in the south—the race law, which no man can override. With something like a panic within he decided at once. He would not witness the meeting. He would give them no chance to touch him by sympathetic pity and by—aversion. It should all come to him by letter, while he was far away! His affairs were in order. The next day he would be gone.

"General," he said, "will you do me a favor? I must return to the city; my coming was altogether a matter of accident, and I am afraid it will inconvenience our friends here at this time to send me back. Let me have your horse and I will send him to you in the morning."

The abrupt interruption filled the old man with surprise.

"Why, certainly, if you must go. But I thought you had no idea of returning—is it imperative?"

"Imperative. I am going away from the city to-morrow, and there are yet matters—you understand, and Virdow is expecting me. I trust it will not inconvenience you greatly. It would be well, probably, if one of us stayed to-night; this sudden illness—the family's condition—"

"Inconvenience! Nonsense! If you must go, why, the

horse is yours of course as long as you need him." But still perplexed the general waited in silence for a more definite explanation. Edward was half-facing the doorway and the lighted hall was exposed to him, but the shadow of the porch hid him from any one within. It was while they sat thus that the old man felt a hand upon his arm and a grasp that made him wince. Looking up he saw the face of his companion fixed on some object in the hall, the eyes starting from their sockets. Glancing back he became the witness of a picture that almost caused his heart to stand still.

CHAPTER LVI.

FRAGMENTARY LIFE RECORDS.

The records of John Morgan's life are fragmentary. It was only by joining the pieces and filling in the gaps that his friends obtained a clear and rounded conception of his true character and knew at last the real man.

Born about 1820, the only son of a wealthy and influential father, his possibilities seemed almost unlimited. To such a youth the peculiar system of the south gave advantages not at that time afforded by any other section. The south was approaching the zenith of its power; its slaves did the work of the whole people, leaving their owners leisure for study, for travel and for display. Politics furnished the popular field for endeavor; young men trained to the bar, polished by study and foreign travel and inspired by lofty ideals of government, threw themselves into public life, with results that have become now a part of history.

At 22, John Morgan was something more than a mere promise. He had graduated with high honors at the Virginia University and returning home had engaged in the practice of law—his maiden speech, delivered in a murder case, winning for him a wide reputation. But at that critical period a change came over him. To the surprise of his contemporaries he neglected his growing practice, declined legislative honors and gradually withdrew to the quiet of Ilexhurst, remaining in strict retirement with his mother.

The life of this gentlewoman had never been a very happy one; refined and delicate, she was in sharp contrast with her husband, who, from the handsome, dark-haired gallant she first met at the White Sulphur Springs, soon developed into a generous liver, with a marked leaning towards strong drink, fox-hunting and cards. As the wife, in the crucible of life, grew to pure gold, the grosser pleasures developed the elder Morgan out of all likeness to the figure around which clung her girlish memories.

But Providence had given to her a boy, and in him there was a promise of happier days. He grew up under her care, passionately devoted to the beautiful mother, and his triumphs at college and at the bar brought back to her something of the happiness she had known in dreams only.

The blow came with the arrival of Rita Morgan's mother. From that time John Morgan devoted himself to the lonely wife, avoiding the society of both sexes. His morbid imagination pictured his mother and himself as disgraced in the eyes of the public, unconscious of the fact that the public had but little interest in the domestic situation at Ilexhurst, and no knowledge of the truth. He lived his quiet life by her side in the little room at home, and when at last, hurt by his horse, the father passed away, he closed up the house and took his mother abroad for a stay of several years. When they returned life went on very much as before.

But of the man who came back from college little was left aside from an indomitable will and a genius for work. He threw himself into the practice of his profession again, with a feverish desire for occupation, and, bringing to his aid a mind well stored by long years of reflection and reading, soon secured a large and lucrative practice.

His fancy was for criminal law. No pains, no expense was too great for him where a point was to be made. Some of his witnesses in noted cases cost him for traveling expenses and detectives double his fee. He kept up the fight with a species of fierce joy, his only moments of elation, as far as the public knew, being the moments of victory.

So it was that at 40 years of age John Morgan found himself with a reputation extending far beyond the state and with a profession that left him but little leisure. It was about this time he accidentally met Marion Evan, a mere girl, and felt the hidden springs of youth rise in his heart. Marion Evan received the attentions of the great criminal lawyer without suspicion of their meaning.

When it developed that he was deeply interested in her she was astonished and then touched. It was until the end a matter of wonder to her that John Morgan should have found anything in her to admire and love, but those who looked on knowingly were not surprised. Of gentle ways and clinging, dependent nature, varied by flashes of her father's fire and spirit, she presented those variable moods well calculated to dazzle and impress a man of Morgan's temperament. He entered upon his courtship with the same carefulness and determination that marked his legal practice, and with the aid of his wealth and reborn eloquence carried the citadel of her maiden heart by storm. With misgivings Albert Evan yielded his consent.

But Marion Evan's education was far from complete. The mature lover wished his bride to have every accomplishment that could add to her pleasure in life; he intended to travel for some years and she was not at that time sufficiently advanced in the languages to interpret the records of the past. Her art was of course rudimentary. Only in vocal music was she distinguished; already that voice which was to develop such surprising powers spoke its thrilling message to those who could understand, and John Morgan was one of these.

So it was determined that Marion should for one year at least devote herself to study and then the marriage would take place. Where to send her was the important question, and upon the decision hinges this narrative.

Remote causes shape our destinies. That summer John Morgan took his mother abroad for the last time

and in Paris chance gave him acquaintance with Gaspard
Levigne, a man nearly as old as himself. Morgan had
been touched and impressed by the unchanging sadness
of a face that daily looked into his at their hotel, but it is
likely that he would have carried it in memory for a few
weeks only had not the owner, who occupied rooms near
his own, played the violin one night while he sat dreaming of home and the young girl who had given him her
promise. He felt that the hidden musician was saying
for him that which had been crying out for expression in
his heart all his life. Upon the impulse of the moment
he entered this stranger's room and extended his hand.
Gaspard Levigne took it. They were friends.

During their stay in Paris the two men became almost
inseparable companions. One day Gaspard was in the
parlor of his new friend, when John Morgan uncovered
upon the table a marble bust of his fiancee and briefly explained the situation. The musician lifted it in wonder
and studied its perfections with breathless interest. From
that time he never tired of the beautiful face, but always
his admiration was mute. His lips seemed to lose their
power.

The climax came when John Morgan, entering the
dim room one evening, found Gaspard Levigne with his
face in his hands kneeling before the marble, convulsed
with grief. And then little by little he told his story. He
was of noble blood, the elder son of a family, poor but
proud and exclusive. Unto him had descended, from an
Italian ancestor, the genius of musical composition and
a marvelous technique, while his brother seemed to inherit the pride and arrogance of the Silesian side of the
house, with about all the practical sense and business
ability that had been won and transmitted.

He had fallen blindly in love with a young girl beneath
him in the social scale, and whose only dowry was a pure
heart and singularly perfect beauty. The discovery of
this situation filled the family with alarm and strenuous
efforts were made to divert the infatuated man, but without changing his purpose. Pressure was brought to bear
upon the girl's parents, with better success.

Nothing now remained for Gaspard but an elopement,

22

and this he planned. He took his brother into his confidence and was pleased to find him after many refusals
a valuable second. The elopement took place and assisted by the brother he came to Paris. There his wife
had died leaving a boy, now nearly 2 years old.

Then came the denouement; the marriage arranged
for him had been a mockery.

It was a fearful blow. He did not return to his home.
Upon him had been saddled the whole crime.

When the story was ended Gaspard went to his room
and brought back a little picture of the girl, which he
placed by the marble bust. Morgan read his meaning
there; the two faces seemed identical. The picture would
have stood for a likeness of Marion Evan, in her father's
hands.

The conduct of Gaspard Levigne upon the discovery
of the cruel fraud was such as won the instant sympathy
of the American, whose best years had been sacrificed
for his mother. The musician had not returned to Breslau and exposed the treachery of the brother who was
the idol of his aged parents; he suffered in silence, and
cared for the child in an institution near Paris. But John
Morgan went and quietly verified the facts. He engaged
the ablest counsel and did his best to find a way to right
the wrong.

Then came good Mrs. Morgan, who took the waif to
her heart. He passed from his father's arms, his only
inheritance a mother's picture, of which his own face was
the miniature.

Months passed; Gaspard Levigne learned English
readily, and one more result of the meeting in Paris was
that John Morgan upon returning to America had,
through influential friends, obtained for Levigne a lucrative position in a popular American institution, where in-
strumental and vocal music were specialties.

It was to this institution that Marion Evan was sent,
with results already known.

The shock to John Morgan, when he received from
Marion a pitiful letter, telling of her decision and marriage, well-nigh destroyed him. The mind does not rally
and reactions are uncertain at 40. In the moment of his

despair he had torn up her letters and hurled her likeness in marble far out to the deepest part of the lake.
Pride alone prevented him following it. And in this
hour of gloom the one remaining friend, his mother,
passed from life.

The public never knew of his sufferings; he drew the
mantle of silence a little closer around him and sunk
deeper into his profession. He soon became known as
well for his eccentricities as for his genius; and presently
the inherited tendency toward alcoholic drinks found him
an' easy victim. Another crisis in his life came a year
after the downfall of his air castle, and just as the south
was preparing to enter upon her fatal struggle.

The mother of Rita had passed away, and so had the
young woman's husband. Rita had but recently returned to Ilexhurst, when one night she came into his
presence drenched with rain and terrorized by the fierceness of an electrical storm then raging. Speechless from
exhaustion and excitement she could only beckon him
to follow. Upon the bed in her room, out in the broad
back yard, now sharing with its occupant the mud and
water of the highway, her face white and her disordered
hair clinging about her neck and shoulders, lay the insensible form of the only girl he had ever loved—Marion
Evan, as he still thought of her. He approached the bed
and lifted her cold hands and called her by endearing
names, but she did not answer him. Rita, the struggle
over, had sunk into semiconsciousness upon the floor.

When the family physician arrived John Morgan had
placed Rita upon the bed and had borne the other woman
in his arms to the mother's room upstairs, and stood waiting at the door. While the genial old practitioner was
working to restore consciousness to the young woman
there, a summons several times repeated was heard at
the front door. Morgan went in person and admitted a
stranger, who presented a card that bore the stamp of a
foreign detective bureau. Speaking in French the lawyer bravely welcomed him and led the way to the library.
The detective opened the interview:

"Have you received my report of the 14th inst., M.
Morgan?"

"Yes. What have you additional?"

"This: Mme. Levigne is with her husband and now in this city." Morgan nodded his head.

"So I have been informed." He went to the desk and wrote out a check. "When do you propose returning?"

"As soon as possible, monsieur; to-morrow if it pleases you."

"I will call upon you in the morning; to-night I have company that demands my whole time and attention. If I fail, here is your check. You have been very suc̄cessful."

"Monsieur is very kind. I have not lost sight of Mme. Levigne in nearly a year until to-night. Both she and her husband have left their hotel; temporarily only I presume." The two men shook hands and parted.

Upstairs the physician met Morgan returning. "The lady will soon be all right; she has rallied and as soon as she gets under the influence of the opiate I have given and into dry clothes, will be out of danger. But the woman in the servant's house is, I am afraid, in a critical condition."

"Go to her, please," said Morgan, quickly. Then entering the room he took a seat by the side of the young woman—her hand in his. Marion looked upon his grave face in wonder and confusion. Neither spoke. Her eyes closed at last in slumber.

Then came Mammie Hester, the old woman who had nursed him, one of those family servants of the old south, whose lips never learned how to betray secrets.

The sun rose grandly on the morning that Marion left Ilexhurst. She pushed back her heavy veil, letting its splendor light up her pale face and gave her hand in sad farewell to John Morgan. Its golden beams almost glorified the countenance of the man; or was it the light from a great soul shining through?

"A mother's prayers," she said brokenly. "They are all that I can give."

"God bless and protect you till we meet again," he said, gently.

She looked long and sadly toward the eastern horizon

in whose belt of gray woodland lay her childhood home,
lowered her veil and hurried away. A generation would
pass before her feet returned upon that gravel walk.

CHAPTER LVII.

"THE LAST SCENE OF ALL."

Mary slept.

The blind woman, who had for awhile sat silent by her
side, slowly stroking and smoothing the girl's extended
arm, nodded, her chin resting upon her breast.

Cambia alone was left awake in the room, her mind
busy with its past. The light was strong; noiselessly
she went to the little table to lower it. There, before her,
lay a violin's antique case. As her gaze fell upon it, the
flame sank under her touch, leaving the room almost in
the shadow. The box was rounded at the ends and in-
laid, the center design being a curiously interwoven mon-
ogram. Smothering an exclamation, she seized it in her
arms and listened, looking cautiously upon her companions. The elder woman lifted her head and turned her
sightless eyes toward the light, then passed into sleep
again.

Cambia went back eagerly to the box again and tried
its intricate fastenings; but in the dim light they resisted
her fingers, and she dare not turn up the flame again.

From the veranda in front came the murmur of men's
voices; the house was silent. Bearing the precious burden Cambia went quickly to the hallway and paused for
a moment under the arch that divided it. Overhead, suspended by an invisible wire, was a snow-white pigeon
with wings outspread; behind was the open back door
and across the vista outside swayed in the gentle breeze
the foliage of the trees. She stood for a moment, listening; and such was the picture presented to Edward as
he clutched the arm of his companion and leaned forward with strained eyes gazing into the light.

Aided by the adjuncts of the scene, he recognized at

once a familiar dream. Such was the dream picture, but in place of the girl's was now a woman's face.

Another caught a deeper meaning at the same instant, as the general's suppressed breathing betrayed.

Cambia heard nothing; her face was pale, her hand trembling. She dropped to her knees and laid the case upon the floor. In the light descending upon her she found the secret fastenings and the lid opened.

Then the two men beheld a strange thing; the object of that nervous action was not the violin itself. A string accidentally touched by her sparkling ring gave out a single minor note that startled her, but only for a second did she pause and look around. Pressing firmly upon a spot in the inner side of the lid she drew out a little panel of wood and from the shallow cavity exposed lifted quickly several folded papers, which she opened. Then, half rising, she wavered and sank back fainting upon the floor. The silence was broken. A cry burst from the lips of the old general.

"Marion! My child!" In an instant he was by her side lifting and caressing her. "Speak to me, daughter," he said. "It has been long, so long. That face, that face! Child, it is your mother's as I saw it last! Marion, look up; it is I, your father." And then he exclaimed despairingly, as she did not answer him, "She is dead!"

"It is not serious, general," said Edward hurriedly. "See, she is reviving." Cambia steadied herself by a supreme effort and thrust back the form that was supporting her.

"Who calls Marion?" she cried wildly. "Marion Evan is dead! Cambia is dead! I am the Countess Levigne." Her voice rang out in the hall and her clenched hand held aloft, as though she feared they might seize them, the papers she had plucked from the violin case. Then her eyes met the general's; she paused in wonder and looked longingly into his aged face. Her voice sank to a whisper: "Father, father! Is it indeed you? You at last?" Clinging to the hands extended toward her she knelt and buried her face in them, her form shaking with sobs. The old man's tall figure swayed and trembled.

"Not there, Marion, my child, not there! 'Tis I who should kneel! God forgive me, it was I who—"

"Hush, father, hush! The blame was mine. But I have paid for it with agony, with the better years of my life.

"But I could not come back until I came as the wife of the man I loved; I would not break your heart. See! I have the papers. It was my husband's violin." She hid her face in his bosom and let the tears flow unchecked.

Edward was standing, white and silent, gazing upon the scene; he could not tear himself away. The general, his voice unsteady, saw him at last. A smile broke through his working features and shone in his tearful eyes:

"Edward, my boy, have you no word? My child has come home!" Marion lifted her face and drew herself from the sheltering arms with sudden energy.

"Edward," she said, gently and lovingly. "Edward!" Her eyes grew softer and seemed to caress him with their glances. She went up to him and placed both hands upon his shoulders. "His child, and your mother!"

"My mother, my mother!" The words were whispers. His voice seemed to linger upon them.

"Yes! Cambia, the unhappy Marion, the Countess Levigne and your mother! No longer ashamed to meet you, no longer an exile! Your mother, free to meet your eyes without fear of reproach!"

She was drawing his cheek to hers as she spoke. The general had come nearer and now she placed the young man's hand in his.

"But," said Edward, "Gerald! You called him your son!" She clasped her hands over her eyes and turned away quickly. "How can it be? Tell me the truth?" She looked back to him then in a dazed way. Finally a suspicion of his difficulty came to her. "He was your twin brother. Did you not know? Alas, poor Gerald!"

"Ah!" said the old man, "it was then true!"

Edward took her hand.

"Mother," he said softly, lifting her face to his, "Gerald is at peace. Let me fulfill all the hopes you cherished for both!"

"God has showered blessings upon me this night," said the general brokenly. "Edward!" The two men clasped hands again and looked into each other's eyes. And, radiant by their side, was the face of Cambia!

At this moment Mary, who had been awakened by their excited voices, her hand outstretched toward the wall along which she had crept, came and stood near them, gazing in wonder upon their beaming faces. With a bound Edward reached her side and with an arm about her came to Cambia.

"Mother," he said, "here is your daughter." As Cambia clasped her lovingly to her bosom he acquainted Mary with what had occurred. And then, happy in her wonder and smiles, Edward and Mary turned away and discussed the story of Cambia's life with the now fully awakened little mother.

"And now," said he, "I may ask of you this precious life and be your son indeed!" Mary's head was in her mother's lap.

"She has loved you a long time, Edward; she is already yours."

Presently he went upon the veranda, where father and daughter were exchanging holy confidences, and, sitting by his mother's side, heard the particulars of her life abroad and bitter experience.

"When Mr. Morgan went to you, father, and stated a hypothetical case and offered to find me, and you, outraged, suffering, declared that I could only return when I had proofs of my marriage, I was without them. Mr. Morgan sent me money to pay our expenses home—Gaspard's and mine—and we did come, he unwilling and fearing violence, for dissipation had changed his whole nature. Then, he had been informed of my one-time engagement to Mr. Morgan, and he was well acquainted with that gentleman and indebted to him for money loaned upon several occasions. He came to America with me upon Mr. Morgan's guaranty, the sole condition imposed upon him being that he should bring proofs of our marriage; and had he continued to rely upon that guaranty, had he kept his word, there would have been no trouble. But on the day we reached this city he gave way to temptation again and remembered all my threats to leave him. In our final interview he became suddenly jealous, declared that there was a plot to separate us, and expressed a determination to destroy the proofs.

"It was then that I determined to act, and hazarded everything upon a desperate move. I resolved to seize my husband's violin, not knowing where his papers were, and hold it as security for my proofs. I thought the plan would succeed; did not his love for that instrument exceed all other passions? I had written to Rita, engaging to meet her on a certain night at a livery stable, where we were to take a buggy and proceed to Ilexhurst. The storm prevented. Gaspard had followed me, and at the church door tore the instrument from my arms and left me insensible. Rita carried me in her strong arms three miles to Ilexhurst, and it cost her the life of the child that was born and died that night.

"Poor, poor Rita! She herself had been all but dead when my boys were born a week later, and the idea that one of them was her own was the single hallucination of her mind. The boys were said to somewhat resemble her. Rita's mother bore a strong resemblance to Mrs. Morgan's family, as you have perhaps heard, and Mrs. Morgan was related to our family, so the resemblance may be explained in that way. Mr. Morgan never could clear up this hallucination of Rita's, and so the matter rested that way. It could do no harm under the circumstances, and might—"

"No harm?" Edward shook his head sadly.

"No harm. You, Edward, were sent away, and it was early seen that poor Gerald would be delicate and probably an invalid. For my troubles, my flight, had—. The poor woman gave her life to the care of my children. Heaven bless her forever!"

Cambia waited in silence a moment and then continued:

"As soon as I could travel I made a business transaction of it, and borrowed money of my friend, John Morgan. He had acquainted me with the conditions upon which I would be received at home; and now it was impossible for me to meet them. Gaspard was gone. I thought I could find him; I never did, until blind, poor, aged and dying, he sent for me."

"John Morgan was faithful.   He secured vocal teachers for me in Paris and then an engagement to sing in public.   I sang, and from that night my money troubles ended.

"Mr. Morgan stayed by me in Paris until my career was assured. Then, in obedience to his country's call, he came back here, running the blockade, and fought up to Appomattox."

"As gallant a fire-eater," said the general, "as ever shouldered a gun. And he refused promotion on three occasions."

"I can readily understand that," said Cambia. "His modesty was only equaled by his devotion and courage.

"He visited me again when the war ended, and we renewed the search. After that came the Franco-Prussian war, the siege of Paris and the commune, destroying all trails. But I sang on and searched on. When I seemed to have exhausted the theaters I tried the prisons. And so the years passed by.

"In the meantime Mr. Morgan had done a generous thing; never for a moment did he doubt me." She paused, struggling with a sudden emotion, and then: "He had heard my statement—it was not like writing, father, he had heard it from my lips—and when the position of my boys became embarrassing he gave them his own name, formally adopting them while he was in Paris."

"God bless him!"   It was the general's voice.

"And after that I felt easier. Every week, in all the long years that have passed, brought me letters; every detail in their lives was known to me; and of yours, father. I knew all your troubles. Mr. Morgan managed it. And," she continued softly, "I felt your embarrassments when the war ended. Mr. Morgan offered you a loan—"

"Yes; but I could not accept from him—"

"It was from me, father; it was mine; and it was my money that cared for my boys. Yes," she said, lifting her head proudly, "Mr. Morgan understood; he let me pay back everything, and when he died it was my money, held in private trust by him for the purpose, that constituted the bulk of the fortune left by him for my boys. I earned it before the footlights, but honestly!

"Well, when poor Gaspard died—"

"He is dead, then?"

"Ah! of course you do not know. To-morrow I will tell you his story. I stood by his body and at his grave, and I knew Edward. I had seen him many times. Poor Gerald! My eyes have never beheld him since I took him in my arms that day, a baby, and kissed him good—" She broke down and wept bitterly. "Oh, it was pitiful, pitiful!"

After awhile she lifted her face.

"My husband had written briefly to his family just before death, the letter to be mailed after; and thus they knew of it. But they did not know the name he was living under. His brother, to inherit the title and property, needed proof of death and advertised in European papers for it. He also advertised for the violin. It was this that suggested to me the hiding place of the missing papers. Before my marriage Gaspard had once shown me the little slide. It had passed from my memory. But Cambia's wits were sharper and the description supplied the link. I went to Silesia and made a trade with the surviving brother, giving up my interest in certain mines for the name of the person who held the violin. Gaspard had described him in his letter only as a young American named Morgan. The name was nothing to the brother; it was everything to me. I came here determined, first to search for the papers, and, failing in that, to go home to you, my father. God has guided me."

She sat silent, one hand in her father's, the other clasped lovingly in her son's. It was a silence none cared to break. But Edward, from time to time, as his mind reviewed the past, lifted tenderly to his lips the hand of Cambia.

* * *

Steadily the ocean greyhound plowed its way through the dark swells of the Atlantic. A heavy bank of clouds covered the eastern sky almost to the zenith, its upper edges paling in the glare of the full moon slowly ascending beyond. .

The night was pleasant, the decks crowded. A young man and a young woman sat by an elderly lady, hand in hand. They had been talking of a journey made the year previous upon the same vessel, when the ocean sang for them a new sweet song. They heard it again this night and were lost in dreams, when the voice of a well-known novelist, who was telling a story to a charmed circle near by, broke in:

"It was my first journey upon the ocean. We had been greatly interested in the little fellow because he was a waif from the great Parisian world, and although at that time tenderly cared for by the gentle woman who had become his benefactress, somehow he seemed to carry with him an atmosphere of loneliness—of isolation. Think of it, a motherless babe afloat upon the ocean. It was the pathos of life made visible. He did not realize it, but every heart there beat in sympathy with his, and when it was whispered that the little voyager was dead I think every eye was wet with tears. Dead! Almost consumed by fever. With him had come the picture of a young and beautiful woman. He took it with him beneath the little hands upon his breast. That night he was laid to rest. Never had motherless babe such a burial. Gently, as though there were danger of waking him, we let him sink into the dark waters, there to be rocked in the lap of the ocean until God's day dawns and the seas give up their dead. That was thirty years ago; yet to-night I seem to see that little shrouded form slip down and down and down into the depths. God grant that its mother was dead."

When he ceased the elder woman in the little group had bent her head and was silently weeping.

"It sounds like a page from the early life of Gaspard Levigne," she said to her companions. And then to the novelist, in a voice brimming over with tenderness: "Grieve not for the child, my friend. God has given wings to love. There is no place in all His universe that can hide a baby from its mother. Love will find a way, be the ocean as wide and deep as eternity itself."

And then, as they sat wondering, the moon rose above the clouds. Light flashed upon the waves around them, and a golden path, stretching out ahead, crossed the far horizon into the misty splendors of the sky.

THE END.